D0417838

What others are saying about this book

Whole Person Learning by Bryce Taylor is a powerful work that attempts to bring forward fields of learning involved with both transformative and holistic education. It presents a closely argued and paradigmatically sophisticated understanding of learning models that makes the case for integral scholarship and practice across a whole range of subjects. A work of considerable merit and acumen, it offers the reader a largesse in perspective that has both visionary and practical significance.

Edmund O'Sullivan, Transformative Learning Centre, University of Toronto.

Whole Person Learning is completely new to me but I love the values it encapsulates and believe we need to honour these values if we are to find a way through the crises humanity now faces.

Rt. Hon. Clare Short MP, House of Commons, UK.

In his latest book, Bryce Taylor addresses in a radical and uncompromising manner, grounded in long-standing and committed practice, a major issue at the leading edge of educational transformation – the integration of autonomy in learning and holism in learning. An important resource for educators with courage and vision.

John Heron, Co-director, South Pacific Centre for Human Inquiry, New Zealand.

Building on the earlier seminal work of Knowles, Heron, Senge and others, Bryce Taylor provides a new landmark 'on the edge of a new chapter for the human potentiality of learning'. This book offers a comprehensive framework and set of skills for all teachers, tutors, facilitators and leaders who are preparing others for a world of complexity in which both the transpersonal dimension and our essential interconnectedness are embraced. We live in times of transition and change. This is a brave next step towards the emergence of co-creative solutions.

Janice Dolley, Executive Director, Wrekin Trust, formerly OU Lecturer.

For too long, we humans have pursued narrow goals of gain, oblivious to any environmental or social fall-out. The resulting social and environmental costs have risen to such enormous proportions that they can no longer be ignored. To deal with these consequences effectively, we need to acquire sight where we have been blind for so long. WPL offers a necessary means of 'tuning into' oneself and the world, of raising an individual's sensitivity and receptivity so that we acquire the breadth and depth of vision we will need to

HD58.82 TAY 2007   Teaching & learning

deal with the challenges that our world now faces.

Anthony Sampson, CSR Specialist and Advisor, Chair UN Global Compact, UK.

This book is a must-read for any instructor who wonders if they are really preparing their students for the complex and nuanced challenges of today's world. But it is not for the faint of heart. For most instructors trained in traditional educational institutions, it will turn your world on its head. It's like looking down a well-known but washed-out mountain path. The village you are trying to reach is within sight, but the route is no longer viable. A new road must be built. The focus is on learning versus teaching, and on letting go versus being in charge. Learning begins with introspection and a realization of interdependence. Only when the instructor takes the Whole Person Learning journey themselves, can they guide others to the same path.

Peggy Cunningham, Marie Shantz Teaching Associate Professor, Queen's School of Business, Queen's University, Kingston, Ontario, Canada.

There are good books that demonstrate practice-related knowledge. Then there are interesting books that begin to make connections between one area and other areas of practice. And then there are really interesting books that make all those connections but which also make you look afresh at the subject area and how it is lived. Bryce Taylor's book falls into that category. It is about Whole Person Learning in the context and experience of practice; as such, it is about empowering the learner in and through the learning relationship. Not only does this develop 'practice' and related skills, it also develops qualities, the capacity to take responsibility for learning, and the capacity to develop significant meaning in and through professional practice. This is a ground-breaking book that offers a creative and mature response to the challenges to corporate and professional responsibility in the twenty-first century.

Simon Robinson, Professor of Applied and Professional Ethics, Leeds Metropolitan University, UK.

I think this book creates a compelling case for WPL as a radically (in today's training-oriented world) new approach. I would certainly commend WPL and this book in particular to anybody open-minded enough to be looking for new approaches to/a new experience in learning, which will make a difference in the future life of organisations.

Mike Hardy MD, Longhurst Housing Association, UK.

Whole Person Learning has a clear message: we, as human beings, each and everyone, have a personal operating system, largely composed by our individual beliefs acquired by previous experiences. If we learn to see – and also find ways to share and explore – those as we go, we may not only become fuller and richer to ourselves and therefore to others, we will also, I believe, be able to unlock much of the potential in today's work-place often built around professional teams. Whole Person Learning introduces us to the theories and practices that enable us to start to navigate in this fascinating landscape.

Björn Larsson, CEO, The ForeSight Group, Sweden.

This book is the best and most sophisticated account I have read of the challenges facing those who seek to facilitate and support the learning of others, learning that has as its goal personal development, not simply the acquisition of knowledge and skills. The approach to Whole Person Learning that it sets out has an important part to play in the development of leaders able to act with authenticity in an increasingly chaotic world. The book will be a valuable resource for those wishing and willing to think in new ways about the design of learning approaches for the leaders of the future.

Peter Stott, Executive Director of Strategy, Home Group, UK.

The chapters on the group dimension of Whole Person Learning make clear both the challenge of a commitment to this mode of learning and its rewards. To paraphrase St Augustine, we travel to wonder at the height of mountains, at the huge waves of the sea, (...) and pass by ourselves without wondering. This introduction to Whole Person Learning shows what is possible when we take time to wonder at ourselves.

Gill Tishler, CEO, YWCA England and Wales.

Learning for Tomorrow brings a depth of understanding and application to the holistic development of the person. It is an essential contribution which helps us come to grips with some of the challenging leadership questions facing contemporary society in preparing people for a world of complexity, uncertainty, new forms of innovation – and responsibility. We need this book and now it is here. Let's read, reflect, learn and take it further.

Anders Aspling, General Secretary GRLI and Dean of Vlerick Leuven Gent Management School.

4

The aim of Whole Person Learning is to promote autonomy
in the person and between persons.

Autonomy and collaboration are interrelated terms.
You cannot have the one without the other

The future enters into us... long before it happens. Rilke

Other books by Oasis Press:

Forging the Future Together

Working with Others

Helping People Change

Where do I go from Here?

How did I get Here?

WITHDRAWN

SAID BUSINESS SCHOOL
EXECUTIVE
EDUCATION
LIBRARY

Learning
for Tomorrow:

Whole Person Learning
for the
Planetary Citizen

BRYCE TAYLOR

Series Editor
HEATHER TWEDDLE

OASIS PRESS

MMVII

First published in Great Britain in April 2007 by:

Oasis Press
Hall Mews
Clifford Road   Boston Spa
West Yorkshire LS23 6DT
UK

Oasis Press is the publications element of
The Oasis School of Human Relations

Tel +44 (0) 1937 541700
Fax +44 (0) 1937 541800
e-mail: info@oasishumanrelations.org.uk
website: www.oasishumanrelations.org.uk

© Oasis Press 2007

Bryce Taylor asserts the moral right to be identified as
the author of this work.

A CIP Record for this book is available from the
British Cataloguing in Publication data office

ISBN-13 978-1-871992-45-8 (Paperback)

All rights reserved: no part of this publication may be reproduced, stored
in a retrieval system, or transmitted in any form or by any means,
electronic, mechanical, photocopying, recording, or otherwise, without
the prior permission of the publisher.

Design and illustration by
Ian Thorp

Printed and bound in England by
CROMWELL PRESS
Trowbridge, Wiltshire.

CONTENTS

Endorsements   1

Contents   7

Acknowledgements   8

Foreword   9

Introduction   11

Prelude   15

Chapter 1:   The Need for a New Paradigm of Practice   19

Chapter 2:   Whole Person Learning: Formative Influences   28

Chapter 3:   The Power of Choice   49

Chapter 4:   What Kind of Person?   58

Chapter 5:   The Emergence of Whole Person Learning   77

Chapter 6:   Whole Person Learning in a Peer Paradigm   92

Chapter 7:   The Group Dimension of Whole Person Learning   119

Chapter 8:   Individual Experiences in
              Whole Person Learning Groups   133

Chapter 9:   Living the Learning Transition:
              Facilitating Whole Person Learning   160

Chapter 10:   Living the Learning Transition:
              Assessment in Whole Person Learning   198

Chapter 11:   Living the Learning Transition:
              Accreditation and Whole Person Learning   226

Conclusion: Whole Person Learning: The Way Ahead   240

Appendix1:   UNESCO Draft of Universal Declaration of Identity,
              Diversity and Pluralism   242

Appendix2:   The Ten Principles of The Global Compact   245

Appendix3:   Globally Responsible Leadership Initiative Partners   247

Bibliography   248

Index   253

ACKNOWLEDGEMENTS

I would like to thank all the many people who have contributed towards enabling this book to grow from an idea into reality. Many people from all manner of disciplines and walks of life have been willing to give their time and energy in discussion of the concepts and offering invaluable advice and suggestions.

Special thanks must go to Henri-Claude Bettignies and Mark Drewell, to Barloworld for its sponsorship and to the members of the GRLI for their support. In addition, I would like to thank the Oasis Directors' group, members of the TLC, those involved in the Facilitator Network as well as Bill Berrett, Steve Dilworth, Kathryn Fitch, John Gray, Hilary Wilmshirst and Judith Catchpole for their essential contribution in reading earlier drafts, and a special thanks to Heather Tweddle, series editor of Oasis Press.

FOREWORD

Whole Person Learning: what a wonderful-sounding phrase it is. How easily it resonates in a world where intuitively we know that something is amiss in terms of the mainstream approaches to education.

We sense that somehow the problem is much deeper and more profound than something which can be fixed through the societal equivalent of adjusting the headlights on the car in order to see the road ahead more clearly. Just take the world of business. How many people do any of us know who have left corporate life to forge their own future and then returned to the corporation because they find being an employee of a large enterprise a more wholesome and fulfilling existence? How many people do any of us know who find their work and the ever-evolving learning processes associated with it profoundly satisfying?

We live in the beginning of the twenty-first century in a world where more and more people in every society experience a level of consciousness in which they profoundly relate to the interconnectedness of themselves to the entire system. This can be understood in terms of an unfolding journey of awareness that every human being is on. It takes us from the self-focussed 'I', through 'we' and eventually in many cases to a world-view of 'all of us'.

The difficulty lies in the fact that most companies operate in a paradigm that of 'we'. This 'we' is expressed as a ruthless focus on the success of 'our company' at the expense of everything else. And to make matters worse, it is operationalised almost universally through an even lower level of focus on recognition and respect for success at the level of 'I'.

This is not an abstract issue. In this book, the problem is beautifully and succinctly expressed:

> It is easy to confuse the person with their individuality as tied together with the narrow concerns of their ego consciousness. And it is this confusion of the person with their personality that helps give rise to and reinforce the economic conditions that are <u>a threat to both the planet itself and to our sustainable survival</u>. It includes a narrowing of focus that brings everything down to the bottom line of desire. Attention is focussed upon the relentless pursuit of narrowly interpreted self interest – so often at odds with the deeper interests and wholeness of the person.

I have been privileged over the past three years to be involved with the Globally Responsible Leadership Initiative. It is a group of leading businesses and business schools from around the world focussing on answering the question 'How do we create a new generation of globally responsible business leaders?' Our core conclusion is very simple. It is that the problem is not primarily WHAT is taught in business education. It is HOW things are taught. Our entire mainstream modus operandi at business schools (or for that matter in educational institutions generally) is to focus on cognitive intellectual learning – in plain English that means filling the brains of learners with facts.

And yet we know that profound change comes from other areas of our being – from the heart and the soul. It is no accident that in English we refer to 'taking something to heart' when a new insight has really been internalised. So this is the challenge that Whole Person Learning seeks to address and is the reason why this book is so important.

It is also an extremely uncomfortable book. It is uncomfortable because the world of learning is filled with extremely intelligent people, many of whom are so confident they know all the answers that they are not open to explore better ways of doing things. If you are one of those people, I would expect you not to get beyond chapter two.

It is also uncomfortable because it challenges the power relationships that are entrenched in the ruling paradigms of learning.

In so doing however, it is like a searchlight cutting a path through a pitch-black sky. My hope is that you will pay attention to what it says and find the courage to explore and experience the magic that Whole Person Learning has the potential to unleash amongst us. It is after all vital if our generations are to leave a legacy for those who come after us of which we can be proud.

P. Mark Drewell MA (Oxon)

Father of Francesca, Christopher, Cassandra and Nicholas, husband to Yolanda, businessman, environmental activist, enjoyer of long walks on the beach and chairman of the Globally Responsible Leadership Initiative.

INTRODUCTION

This book is important for several reasons to be developed later. But because produced in Europe, it is of great relevance; because it comes in 2007, it is very timely. Let me explain.

Under competitive pressure to achieve results or just to survive, prisoner of a globalization process that we do not fully understand, we in western societies seem to be running after time. We try to control it rather than being in its hands, we dream to master the time of birth and the time of death, and in between we spend it running, to catch it.

This race for time, though not necessarily rewarding, is supposed to be rewarded. Not with time. It is supposed to make possible for us to have. Not creatures of needs, but creatures of desires, we want to have, to have what the other has. This mimetic desire drives us to have, to own.

In this competitive world, running after having we forget about being. Our thirst to have is exploited by providers of goods and services and turns us into consumption machines or into a 'commodity'. A commodity with purchasing power, hence a valuable commodity to be bought by skillful advertisers who manipulate and buy our propensity to consume.

We accept to be pawns in a game the rule of which we have not defined. In a world where everything is turned into a commodity: blood and body parts, human cells and works of art, nature and culture, education and science, there is a market for everything, there is a price (even if we do not know the value), there are exchange possibilities under the – supposed to be effective – control of its invisible hand.

It is in the context of such market-driven-consumption-society that we see the development of an individual keen to have, self-centered, more concerned about self-interest than common good, in search of quick, immediate satisfaction in a world where everything is increasingly seen as temporary: job, residence, partner, etc… Uncertainty induces a short-term orientation, encourages mobility, and nurtures self-interest and perhaps short-term relationships.

Religion that used to help find meaning in life – or the meaning of life – does not play such a role and the family that used to anchor relationships has become very fragile and often de-structured.

Modernity has brought up a deterioration of many social indicators that made it possible to monitor change in our society: gaps (e.g. rich-poor), divorces, suicides, drug-addiction, mental problems, violence etc... Violence in sport events, in the schools, in the corporation, in cities, in the family…

In such a context the need to reconcile man with his brother is there; we need to re-develop a basic human attitude, beyond respect: the 'care for the other'. However, first and foremost we need to reconcile man with himself, with his/her whole self. The heart and the mind, the body and the soul, the yin and the yang, the I and we have to be reconciled, sometimes re-constructed.

Oasis is a Path

In this book, we are reminded that over the last 50 years, in the United States, theories, models, approaches, and tools have been proposed to deal with the development of the person, not necessarily with the whole person. Along these years, from Kurt Lewin and its group dynamics to Abraham Maslow and his Humanistic Psychology, from the National Training Laboratories and its sensitivity training (T Group) to Will Schutz and his Esalem Institute, we could observe a long search for growing, nurturing the whole person.

Carl Rogers in California (whose work I introduced across the Atlantic in 1960), John Heron in the UK, Max Pages in France have been perhaps among the precious sources that have opened the road to Whole Person Learning, a path taken now so effectively by Oasis.

WPL is not old wine in new bottles, but it is an effective attempt to go through the painful process of a paradigm shift, and to propose an original way to transform education not only as a process to know more or better, but as an exercise to be better.

WPL, beyond the 'what' and 'how', is addressing the why, getting into fundamental questions that our society, our organizations need to address to survive as the 'community' they need to be.

Whole Person Learning is a journey. It is a journey that starts with an original concept of man, not as a set of interdependent parts that have to efficiently and effectively relate together, but as a holistic whole that actualizes its potential in and with the other. WPL goes beyond knowledge of oneself and/or interpersonal competence. These are indispensable ingredients of an effective actualization of one's own potential as an addition of skills that help a person to work effectively in society, to integrate well in a community, and/or to achieve an organization's objectives.

WPL engages in a peer-based process where – with and through the other – the individual takes responsibility to become an autonomous person and in so doing contributes beyond his/her own good to the 'common good'. WPL is a risky but rewarding adventure into building a better world through leveraging one's own whole self to make a better use of it while respecting the other as the source of our identity in the community.

Over nearly two decades, at INSEAD, working with business leaders (900 from 50 countries), in small groups of 15, I have learnt that if one can induce a paradigm shift – hence influencing or changing their mindset – and have them internalize a globally responsible leadership model, then their corporations will be different corporate entities.

For that purpose one needs to go beyond awareness (of our interconnectedness, for instance), beyond the discussion of alternative visions (of Chinese or European CEOs, of Moslems or Buddhists leaders, for example), to an effective stimulation of imagination (to escape from the prison of their current definition of problems), while inducing a genuine internalization of responsibility (avoiding passing the buck to one or several other stakeholders), and enhancing the obligation of action.

It is a long, often painful journey but rewarding if behind the model we have a conviction that to climb the mountain if the top is in the haze, it is only the next step which counts. Inherent in the model is a holistic view of the person, the manager, the leader as autonomous individuals with both influence and power, committed to the concept that if change is indispensable and starts with oneself, it needs the other.

This book is an important one: it is clear, well-documented, addressing a real problem, today. It is important as it will give the necessary additional visibility to the WPL approach and to its potential achievement. It is also important as it will be of great relevance to practitioners, change agents, educators, coaches, managers and leaders keen to go into action once they have realized how much more could be used of their potential and talents.

Our planet is in real danger. Beyond climate change, global apartheid, violence and clash of cultures, are we also going to leave to the grandchildren of our grandchildren a world where a selfish gene will have corroded the altruism we had initially inherited, as a person, a Whole Person?

Henri-Claude de Bettignies

The Aviva Chair Emeritus Professor of Leadership and Responsibility, INSEAD, Fontainebleau and Singapore. Distinguished Professor of Globally Responsible Leadership, CEIBS, Shanghai.

PRELUDE

The Three Laws of Globally Responsible Leadership

The Law of the Environment
The natural system is not a stakeholder in our businesses;
it is the ultimate foundation of the rules.

The Law of Interconnectedness
Everything, everywhere is linked in a single system.
Therefore every action must be considered in the context
of its effect on the whole system.

The Law of Engagement
Globally responsible leaders must become engaged in solving
the dilemmas that confront us as a consequence of the first two laws.

Globally Responsible Leadership Initiative [1]

We are living in times when the urgency of action is upon us and more people have more decisions to take than ever; decisions which themselves are more difficult than ever. There are many people in circumstances who possess all the knowledge they could ask for but who haven't learned enough about themselves and how they operate as the instrument[2] employing that knowledge with confidence. We need to do something about this state of affairs urgently in order to help decision-makers become more 'integrated' in how they join theory and practice usefully together and enable them to act more 'congruently'. That is the domain of Whole Person Learning[3] (WPL).

For things to change in the world we have to *enact* any decision we make and that, too, involves us fully. We have to do something to make the decision move from an idea, a wish, or a possibility into an action with consequences in the world.

---

[1] Developed from work by Mark Drewell as part of the GRLI: www.globallyresponsibleleadership.net

[2] The concept of the 'self-as-instrument' is discussed more fully in this book in *Chapter 9: Living the Learning Transition: Facilitating Whole Person Learning,* and in great depth in *Working with Others,* Bryce Taylor, Oasis Press, 2004.

[3] Whole Person Learning, peer approaches and experiential learning are terms used through this book to describe certain styles of learning. Experiential learning is the approach that is a forerunner to WPL (the terms WPL and peer learning can almost be used inter-changeably). Each of these styles and terms is discussed in *Chapter 5: The Emergence of Whole Person Learning.*

When looked at like this, or better still remembered through an example of your own (of a time when you made an important decision – especially a recent one), it soon becomes obvious that acting in the world is a *whole person* activity. It involves all of us. And we know, too, that how well or how soon we make a decision, how carefully or how casually we consider its implications or measure its impact, is important in what it brings about. It is connected to how far we are willing not only to 'enact' the decision – to be 'in' the decision whole-heartedly – but how far we are willing to live out the consequences that flow from the decision as an expression of who we are.

All this makes being in the world a whole person activity.

It makes learning about the world, in an important sense, a whole person activity.

But we do not, by and large, help people learn as a whole person activity.

There have been a number of radical ventures in WPL that aim:

- To engage learners not only in the content in more imaginative ways, but to provide learners with the opportunity to create the very process of the learning

- To engage learners in structuring the events that will provide the learning material.

A major part of such a whole person approach is to be more *holistic*; to take in more of the context and to involve more of the whole person in their relationship to the learning. The more we approach such forms of learning, the more we are looking at learning as a holistic activity and the more we need a holistic account of how it occurs.

The Bicycle and the Ball – a Parable of Holism[4]

When I see the bicycle against the wall I observe it as an object – as a whole that is made up of its parts. If I look carefully, I can separate the parts out: wheels, chain, brakes and so on. If I want to ride the bike, I need to know which parts do what. If I want to build a bike, I need to know even more about which parts are fitted where and how; I take the parts and put them together.

If I want to 'look at the bike' however, really look, then I need to be more receptive than merely 'seeing' it. There is an inner dimension to experiencing anything and that is in part what WPL is centrally about. It invites the person to develop their internal sensing of how they experience the what it is that they are experiencing. In other words, to be conscious as far as possible of their personal relationship to both their experience and the object of that experience; something not strongly emphasised in traditional cognitive based forms of learning.

When I see the planet floating in the dark night of space, the blue jewel, wreathed and swathed in clouds, I know I am looking at a complete entity. It is a oneness. I know, too, that it has component parts; there are land masses, rivers and forests (though less of them), people (more of them), cities (growing) and huge areas of sea (and yet not enough water). When I look at the world I can only see it as a whole. I can only see it as whole until I want to get on with my life upon it, and then I can readily separate it into the bits and pieces that I need and find useful to meet my purposes. Then I can treat the world like a bicycle and think of it as simply a mechanical object that has a lot of spare parts; spare parts for me to make of them what I choose.

And we know, now, the cost of having lived and acted with such a view. The world is not a ball; it is a living entity. Unless we treat it accordingly, it will further unleash its reaction at our ill-treatment of it.

It is not that the 'mechanical' way of seeing the world and separating it out into functional parts has to be replaced, but we have urgently to develop a way of regarding things more holistically and in context – including ourselves and how we operate.

We learn 'to see' at the cost of 'really looking' if we are not careful, or we reserve really looking for moments 'off duty' and for

---

[4] Holism: the innate tendency in nature to create something greater than the sum of its parts. Oxford Concise Dictionary.

contemplation. But we need to relearn (like the Australian Aborigines never forgot) how to be perpetually aware that we are here as guests like every other life form and that we, too, share in the bounty and danger that is part of the earthly inheritance.

A whole person approach is in balance with a holistic view. We do need to see the parts as we work them. We cannot be expected to keep every aspect of the context in mind when we 'interfere' in making a decision or taking action, but we do need to keep revisiting the fact that it is all of apiece. It is all interconnected; all ultimately one and we are part of that unity.[5]

To look at any thing

To look at any thing
If you would know that thing,
You must look at it long:
To look at this green and say
'I have seen spring in these
Woods,' will not do - you must
Be the thing you see:
You must be the dark of the snakes of
'Stems and ferny plumes of leaves,'
You must enter in
To the small silences between
The leaves,
You must take your time
And touch the very place they issue from.
Moofit in Moustakas, 1990:12.

---

5 Unless attributed to other sources, all material in this book is by the author.

CHAPTER ONE

The Need for a New Paradigm of Practice

It is not until I am my real self and I act my real self that my real self is in a position to grow. One's self grows as a consequence of being.
Sidney Jourard, 1971: 32.

In almost every area of our lives there is massive change; there are changing expectations in the social world and in the world of work. These factors are hugely influential upon how we live our lives, how we relate to other people, how we view ourselves in relation to the planet and our concerns for the future. This chapter explores the need for a different way of being – a new paradigm.

Social Change and Transition[6]

A traditional view of the social order rests strongly on four interlinked social mechanisms:

1. Stable hierarchies.
2. Institutional continuity.
3. Widely accepted sources of acknowledged authority.
4. Clearly demarcated gender differences.

From the sixties onwards, all these have come under increasing question and their unchallenged pre-eminence in determining how the social order evolves has begun to undergo major upheaval, with the kind of far-reaching consequences we see around us today. Indeed, even in traditionally ordered theocratic societies, such as present day Iran, where hierarchy, religious institutions and authority have reasserted themselves, a massive social change is nevertheless unstoppable as a result of the education of women and their access to a view of the wider world obtained via modern media and the internet.

No society is immune from the tensions generated by the transition into new forms of social and economic organisation. The process inevitably

---

6 *Forging the Future Together: Human Relations in the 21st Century* (Bryce Taylor, Oasis Press, 2003) is an excellent resource for gaining insight into the world of human relations and how social, political, work, cultural settings all influence the ways in which these relationships are lived.

weakens stable hierarchies, bringing with it a loss of faith in traditional institutions, and in their capacity and willingness to respond to the challenges of the modern world. Sources of established authority give way to the onslaught of new arrangements that are often most noticeably observed in the changes that take place in the position and roles of women, and the consequent shifts in the way gender relations are demarcated.

Gregory Bateson was one of the first people to recognise that when a person enters a new context or when a context changes radically, individuals tend to find meaning by equating the new context with the nearest equivalent with which they are already familiar. This may or may not be helpful because the actual context and their previous experience might be poles apart. As contexts change more rapidly, meaning is not stable, nor is it predictable, and shared agreement between people gives way. This is a recipe for controversy, dispute and fragmentation.

These were some of the influences that inspired Carl Rogers to see the need for a 'person-centred approach' as far back as the sixties. In an atmosphere of such rapid and on-going change, you cannot rely on traditional teaching to help people adapt and find a place in the world. You need to help them acquire skills and understanding that is ever-renewable, and enable them to evaluate information according to its use and its currency. Learning becomes about having the skills and awareness to respond to the context much more effectively rather than the simple acquisition of information.

The structures within which people do their work are changing: they are getting 'flatter', less hierarchical. Similarly, the nature of work is also changing; it is moving away from work-as-labour to work-as-attendance. Much modern work is not labour intensive and does not require muscle power and physical attributes, but has moved to brain power. It can often be done in a variety of places (home, for example) and at a time convenient to the worker (i.e. flexi-time) – a feature that could grow.

> Change is in the world…The world for me may not appear to change; but rather it may seem congealed, constant, fixed. I may also experience my own being as unchanging. In fact, people strive to construct a stable world, a world they can control and get their bearings in.
>
> Sydney Jourard, 1968: 153.

We are entering an era where human relations are no longer something that can be taken for granted: whether in personal, social or organisational life. The changes described above are fast permeating every relationship and grouping. The increase in 'ethical' aspects of business, in the 'stakeholder' society and in the various forms of 'social audit' for organisations, all indicate a shift to include other costs and other effects of the organisation's efforts. 'Ecological responsibility' is gradually forcing its way onto the organisational agenda, as are other forms of social responsibility and corporate responsibility.

Features on the way from Change to Chaos			
Modest Change			Extreme Change
Change	Uncertainty	Unpredictability	Chaos
Structure	Direction	Clarity	Flexibility
Mechanisms	Firmness	Roles	Creativity
Order	Resolve	Contracts	Values
Authority	Position	Negotiation	Relationships

Table 1 ◆ The Features of Chaos

Change, uncertainty and unpredictability are, therefore, experienced by many of us in diverse areas of our lives. This condition is accompanied by an increasing sense that there are fewer and fewer reliable 'givens' – fewer certainties and more unknowns – thereby creating greater insecurity. And then we hit chaos.

One reason for this is that chaos faces human beings with the most unsettling of experiences – the *unknowable*. It is one thing to recognise that there are some 'unknowns' but to work with the *unknowable* brings us face to face with our ultimate limitations; i.e. we do not run everything and we cannot actually predict what will happen – only forecast with more or less accuracy. We are reduced down to size.

Such times will continue to place the relationship between individuals as the central point of departure for developing an understanding of the dynamics and issues of relationship as a major influence on all other aspects of our wider life – be that at work, in our domestic arrangements or in our social world. Human relations are on the agenda for us all, whether we choose it or not.

The World of Careers

In such circumstances, career development, training and educational opportunities become more crucial. As we move towards a world of work in which each individual carries their own portfolio of experience, training and development, and has to present it in relation to a future post they may be seeking, the onus is much more strongly on the individual to carve out their own economic destiny. Life-long employment with a company is, for most of us, a dream of the past.

At a time when groups of staff are expected to work in 'self-managed teams' and when organisations expect their members to become more and more accountable, experience in how these processes and ways of working actually operate in practice will be more and more necessary and required. Individuals with this kind of expertise and the skill to manage themselves will be at a premium; those who have a real understanding of the complexity of facilitating the learning of others in such processes will be more and more prized.

The major paradigm shift is in the change from problem to process thinking. Process demands new criteria and process is the foundation of WPL. The politics of the workplace will have to change or many organisations will simply fold for lack of responsiveness on the part of those working in the enterprise. Implications include:

- More collaborative styles of work
- More flexible responses
- More willingness to experiment
- The recognition of the value of the process of differentiation in organisational life
- Dealing with 'information anxiety'
- Changing our beliefs about what and who we are
- Recognition that the 'culture' and/or 'climate' will influence everything.

The management of ideas is perhaps the most difficult challenge facing most organisations. Many people can respond to tangible difficulties, practical problems – either well or badly – but having to change the way we understand what we do and therefore how we approach what we do is not yet something that is familiar to many in the contemporary workplace. Managing information, deciding what is important and what is not, learning the art of managing temporary decisions and not getting too invested in being 'right' but in getting it 'right enough for now', are all attributes that do not come from a brief seminar.

A Second Renaissance?

We are used to talking of 'paradigm shifts' and 'changing world-views' but we are often less clear about just what they mean. The sixties began the process that made those terms become a part of the currency of everyday thinking.

A world-view is not something that everyone in a society is likely to sign-up to in detail, or even in overall view. People have their personal idiosyncrasies, blind spots and areas of primitive thinking; but a world-view is a prevalent system of understanding for explaining 'what is going on' across many facets of life. When a world-view changes, it is much more pervasive than a paradigm shift; it is much more disturbing. After all, it may be upsetting if your pet theory no longer holds the key to understanding the part of the world you study and in which you are invested, but it doesn't usually unsettle the very basis of how you understand your day-to-day reality.

When your world-view is shaken that is very much the experience; your whole world is unsettled. It feels as though you are now floating in a world of such unstable forces and potentially diverse explanations that an incorrect choice of view to replace your former secure one could have potentially devastating consequences.

When you then take into account that the world-view you once held with such conviction was actually a delusion all along, it further undermines your confidence in selecting another with any degree of success! So losing a world-view is much more formidable an experience than a paradigm shift. Nevertheless, even in the realm of personal beliefs, a paradigm shift can be threatening enough.

Agreement over just what constitutes a satisfactory performance in something as essentially co-creative as relationships is itself, of course, open to dozens of interpretations. Those interpretations will depend upon the values, beliefs, attitudes and frame of reference held by those in question; not to mention the purposes they see as fitting for human relationships.

There are matters of great anguish as world-wide conflicts testify. The following questions highlight differences that cannot be willed away in classroom discussions or on training courses; they are lived with agony and sacrifice unto death in many places upon the earth.

- What kind of place do we want to dwell in together in a world getting smaller by the day?

- What ways do we want to find to relate together, to reach across our differences and find our blessedness in our diversity in a way that is genuine?

- How do we find ways to live beside one another and share the planet together without feeling overpowered by the other or subjecting the other to our own dominion?

- How are we to find the means to make those differences that seem unsupportable and unbridgeable nevertheless manageable?

This challenges us to evolve our consciousness to include a true recognition of those things about which we are not at one and never shall be whilst also attempting to avoid eradicating difference by calls for pious solidarity that has no meaning. Further, it requires us to learn how to meet in ways that both include and transcend conflict to find new forms of co-creative development.

The nature of how we understand and exercise such features as power, charisma, seductiveness, skill, knowledge and so on, all shape and help determine what we make of our relationships and how we 'use' ourselves when we are relating. Relationships are not simply a matter of skills. Indeed, there are many who recognise that the *skills of relating* are amongst the least important aspects of real relating.

Skills can be adopted by anyone with a modicum of ability to mimic another and then perform as though they are sincere, even when they patently are not. Adding phrases like 'acceptance', 'positive regard' and other specialist terms can make someone who has no interest in others *appear* to be empathic – a very different thing from *being* empathic.

Educating Professionals

There is a major anomaly in our current methods of educating professional people. Many people would recognise that deliberate self-aware action and accountable competence are reasonable expectations of any educated professional. As John Heron says:

> ...a fully educated person is, among other things, an awarely self-determining person, in the sense of being able to set objectives, to formulate standards of excellence for the work that realises those objectives, to assess work done in the light of those standards, and to be able to modify the objectives, the standards or the work programme in the light of experience and action; and all this in discussion and consultation with other relevant persons...

Unfortunately, the educational process in most of our major institutions of higher education does not prepare students to acquire this kind of self-determining ability. For the staff in these institutions unilaterally decide student objectives, work programmes and assessment criteria, and unilaterally do the assessment of student work. This goes on until graduation, so that fledgling professionals are undereducated so far as the *process* of education is concerned: they have had no experience in setting objectives, planning a work programme, devising assessment criteria, or in self-assessment; nor have they acquired any skills in doing any of these things co-operatively with others.

John Heron, 2000: 131.

What this all means is that many professionals emerge from their training having been immersed in an educational system which has failed to equip them with the basic self-determining and co-operative competencies that are required for the effective practice of peer review and audit. The education system is slowly changing; more student autonomy in learning is slowly gaining ground. However, there is still a long way to go.

'Professional education' implies much about the training: about examining oneself, investigating the nature of the activity, its utility, its value to those served and its ultimate relationship to the wider society. However, unless it is embraced as an autonomous expression of personal commitment, there is a danger that it becomes little more than a form of socialised training and an induction into corporate rituals and routines. An aspiring professional requires these rituals and routines in order to function in a world governed by a range of professionals each elaborating their own codes and standards of practice to reassure the public; a public that is largely unaware and which finds its own uncertainties not much reflected in the confidence offered by the professionals themselves.

The advent of the professional 'spokesperson' further removes the direct relationship between those who do the work and those who speak about the consequences. Many professional organisations, of course, employ public relations experts to manage their crises in order to mollify the concerns of the questioning public. The direct engagement between professional and critic is less and less seen. Schon,[7] as long ago as 1984 was advocating a change to the existing arrangements – a radical change.

Professional education should be redesigned to combine the teaching of applied science with coaching in the artistry of reflection-in-action.

Donald Schon, 1984: 13.

---

[7] In his book, *Educating the Reflective Practitioner*, Donald Schon highlighted many of the issues surrounding professionals, professional practice and how attitudes and stances towards the 'expert' were fast changing – but not within the professions themselves. It is a situation which continues.

The Future Agenda

The crisis first described so ably by Schon has hardly lessened. The complexities of shifting the emphasis of professional training towards the real world of practice still eludes most training courses, and the academic and the theoretical still triumph over the applied and the practical. Re-focusing professional practice has not kept pace with the changes forced upon the professions themselves. Integrating the contributions of different disciplines still remains the hope of most inter-disciplinary initiatives.

The irony of Schon's contribution is that in order to gain a great victory, little would have to be done, little would have to be spent – only a great deal would have to change. What Schon described most importantly of all was that major improvements to practice were obtainable, not by expensive programmes of curriculum reform and not by re-shaping programmes of study, but by giving up a lot of the separation of disciplines and fields of knowledge for the more demanding exploration of reflection-upon-action and moving to the reflection-in-action that is the hallmark of the artistic professional. In other words, it is a move, in short, towards more of a whole person approach; a more engaged dialogue between all those related disciplines whose work inter-connects. Multi-disciplinary work could and needs to be a crucible[8] for practitioners developing new models of collaboration, negotiation and new forms of integrated practice that cross traditional disciplines. No easy challenge, but one that will not go away.

However, combining them together immediately raises an assault upon the traditional forms of authority that hold professional education and practice and their social standing in place in the wider world. The very changes that Schon advocates are themselves indicative of a paradigm shift; it asks of those involved to become partners in the enterprise of learning alongside their juniors. It changes the nature of the 'learning contract' and establishes a form of *collaborative approach* to learning that would revolutionise the power structure within professions and between its members.

Taken together, we are in 'New Times', and we can find the scale of what we have to tackle together overwhelming, or we can respond with the energy of interest and engagement. We certainly need more flexible and responsive ways of beginning the job. Ever since the explosion of consciousness in the sixties there have been explorations into how people could relate to each other differently, and a diversity of expressions of

---

[8] A crucible refers to an alchemical vessel which takes some raw material and transforms it into something richer. Group process work provides opportunities for personal transformations to take place.

learning and 'being' began to appear, many of which can help inform us on our way to tomorrow.

The new paradigm being offered here is Whole Person Learning. WPL involves, as its name implies, all aspects of what it means to be human: feelings, senses, intuition, connection to others and the cosmos, as well as the more familiar ground of the mind and intellect. WPL is intimately linked with how the individual sees themselves and, supremely, how they view others.

Concepts of the person and personhood are, therefore, crucial aspects of coming to understand WPL. WPL calls for a fundamental transition from traditional, hierarchical and 'power over' styles of leadership and management to a more collaborative, peer-based, self-generating approach in all forms of relationship. It is a change to process thinking and working, a major paradigm shift; a change from just 'following orders' to being part of the process and having influence.

WPL is *future directed* and is a way of preparing people for a world of complexity and deep and 'blessed unrest'. In the book, we explore the concept of the whole person, the peer[9] principle, WPL, learning groups, and address those issues involved in living the transition from traditional ways of operating and being into that of a new paradigm. The approach is new; it is about change and evolution, and it is in flux – awareness, experience and understanding are constantly shifting and deepening. This is very much a live and on-going process. This book is an invitation and a call to engagement; it is not a substitute for the real thing.

It invites you, the reader, at whatever stage of life you find yourself currently, to be part of the emerging story that is WPL; to be part of the transition to collaborative and co-creative forms of working, learning and living. In order to encourage this, we will explore:

- What WPL entails
- Why WPL is so important
- How WPL might be implemented
- The implications of implementing WPL.

---

[9] Throughout this book, we are using the term 'peer' to describe people meeting on terms of parity, equality of potential contribution, no matter what their roles. It also indicates willingness to examine and reformulate power, authority and gender relations to reflect that commitment to equality and the celebration of genuine diversity.

CHAPTER TWO

Whole Person Learning:
Formative Influences

Meaning is in people. Without people there are no meanings.

Anonymous.

The Early Pioneers

Kurt Lewin and his colleagues in the USA in the late 1940s are often hailed as amongst the early pioneers of the movement that led to experiential learning methods and participative learning approaches. E C Lindeman (1926) had also seen the importance of the learner's own experience in adult learning:[10]

> The resource of highest value in adult education is the learner's experience. If education is life, then life is also education. Too much of learning consists of vicarious substitution of someone else's experience and knowledge... Experience is the adult's learner's living textbook.
> In K Knowles, E F Holton and R A Swanson, 1998: 37.

He went on to describe *androgical assumptions* that highlighted the shift from a pedagogical style of conventional education:

> The androgical model focuses on the education of adults and is based on the following precepts: adults need to know why they need to learn something; adults maintain the concept of responsibility for their own decisions, their own lives; adults enter the educational activity with a greater volume and more varied experiences than do children; adults have a readiness to learn those things that they need to know in order to cope effectively with real-life situations; adults are life centred in their orientation to learning; adults are more responsive to internal motivators than external motivators.The pedagogical model is an ideological model that excludes the androgical assumptions. (ibid: 72.)

It was Lewin and others who created ways of working with people that established the field of group dynamics and interpersonal skills development which has grown so substantially and which now influences a wide variety

---

[10] The discussion throughout this book is based upon adult to adult education.

of arenas of practice. Once it was recognised that learners would often internalise learning more deeply and go on to apply it more fully if they were engaged in the learning, many educators of adults have sought to involve learners in the learning – even if it is simply to offer a group discussion instead of an information-based presentation.

Carl Rogers, another early pioneer of what has become WPL, pointed out in his book *Freedom to Learn* that experiential learning:

> *...has a quality of personal involvement* – the whole person in both his feeling and cognitive aspects being in the learning event. *It is self-initiated.* Even when the impetus or stimulus comes from the outside, the sense of discovery, of reaching out, of grasping and comprehending, comes from within. *It is pervasive.* It makes a difference in the behaviour, the attitudes, perhaps even the personality of the learner. *It is evaluated by the learner.* He knows whether it is meeting his need, whether it leads toward what he wants to know, whether it illuminates the dark area of ignorance he is experiencing. The locus of evaluation, we might say, resides definitely in the learner. *Its essence is meaning.* When such learning takes place, the element of meaning to the learner is built into the whole experience.   (Italics in the original.) 1969: 5.

Rogers, like many others since, pointed out that teaching works best when the world is relatively stable and it is continuity of knowledge that needs to be passed on. In his example, he admired the Aborigines of Australia as a great example of the successful transmission of their culture from one generation to another via the teaching of its traditions and its culture in such a way that it had been enabled to survive uninterrupted (and largely unchanged) for tens of thousands of years.

In the modern world, however, when knowledge moves fast, conditions change unexpectedly and unpredictable forces are at play, teaching is less important than learning and learning that involves more of the whole person needs to be fostered especially. We lack adequate descriptions of what is involved in that process and this book aims to help by beginning to provide some of the building blocks of WPL. WPL is already a growing area of exploration and one upon which we will come to rely more and more if we are to develop people capable of managing the kinds of stresses the future is already generating.

Rogers stressed the importance of the learner developing a real (authentic) personal engagement with their world in order to generate meanings – meanings that are not simply subjectively appealing, but which have social weight, personal impact and can help make the circumstances of the person more useful both to themselves and those around them. Without such engagement, and the development of internal self-direction, we know we will struggle.

Mind/body/soul/spirit (or however you conceptualise the elements that make up a whole person – and they do matter in the end) is, in part, an element of the strenuous inquiry all learners have to be willing to undertake as part of the process of learning in a more engaged way. So this book is, in part, an inquiry into just what you, the reader, take to be the elements of what goes to make up a whole person – like you.

The difference between academic interest and personal involvement was dramatically manifest to another of those pioneering figures, Will Schutz, when he began to attend experiential learning events:

> ...there I found what I had been missing. As a group member, I was admonished to tell the truth, hear feedback, and open myself to the world of feelings.... The discovery of the world of feelings was a frightening delight. In addition to letting me gain personal growth, the group experience helped reduce (but did not eliminate) my feeling of being a phoney in my teaching.   1994: 3.

Schutz continued his search:

> T-groups were being conducted by many people who, from the traditional-professional viewpoint were 'unqualified', used 'untested' methods for 'too short a time' with 'inadequate screening and follow-up'. In short, they were 'outlaws' – they intrigued me.

> ...At Esalen, I entered the heart of the Human Potential Movement. I studied and experienced a variety of approaches, drawn from many periods of history and from many countries to develop the full potential of each person and each interaction between people. I tried everything physical, psychological and spiritual – all diets, all therapies, all body methods, jogging, meditation, visiting a guru in India and fasting for thirty-four days on water. These experiences counterbalanced my twenty years in science and left me with a strong desire to integrate the scientific with the experiential.   1994: 6.

Providing opportunities for group members to discuss the implications of what they were learning and inviting them to think ahead to how they might apply it in their own circumstances (essentially a more *participative* involvement) is familiar to many of us now but was radical at the time. From there, participants were soon being enabled to shape some of the learning itself (*experiential* methods) in events such as interpersonal skills training. As methods developed and the role of Humanistic Psychology became a stronger influence, the challenge of involving learners at all stages of the learning process began to become open for exploration. Thus the foundations for WPL itself began to appear.

Organisational developers have long been supporters of new ideas and new methods of doing things, keeping abreast with developments in learning methods and their potential application to their own concerns as a way of keeping pace with change. Action Research (AR), Appreciative Inquiry, Action Inquiry (AI) and Participatory Action Research (PAR) have all been seen by business educators as having potential and they have been effectively implemented.

The growth and development of Humanistic Psychology and the Human Potential Movement in the sixties were two of the most essential influences on the ethos out of which WPL approaches have evolved. Hywell Williams is only one of several commentators who have pointed out that in the 1960s something shifted in our understanding of our place, not simply in the world, but in the cosmos as a result (he argues) of the US and Soviet space programmes. He writes:

> Other earlier civilisations and empires established a dominant culture within their boundaries. Those boundaries seemed to them the limits of culture itself, but the capacity to see a single world with one pair of eyes – a moment that perhaps first arrived when humans went into space in the 1960s – did have a deep emotional impact on such parochialism.
>
> Hywel Williams, quoted in the New Statesman Review, 2005.

The United States was the place where the experiments with personal direction and the wish to explore the inner world were soon to match the need to explore outer space now that the terrestrial frontiers were all but exhausted.[11] Once you had arrived in California, there was nowhere else to go except 'up and out', or 'down and in' and there was no shortage of volunteers to try either or both. It is no wonder that the growth movement found its home in a state that already had Disneyland, Hollywood, the Space industry and a society that had achieved the most prosperous standard of living on the planet.

Existential philosophy also had a radical influence upon the developing counter-culture. It placed freedom at the centre of the individual project,

---

[11] No account of the development of the human potential movement would be complete without acknowledging the contribution of Esalen Institute in Big Sur California, regarded as the first 'growth' centre. Esalen has had world-wide influence and was the venue for those who sought to work with leading figures of the emerging discipline of humanistic psychology.

choice as its expression and authenticity as the impulse that drives humanity forward in its attempt to act in good faith, in real contact with oneself and one's deepest needs.

This experiential approach to learning puts participants and their own process central to the learning they achieve. It seeks ways to enable them to learn how to 'use' them-'selves', (the 'self' that is theirs, that is), in their various roles and relations. Thus, the person is seen as the crucible for development. The person has the capability of moving beyond their often self-imposed limits into new realms of freedom and potential. Whilst many existential thinkers saw, too, how routine and banal much of what passes for modern life actually was, nevertheless the movement aimed to reach out beyond the prosaic and make contact with the deeper reaches of human nature.

Underlying Values of the Human Potential Movement

Humanistic Psychology became concerned with exploring the individual's potential and capacities in order to enhance the individual, their inner life, as well as their social world. It is also sometimes referred to as 'the third force', to distinguish it from behavioural and psychoanalytic approaches. It transcends the traditional academic boundaries and is as much educational as it is clinical. Amongst its key figures were:

- Abraham Maslow, who became interested in 'peak' experiences and how individuals could function in more highly effective states
- Stanislav Grof, who brought a serious interest in altered states of consciousness and the domain of the transpersonal as a field of investigation
- Carl Rogers and his developing understanding of what was to become known as a 'person-centred' approach to helping and educating
- Will Schutz who brought together a range of body/mind methods in his development of 'Open Encounter'.

The early founders of the Human Potential Movement developed methods, techniques and ways of working that have become much more widely adopted but the philosophy and underlying belief system has not always travelled so well. Many of the methods and approaches of Humanistic Psychology have been adopted within conventional educational practices; experiential learning, for instance, owes a great deal to humanistic educators.

Some of these approaches have very different techniques, and at first glance it may seem difficult to identify any common ground. An Encounter approach, for example, superficially seems to work very differently from a transpersonal approach. However, the Human Potential Movement enshrined a common cluster of important values that enabled it to distinguish itself from other contemporary enterprises. WPL wasn't conceived at this stage, yet the values enshrined within WPL were developed and deepened out of the values given here:

- An openness that encouraged individual willingness to risk
- Acceptance that those who came into its orbit would take what they needed and move on
- The valuing of personal experience
- Validation of the importance of subjective experience as the basis for development and change, rather than the interpretations and judgements of external experts[12]
- Learning in a collaborative way
- Approval of the desire to enhance one's own capabilities
- Openness to work with the struggles that arise in any group of people working together
- The effort to explore authenticity
- Emotional competence was encouraged instead of elevating intellectual understanding.

'Know What' to 'Know How' – the Question of Application

A good deal of the energy of the Human Potential Movement was spent in getting to *know how*, rather than in learning more about *knowing what* (learning more *about*) or learning more about *knowing why* (*theorising*). The focus was on *knowing how* to go about bringing more useful or more satisfying results in the world – usually the world of the participant. Not all those taking part in workshops throughout the land were narcissistically self-absorbed; there were many who had a deep concern that the newly-

---

[12] Subjective experience is not placed over and above other forms of knowing, but is the starting point for developing personal knowledge. Many of those involved in this work were themselves very gifted academics who found that academic explanations were not the whole story and that the implicit view of the person taken by much contemporary thought was restricted, pessimistic and unadventurous.

developing process of learning would result in beneficial changes in the world.

This is the beginning of a key transition point in approaches to learning.

With little support or encouragement from the conventional world, individuals and groups began to explore and experiment with putting together things that, at the time, had no obvious direct relationship: meditation and dance; martial arts and communication skills; biofeedback and fire-walking; mind control techniques and bioenergetics; shamanism and hypnotic training; yoga and the Enneagram; working with posture and movement linked to art and poetry.

The potential combinations were limited only by the willingness of someone to put together a way of exploring these apparently unrelated fields of activity and a group of people willing to experience the impact they had. Opportunities were practically endless, limited only by the human imagination as the interest in exploring the farther reaches of human nature exploded.

People learned by first hand experience that physiology is, indeed, 'the key to consciousness'. They learned that states of awareness are linked to positions, posture, breathing and muscular holding-patterns and that all of these help to create a cluster of mind-body associations that contribute to the overall state itself. To change the state you need, at the very least, to change the activity. This can be summarised as recognising that the mind-body is all one system: what happens in the body affects the mind. How you feel affects how you think. (You can at times override it, or think you can.) What you think influences how you feel. You are a holistic operating system.

Many of those who took up an interest in experiential learning had already tried social action and found that, without some self-understanding and some awareness of the unresolved nature of the impulses and internal conflicts that drove the crusader with such passion and zeal, most social action brought little serious benefit. Many saw the need to begin to attend to the instrument of the self before going around polishing that of others. Unless one had an understanding of one's own dynamics, how could you possibly really change systems for any longer-term benefit?

Given this kind of impulse, it was not surprising that in the early days theory wasn't a strong feature; experiential learning was about exploring:

- Knowing how to influence
- Knowing how to change people (starting with oneself)
- Knowing how to change systems (starting with those you encountered).

Although this can and does become highly subjectively focused, it also leads to a more attentive gaze on those things that the individual is bound to encounter rather than what they might theoretically understand.

Nothing was taken for granted. Individuals were encouraged to build their own frameworks of understanding. Rigour came by making clear what was being attempted and how it fitted together. It wasn't necessary to find acceptability within an existing body of theory or method. Canons of respectability were still largely unknown.

Because of its ready interest in application, the findings from Humanistic Psychology and the Human Potential Movement drew considerable interest from those involved in the training and education of managers and leaders in the world of commerce and business, for they too are concerned less with 'Why it works' and more with 'Does it work'? And if not, 'How do we get it to work?' T-groups themselves had originated as a means of improving the interpersonal sensitivity of those taking part – drawn largely from industry and commerce. Macgregor's Theory X and Theory Y from that period[13] was well regarded as offering an alternative account to influence both the way in which the world of work could develop and the way in which people could be motivated to reflect the kinds of social shifts that were already taking place.

Gregory Bateson's influence can be found in different forms in so many of the disciplines and activities that began to emerge as the sixties progressed. He is perhaps most well-known for his work on the 'double bind' theory, but the contribution of his work establishing the relational nature of the way people develop is inestimable. NLP, to give another illustration, took a great many of his ideas and reshaped them. The discipline of Ecology owes a great deal to him and so it goes on. Bateson was someone who had already recognised that the traditional division between fields of study were not going to survive the shifts and changes of consciousness and experience that people were beginning to encounter.

As the current of inquiry and development that Humanistic Psychology reflected got underway, its influence could be seen in the work of people like Argyris and Schon. There was, too, an increase in its application to people in organisations in addition to those original pioneers of human consciousness. Gerry Egan developed his organisational perspective during this period; linking the work of counselling to a greater understanding of context and system in a series of influential publications.

---

[13] Theory X and Theory Y were two styles of management: one traditional and one that reflected the 'new realities' (to quote a phrase that management thinker, Peter Drucker, used as the title of one of his books).

Whole Person Learning Formative Influences: the UK

Interest in what was happening in California had led to some sporadic efforts to create a groundswell of involvement in the UK, but it was not until a team of Encounter group leaders and workshop facilitators from the USA came to a gathering organised at *The Inn on the Park* in 1970 that the movement really begin to take off in the UK.

Over a period of several days, European enthusiasts and pioneers had a first-hand opportunity to work with and explore the methods that were generating such interest. Out of that gathering, and the momentum it helped create, came a number of initiatives that took hold not only in the UK but in other parts of Europe too. Two important developments concern us here:

1. The opening in March 1970 of the first privately-owned growth centre in the UK and Europe, Quaesitor, based in London.

2. The establishment in November 1970 of the first university-based growth centre in the UK and Europe, the Human Potential Research Project (HPRP) at the University of Surrey under John Heron's guidance.

The HPRP pioneered major innovations in applying whole person experiential methods in a wide range of courses and workshops in the fields of tertiary education, adult education and the continuing education of diverse professions. This work included: intensive facilitation training, interpersonal skills training, peer self-help counselling, organisational change consultancy, participative research in the human sciences, group dynamics, academic tutoring and teaching, the development of student autonomy and holism in learning, self and peer assessment and accreditation, the training of GP trainers of new entrants to general practice, and more.

Quaesitor was a focal point for anyone interested in experiential approaches. It was successful in its early years until one of its guiding lights, David Blagdon Marks, drowned in the Irish Sea as a result of a boating accident. The shock and the resulting impact upon the newly-emerging group of practitioners was immense and losing one of its most entrepreneurial figures at so early a stage proved to be a major set back for the movement.

Since the community of practitioners and participants (who were one and the same for most purposes during this early period) was still in its infancy, discussion about the future of the work took place largely amongst the same group of people in the different arenas in which they met and peer self-help was the model. This led to a number of experienced facilitators forming the Institute for the Development of Human Potential (IDHP) in 1976.

John Heron was part of all these discussions and played a key role in the formation of the IDHP. His academic background helped create the intellectual foundations for the rationale that brought assessment and accreditation processes to a clear and rigorous expression and which, in turn, helped strengthen the guidelines and conditions for course development. Whilst by the 1980s there was some form of growth centre operating in most larger cities[14] in the UK, they largely offered short-term events that didn't require any great theoretical underpinning in the way that a two year diploma in Humanistic Psychology required – especially one that was to claim parity with other post graduate programmes.

The IDHP was a self-managed peer-based entity established on a not-for-profit basis to promote peer-based experiential learning at Postgraduate level. Under its auspices, programmes of Humanistic Psychology were approved and supported. All of its Advanced Diploma courses were taken through a rigorous self and peer assessment process along with a similarly rigorous self and peer assessment process for intending facilitator teams – which had to be a man/woman working partnership (to manage gender differences). Programmes had to demonstrate a commitment to:

- Individual personal development
- Group process
- Social action.

Initiating facilitators were expected to facilitate the group into its own empowerment. By the second year, the learning group would manage its own life, including: finances; securing staff for the visiting facilitator weekends; organising residentials; paying for the use of venues and so on. Final assessment was based on self and peer assessment with facilitator assessment as a guide and a check, and the whole enterprise was supervised and supported by the IDHP itself, which met regularly in London.

An IDHP course was a form of WPL in earnest, taking place, as it did, part-time over two years with something like 430 hours of facilitated experience, in a mixture of one-day, weekend and five-day meetings.

Each course was expected to find some link to a major institution of Higher Education with the aspiration that, through such a link, IDHP programmes might begin to develop a dialogue with mainstream faculties (something that rarely happened).

---

[14] The Rajneesh movement was a major provider of short-term experiential events for a decade or so between the early seventies and eighties. Although still in operation, it is on a much reduced scale.

Many IDHP graduates went on to work in the world of organisations where the interest in finding effective ways of applying new ways of learning, as we have pointed out, was strong. Learning Edge, Chrysalis, Leading Edge, and The Oasis School of Human Relations (Oasis) in the sphere of social organisations are just four such examples. In addition, individuals often offered themselves as coaches and mentors long before these terms had the ready understanding they do now.

Following John Heron's departure in 1984, the HPRP came under the guidance of new figures and the Human Potential Research Group[15] (HPRG), as it became known, later began to offer a mainstream MSc in Managing Change. This course had a strong component of WPL and self and peer assessment that attracted people from organisational backgrounds. Lancaster University offered an MA in Management Learning that was based on a model of peer learning. Peter Reason's work at Bath led to the formation of CARPP (Centre for Action Research in Professional Practice) that also involved participative and experiential methods strongly linked to the WPL approach and values.

In addition to his role in the IDHP, John Heron was a founding member of the UK co-counselling community. John was a strong supporter of the techniques of co-counselling (a peer model for emotional self-help), but his conceptual clarity identified a fundamental contradiction between the methods devised and how the community of practice – Re-evaluation Counselling (RC) – was subject to control by its founder Harvey Jackins.

John Heron thus broke with RC early in 1974 and helped inaugurate a more radical and peer-based model of organisation and practice, which became known as Co-Counselling International (CCI). This was launched in the summer of 1974 by John Heron with Dency Sargent and Tom Sargent from the USA, who had also separated from RC. The first CCI workshop was run in the UK in September 1974 and there are still regular workshops in many parts of the world. The break from RC is an indication of a deep commitment to the peer principle and the concepts of mutuality and parity.

Between 1977 and 1985, John Heron – while continuing on as Honorary Co-Director of the HPRP (until 1984) – was also Assistant Director of the British Postgraduate Medical Federation, University of London, where he held responsibility for the continuing education of doctors. Here he introduced whole person educational methods into postgraduate courses for

---

15 The Human Potential Research Project (HPRP) underwent a succession of transformations after John Heron's departure in 1984 including a change of name to the Human Potential Research Group (HPRG), and has now been absorbed into the School of Management at the University of Surrey.

hospital doctors and GPs; launched a co-operative inquiry into whole person medicine – which led to the founding of the British Holistic Medical Association; and pioneered peer review audit among GPs using self and peer assessment to monitor and maintain standards of medical practice. All this has had a considerable long-term influence upon many doctors.

One of John Heron's major contributions to the evolution of WPL at this time (and they continue to this day) was to bring a critical rigour to the deep exploration of both theory and practice. As we've acknowledged in this account, theory was not a strong focus in the early days of the Human Potential Movement. Indeed, if you read Will Schutz's own account, it was an overdose of theory and academic discipline that drew him to question the whole basis of learning as an adult and that, in turn, led him to design his approach, which he termed Open Encounter.

WPL needed a theory and it needed a theory that was congruent with its practice. As much as anyone in the UK, John Heron, in a succession of publications, provided much of that thinking. Throughout the eighties, culminating in his book *The Complete Facilitator's Handbook* in 1999, John Heron has continued to revise and extend his thinking about the implications of a whole person approach in a contemporary setting – as the Bibliography illustrates.

A fundamental application of this approach has been in whole person research in the form of co-operative inquiry, developed by John Heron between 1971 and 1981, after which he invited Peter Reason, a fellow member of the IDHP (and now a professor at CARPP, the University of Bath), to collaborate in initiating three co-operative inquiries and in co-authoring several introductory papers on the method.

Another leading figure at the time was John Rowan, a member of the Association of Humanistic Psychology in the UK and author of one of the earliest and most comprehensive summaries of the newly emerging field of Humanistic Psychology, *Ordinary Ecstasy* (1976). The book was one of the few texts written in the UK (updated several times since its first publication in the late seventies) that outlined what new forms of experiential learning involved and described many of its influences. Rowan went on to write *The Reality Game* (1983), which outlined many of the features of a humanistic approach to the practice of therapy and he has been a significant influence in bringing the ideas of Humanistic Psychology to a wider audience.

These three, Heron, Reason and Rowan, were also members of an informal collective, the New Paradigm Research Group. Out of this group came the beginnings of a more clearly and rigorously formulated experiential research methodology. This methodology was detailed in the influential publication *Human Inquiry – A Source Book of New Paradigm Research* (1981) edited by Rowan and Reason. *Human Inquiry* was, and remains, a foundational text both in the level of seriousness and the range of papers it contains. Contributors to this publication explored the theoretical implications of the emerging field of experiential inquiry from a number of positions. Contributors included John Heron (whose two chapters further developed the founding theory and method of co-operative inquiry), Rom Harre, Don Bannister (personal construct theory), Judi Marshall, and William Tobert from the USA (still a leading figure in the world of Action Research and who is quoted later in this book) along with contributions from the editors.

The Open Centre and the Minster Centre were both important focal points of the emerging body of practice in the UK based in London.

The author of this book was involved in the foundation of the Leeds based IDHP Diploma in Humanistic Psychology[16] (1981), first as a participant before jointly facilitating two further diplomas. During 1981-87 he was also a committee member of the IDHP and participated in the developing IDHP approach. Visiting facilitators to those IDHP programmes included John Heron,[17] Peter Reason, and John Rowan; along with Tom Feldberg (another IDHP founder), Brian Coombs, Eva Chapman, Alix Pirani, Frank Lake, (founder of the clinical theology movement) and Peter Hawkins (a founder of the Bath School of Counselling and Psychotherapy). Many of the founding figures of the Humanistic movement, including most of the above, also came to offer workshops in the earliest days of what was later to become the Oasis School of Human Relations.

In retrospect, the efforts of the IDHP in promoting the Diploma as a long-term educational venture provided an important base for deepening the theoretical framework and methodology of emerging WPL.

---

[16] The Leeds-based IDHP Diploma in Humanistic Psychology was initiated by Beryl Heather, an associate of the Career Counselling Development Unit (CCDU) of Leeds University. The CCDU, a semi-autonomous institute of the University that promoted participative approaches in education, was founded by Barry Hopson and his associate Mike Scally. They were amongst the first, and certainly the most well-known, developers of what came to be known in the UK as Lifeskills material. Indeed, so successful were they that they left the auspices of the University to create 'Lifeskills', a thriving training organisation that works largely within the commercial sector.

[17] The author's long-standing and continuing relationship with John Heron has had a significant influence upon the ideas discussed throughout this book.

The Appearance of Whole Person Learning

As more strands, insights and ideas about how adults learn most effectively emerged, WPL began to appear. These strands included the awareness that:

1. The more involved the learner is required to become in their own learning, the more the conditions of that learning need to reflect the nature of an adult to adult relationship.

2. 'Communities of practice' are successfully able to evolve without hierarchical authorities.

3. Individuals can be involved not only in what they are learning, but in what they are going to learn, in how they are going to do that learning and also in assessing how successfully they have accomplished their learning.

Communities of practice can explore all these ideas in a non-hierarchical way as the basis for any collaborative endeavour, especially in developing effective working relationships and active citizenship in general.

These three features listed above are useful ways of learning on the way to WPL. But WPL includes all these and goes beyond them, because it includes the person in a much wider network of influences and within an overarching view of the person and those influences. Why, you may ask? Because WPL has an underlying and developing sense of the nature of the person and what it might mean to be a 'whole person'.

Any educational endeavour is based on some premises about the nature of the person being educated, and that's the place where the WPL account starts. John Heron writes about the person in the following way and it is in this sense that we too use the term throughout this book:

> A person is a particular focus of development within the field of universal life and consciousness, unfolding a unique creativity within it, and emerging though progressive differentiation from germinal to transfigured states. In Reality there is no separation between a person, this unified field, and all the other beings embraced within it. A person manifests through a self or ego, which is the focus for choices made in everyday life. The ego can become contracted, isolated and alienated from the wider field of being; such a contracted ego within the person is a rigidity shaped by psychological wounding, the way our use of language splits subject from object, and deep tensions inherent in the human condition. Loosening that rigidity and liberating the ego for openness in living, means that a person can uncover her or his true heritage, becoming both creatively distinct within, and participating in, the universal field of being and its constitutive beings. John Heron, personal communication, 2007.

Education and an Educated Person

'What is the nature of the person?' is, therefore, the question that stands at the heart of any educational venture. How we view the role of the person and what we consider to be the obligations, privileges, rights and duties of the person all underpin our view of what makes up an educated person. As the inspiring being Thomas Merton wrote:

> Personalism and individualism must not be confused. Personalism gives priority to the *person* and not to the individual self. To give priority to the person means respecting the unique and inalienable value of the *other* person, as well as one's own, for a respect that is centred only on one's own individual self to the exclusion of others proves itself to be fraudulent.
>
> Thomas Merton, 2004: 5.

These considerations should inform the educational process that we provide if we aim to encourage the person to emerge more able to fulfil their personhood as a result of their educational experience.

Indeed, criteria for a successful educational experience could include:

'How far does it enable individuals to experience themselves as persons in their own right?'

'How far do people engage with the implications of being a person in relation to others?'

'How far are they encouraged to explore themselves as persons alongside and with other persons in relation to them as persons?'

Put like this, a good deal of present-day educational activity assumes much of this can be left to itself. And yet the above issues matter more than just about anything else in an age when more straightforward ways of learning can be gained from such an amazing range of sources.

The focus on content and the ability to absorb and then to reproduce the given subject matter in examinations is of little value given the nature of the transition taking place that we described earlier, something noted by EC Lindeman as far back as 1926:

> Our academic system has grown in reverse order: subjects and teachers constitute the starting point, students are secondary. In conventional education the student is required to adjust himself to an established curriculum; in adult education the curriculum is built around the student's needs and interests... Texts and teachers play a new and secondary role in this type of education; they must give way to the primary importance of the learners.
>
> E C Lindeman (1926), in K Knowles, E F Holton and R A Swanson, 1998: 37 (6th ed).

A system based on the accumulation of knowledge often rightly claims to create a certain attitude of mind, a respect for clarity of information and the ability to absorb the fundamental aspects of the tradition upon which the knowledge base is built. But it also fails many people very badly. It does little to help people work out those aspects of practice that rely upon the integration of knowledge and application; i.e. theory and skills brought together in the performance of the task to be done. In any consideration of what needs to be done there are at least four strands about which the individual needs to know more:

1. Themselves.

2. How they relate to others – colleagues, customers, stakeholders.

3. The processes that are taking place between them and others – the micro and macro dynamics of the 'system' in which they are operating.

4. Any contextual shifts are taking place and the potential implications they have upon whatever course is decided upon.

These four areas indicate a radically different starting point compared to most traditional educational provision. They are also especially crucial in organisational life, particularly in global organisations or those whose

Attributes of a Contemporary Educated Person might include:

- Having a grasp of themselves as whole persons: inheritance, mind/body/spirit; we can term this 'self-awareness'

- Having some notion of the social roles they perform and how they interact with others

- Having some level of due regard, recognition and consideration for others

- Having developed some moral imagination that enables them to enter into the world of the *other*; albeit tentatively and even inaccurately at times

- Having a set of values that they can articulate with more or less fluency, given the complexities and choices that make the human condition the exciting and exacting project that it is

- Embracing the capacity to contribute to the decisions that effect their lives.

members come from more than one culture. Yet it is precisely these areas that a primarily conceptual and cognitive approach to learning leaves largely unattended. These four areas are also linked to the qualities an educated person would display as described in the box on the previous page.

Whilst most of those attributes outlined above would pass uncontested in most conversations about what constitutes an educated person, the implications that flow when any one of them assumes priority over others takes different thinkers in widely different directions and therefore to widely different destinations. Depending upon the emphasis and priorities selected, programmes are constructed, curricula designed, methods developed, all of which leads to a system being created with a particular *ethos*.

If you assume, for example, that an educated person is someone:

- Who has both a right and a duty to take part in the decisions that affect their lives

- Who plays an active part in the community to which they are attached

- Who displays an involved concern toward those people and things they care about,

then much current educational practice falls outside the task of the preparation of persons.

A dilemma is apparent: if you are not fit to be regarded as an educated person in relation to your own learning until someone else tells you that you have achieved the desired state, then how and when do you assume authority over the bigger and more complex matters that affect your life? If you are only qualified to make judgements because someone else decides you are, how do you develop an authentic understanding of your own personal authority? If the only way to take up a role is by having to conform to the expectations of others who dictate the terms of how one is to operate, then how do we learn to influence the events that affect us elsewhere in our lives and develop a sense of personal authenticity about what we value and how we promote it?

The internal commitment of the learner to follow their own standards of practice and to articulate their own values about what happens to them is thus largely incidental to the educational process and largely excluded from playing any major part in the learning process – and deliberately so. Herein lies a further contradiction: an educational process that sets out to promote the educated person, and yet goes about it by a method that violates one of the most fundamental aspects of the definition, i.e. that a person has the capacity to play a part in the assessment of their own learning and has a right to be fully involved in and responsible for their own learning!

If you have authority and you exercise it, you employ power – well or poorly. Power is often wielded through the benign disguise of 'influence' (but always in the knowledge that the power stands behind you, should you need it). Asking a class of students to do something rather than ordering them, say, is just one example of the use of apparent influence, but it is a form of influence that draws upon a power structure which lies only just below the surface. You can have authority and not exercise it. You can also know you have it, others know you have it and you can refrain from employing it – but you nevertheless still have it by virtue of the position you hold within the hierarchy of relations of those involved in the endeavour.

Power involves the exercise of the will. You can use power with no authority from anyone else in an unaccountable and degenerate manner. You can use power judiciously, accountably and in proportion to the needs of the situation without having formal authority to act. You can also use the power of office with little degree of self-awareness and little regard for the consequences. The employment of effective personal power, whether or not it rests alongside positional power, is to use power awarely, discriminately, responsibly and with a willing accountability.

Organisations ask people to use personal power in ways outlined in the duties attached to the position to which they have been appointed. They may also hold a degree of authority that goes with the position but it may not match the individual's internal sense of their own authority. Here lies the dilemma. People who do not know how to use power are put in positions of authority: some overuse it; some refuse to use it until they absolutely have to – the point at which it is usually too late. Power needs to be exercised *with* people, not over them. WPL provides a process by which people can become more self-aware, more self-generating and therefore more able to use power appropriately and with awareness.

The Challenges Ahead

It is becoming more apparent that the individuals emerging from our current educational institutions often gain educational qualifications[18] that do not equip them for the demands that are increasingly made upon the citizen of the twenty-first century. This is the person who is hailed as '*the*

---

18 In July 2006, the author attended a conference (*Beyond Reflective Practice*) of some 100 academics who were very concerned about the difficulties the academic curriculum places upon their ability to prepare their students for real-world practice.

self-managed learner', for example, or who now needs to '*work in teams*'. It is the profile of someone who is required to possess a range of attributes that have never previously been required; someone who is suddenly expected to look forward to taking up a place in the great *collaborative* adventure that is to be our future. Such fashionable notions are promoted as though they are no more than simple adjustments to action, slight modifications to practice when we know they stand at a fundamental divergence from the educational experiences individuals receive.

People do not learn to assume their internal authority at the command of others, nor do they learn how to become 'self-managed learners' or 'good team players' because there is a new social requirement for these attributes. What they learn, all too frequently, is how to absorb the rhetoric, and how to manufacture a 'performance' that leaves the incongruity, the doubt and the difficulty of internalising the new requirements with their existing value-system all unresolved. The result is that there are large numbers of people, some in influential positions, who have an idea of what they are promoting, but little internalised experience of what it really involves and no safe place to explore it!

The Role of Whole Person Learning

If there is a need for people to possess these attributes (rather than understand what they are and why they might be important) then people have to be given opportunities to practice what is involved. They need opportunities to learn, from reflection and discussion, what the implications are – for them. They have a right to participate in the discussion, at the very least, about how these will impact upon them rather than be sent the command from mission control with the full expectation that in due time these new social attributes will be displayed. Such a shift requires some form of experiential learning and some form of greater participation in the nature of the enterprise than is usual in a traditional system.

Carl Rogers realised some time ago that traditional learning is restricted and restricting, and that there were possibilities for more; something more comprehensive and embracing:

> It is learning which takes place 'from the neck up'. It does not involve feelings or personal meanings; it has no relevance for the whole person. In contrast there is such a thing as significant, meaningful, learning.

> Let me define a bit more precisely the elements which are involved in such significant or experiential learning. It has a quality of *personal involvement* – the whole person in both his feeling and cognitive aspects *in* the learning event. *It is self-initiated.*   Carl Rogers, 1969: 4/5.

This personal involvement and quality of self-initiated learning are, however, part and parcel of what goes on in a *Whole Person Learning Community* (WPLC).[19] All those questions raised by the future we face are well practised and deeply entered into in a WPL programme that works on a WPLC model. And arduous and rigorous it is. It is nothing less than a radical alternative paradigm.

> Self-initiated learning which involves the whole person of the learner –
> feelings as well as intellect – is the most lasting and pervasive... It is the
> whole person who 'lets himself go' in these creative learnings. An important
> element in these situations is that the learner knows it is his own learning and
> thus can hold to it or relinquish it in the face of a more profound learning
> without having to turn to some authority for corroboration of his judgement.
> Carl Rogers, 1969: 162/3.

WPL as a form of education, as advocated here, will never be cheap. WPL is people and resource intensive, or, to put it more elegantly, it will always require those involved to spend a good deal of time together, to meet and to engage with one another and not simply absorb some aspect of the subject matter, area of knowledge or practise some skill. In this respect, and others, it is at odds with the prevailing ethos of our culture: a culture that elevates materialist ambitions and which views education as a passport to gain access to the wealth of commodities that are in abundance everywhere. In such a society, education itself has already become a commodity to be consumed and a means of self-advancement in the economic race against those around you.

One result of this overview is to provide a guide to the implications for those involved in designing educational provision. Another is to emphasise the link between educational practices and how they reflect and reproduce the nature of the relationships between the citizen and the state, the individual and society; and to remind us that the way education occurs is an implicit but very pervasive model of how many other things get done.

We need to encourage learners to explore how to manage the uncertainties of planning their own learning process, how to collaborate with others in a similar endeavour and how to take shared responsibility for the outcomes. These are things that must inform classroom activity if we want citizens who are self-critically aware and responsive to those around them.

WPL methods have a future simply because it is only in peers meeting, collaborating and exploring together that useful answers to many pressing

---

[19] A WPLC is where we meet WPL in its most collaborative form in the spectrum of the peer paradigm possibilities.

social problems will be discovered. In the field of research, qualitative methods and participative approaches are increasingly undertaken. More and more individuals expect to be consulted and involved in decisions that affect their lives. Indeed, this is now a statutory duty for many public services; a duty that is fulfilled in many ways, ranging all the way from efforts that merely pay lip-service to the process to genuine comprehensive attempts to involve the person more fully.

A peer approach to learning is a hugely useful way of enabling individuals to begin to manage some of the complexities, the ambiguity and ambivalence that inevitably arises when individuals are pursuing a variety of contending directions. Increasingly, groups, teams and gatherings of folk will have to work out their priorities *together* and will have to learn how to integrate needs, share time and arrange useful ways of working things out.

The place of power and authority are crucial aspects of how easily – or otherwise – WPL can be transferred to traditional systems, or establishments, hierarchical organisations of all kinds, and many of the other groups to which we belong. How these twin forces influence and control how free we are to make our own autonomous choices is taken up further in the next chapter.

Chapter Three

The Power of Choice

The truth is that as a man's real power grows and his knowledge widens, ever the way he can follow grows narrower and narrower until at last he chooses nothing but does only and wholly what he must do.

Ursula le Guin, 1993.

Presence and the Whole Person

Inherent within this concept of being a whole person is the notion of presence: of a person striving to be wholly present to oneself, whilst also being wholly present with and to the other(s). Engagement with others is a prerequisite for such presence to be both valued and for it to develop.[20] Because in so many aspects of our cultural life our feelings of embodiment are suppressed and we are required to adjust and conform to external requirements, enriching the possibilities of embodied experience are rare and often become distorted.

Presence is influenced enormously by our ability to manage ourselves, especially when old patterns of behaving and habitual ways of being threaten to engulf us. It relates to how we present ourselves to others, how we feel about ourselves and, crucially, our willingness – or not – to bring our whole being into relationship with the other. It has, therefore, huge implications when examining issues of power and authority, and how they are exercised.

The place of presence is not found once and then held in perpetuity, although it does have a sense of continuity about it. It is about expressing one's fullest capacities whilst not shrinking or hiding; it is not about attempting to gain a position, out-compete someone or making use of one's power in a manipulative manner. It is a process of learning and discovery which is life-long – and beyond, depending on your belief structure.

---

[20] Every meeting has the potential for meeting at three levels – intra-personal (within oneself), interpersonal (between one or more people) and transpersonal (that which is beyond the person, the spiritual, the numinous). It may be that the focus of some meetings takes place at a purely intra-personal level without the other elements being present, but when working from a transpersonal perspective it is inevitable that each element will be present in some degree. In other words, some things are an expression of my intra-personal experiences and can be seen as independent of my interpersonal and my transpersonal experiences. There is a sense that things are reflected in other levels and of how the 'whole is greater than the parts'.

Whole Persons and Choice

Choice is both a foundation and an expression of personhood. Choice is one substantial way in which we experience ourselves as persons. The more sophisticated our understanding of how choice operates (rather than holding to a simple notion that choice = 'getting what I want'), the more it leads us to consider the whole question of *presence*[21] and how we bring ourselves 'present' to an occasion or an experience.

Effective choice is based on the growth of healthy self-esteem. Someone with a secure sense of self neither avoids choosing for fear of causing offence (because they can deal with any differences they create by demonstrating their emotional competence), nor needs always to ensure that they have their wishes fulfilled each and every time they express them. They can negotiate and modify their choosing in the light of new information, especially in the light of unexpected or previously unclear consequences that may be pointed out by others. Working out how to deal with one's choices openly with others is therefore a major crucible for learning about how to become a whole person.

In conversational usage, we easily speak of 'freedom of choice' and use terms like the 'right to choose'. When we start to examine how far we are actively responsible for the choices we make and how clear we are about what they are, we soon learn we are much less free than we generally claim we are. We discover we make far fewer *real* choices than we would like to believe. It is almost a self-deception to believe that habitual behaviour is a result of 'choice', or that compulsive actions are somehow 'freely adopted'. Only when I bring choice, action and consequence together does it start to take on the kind of meaning being described here.

It is fairly easy to sit around a restaurant table and discuss political, social or economic ideas. In such circumstances, it is not difficult to be as radical as you like. Other people might disagree with you vehemently but nothing is likely to change as a consequence – not even a change of mind because these tend to be well-rehearsed social exchanges. In our educational experiences, our views about what to do and how to go about it are largely irrelevant to what will happen. Not so in a WPL group; in a WPL group they are the essence of the enterprise.

All of us live with a degree of freedom, but it is not a freedom that requires much in the way of accountability, unless we establish a way to become accountable (a theme which runs throughout this book). All of us can make

---

21 The notion of presence described in Chapter 12 of *The Complete Facilitator's Handbook* (John Heron, 1999) is a really valuable resource in the exploration of presence; it works from the ground up, building different layers and capacities out of the human condition as an embodied being.

> Suddenly choice takes on a much more immediate and electrifying significance. What is decided and how it is decided become highly meaningful because it affects *me*.
>
> > It is no simple matter, for example, to recognise and then challenge some form of alliance taking place between a number of people, who always seem to come up with a similar pattern of behaviour or kind of suggestion.
>
> No decision is taken for granted in WPL and neither does it have to pass by unnoticed or unacknowledged. The commitment to attempt to increase the intentionality and awareness of all is a powerful motivator for unravelling *how* things happen rather than *what* happens.

choices, more or less consciously, with more or less intentionality, but no one needs to know either what the choice was or how it turned out unless we speak about it. Even then, we can speak about it in any number of ways according to the audience we are addressing and the way we wish to present ourselves.

Individuals can be in the present in such a way that past concerns do not intrude. Therefore they are managing their past; they are not governed by it or ignoring it. When this state is reached and when they are not disabled by anxieties that the future may fail to live up to their demands, then they begin to have a greater freedom of choice about a good many things.

Learning with others, deciding what to do in what order, facing the prospect of talking before my peers, introducing ideas, sharing experience, leading a group through a process – all are potentially daunting prospects for most people entering into WPL for the first time. Understandably, they need support and facilitation if they are to overcome those inhibitions and self-limiting beliefs. They need encouragement and assistance if the group is to develop a climate where individuals genuinely believe that they are there to facilitate each other – a belief that is a fundamental prerequisite to WPL.

Until we meet our own experience of these things we are only in the land of speculation. Much of that speculation will be all too accurate – ensuring we generate the very experiences we expect. All of which makes some change very difficult to contemplate, let alone attempt. On the other hand, people also discover they have many fears that have no real substance at all and they take delight and enjoyment in the possibilities for influence that their new-found freedom opens up for them. No one can know about these things for sure in advance. It is one of those things like life: there is no rehearsal.

The fear for many is that the group will let them down, inflict familiar painful distress-laden experiences, or worse. For some, facing their lack of control over events in the group is a major issue to work through. For still others, the realisation that they are not as free in disclosing really important aspects of their inner life as they had always believed is a deeply disturbing revelation. Of course these things can and do also bring great delight to many. Realising that long-held fears of what can happen in a group have no real place in the present, or that an over-concern about what others might think of oneself can actually be faced and overcome, or that efforts to disclose or challenge oneself will find support and appreciation from others – all these things and more are amongst the benefits. For each person it will be a surprise which learning comes with which experience.

People can only learn what is there for them to learn at the time: another reason why WPL has to be self-chosen and cannot be prescribed.

The Benefits of Choice and Commitment

All these forms of insight and awareness are a vital aspect of learning about the possibilities of personhood. They can only be done in company with others committed to the same enterprise. Indeed, *commitment* is the critical foundation for the enterprise to get underway.

There are many people who choose to enter programmes that are peer-based who are certainly there by 'choice' as conventionally understood. In other words, they have elected to be there, are willing to pay for their place and to take that place up; however, some do not remain because the level of commitment to sustain their involvement proves too great.

The process of decision-making in company with up to fifteen or twenty others can turn out to be too daunting and some individuals face major difficulties. These difficulties concern aspects of relationship about which we may be more or less aware and they relate strongly to essential *interpersonal needs*[22] that all persons have. This includes the need for *inclusion* (how much we seek to belong), the desire for *control* (how far we need to influence people and events) and the degree to which we can face *openness* in relationship (how self-disclosing we can be and how far we can share intimacy with others).

---

[22] This is a truncated account of the work of Will Schutz, author of *Profound Simplicity, FIRO-B, The Truth Option* and other books. FIRO-B is a theory of interpersonal behaviour that looks at three major aspects of human interaction. The theory was developed by Will Schutz in the late sixties and seventies and it is still widely used as a reliable method of establishing individual performance within the realm of interpersonal relationships. It fits well within the theory of group development. These interpersonal needs and the social drives we all experience are explored more fully in *Chapter Eight: Individual Experiences in Whole Person Learning Groups.*

Every individual has these needs to a greater or lesser extent. We each have varying ways of seeking their fulfilment and expressing the degree of the need. Together they make up our interpersonal style of relating.

Choice is not easy when it requires a willingness to share the power with others. Amongst all the other things you are going to be learning, you are likely to learn that:

- You will not always get your own way and you may well come to learn how it feels to put great energy into something few others care that much about

- Unless you are willing to have some enthusiasm to start with, then you are unlikely to get much of what you want even discussed

- Even if everyone else knows your interest, unless you promote it they will be too busy promoting their own views.

Selfish? Perhaps, but it is the result of everyone seeking to make real choices for themselves and reflecting the reality of the commitment required to ensure all are fully engaged. The struggle and the rich harvest make WPL groups a uniquely valuable experience.

Power and Authority

Choice, in the end, is about power. What power do I have to influence what happens to me? What power do I believe I have to influence what happens to me? And what may befall me if I venture to have aspirations, voice them and work towards attaining them? None of us is without painful experiences at the hands of those who have misused their power – either deliberately or unconsciously. Given the level of unawareness on the part of those who hold authority in our culture, the exercise of benign *power with* others is one of the major areas of learning in any WPL group enterprise.

Power is a very difficult force to manage. By and large, society prescribes who has power, how much and how it is to be managed. But power and authority of that kind are increasingly becoming de-coupled. The sixties, for all they are reviled or revered, saw the beginnings of a major shift in the development of the Western world that is likely to be every bit as important as the Renaissance was five hundred years ago. In the sixties there came a gradual dawning of awareness that individuals could, should and must learn to take increasing responsibility for themselves in all aspects of their personal, social and political life.

For the last part of the twentieth century, the idea of *personal responsibility* has extended to cover more and more areas of our conduct and in more and more parts of the globe – though not everywhere as yet. The increase in individualism is a mark of this shift. Most adults now regard it as unsurprising that they are responsible for their own actions, even when they have not considered all the implications. Investigations are now made into people's conduct that goes back years as a result of the socially understood belief that we are always responsible for what we did.

A mature society recognises that citizens are free beings who are accountable; that those who serve society, those who hold power and position, are answerable to those who elect or appoint them. No one is exempt from being accountable and having to take responsibility: corporate executives or Boards, medical specialists, leading religious figures, political leaders – all come under the same potential for scrutiny. This represents a major turning point in human society.

In all this, we are describing the transition from externally authorised, appointed and designated forms of authority to a future in which the norms will be much more those of negotiated, democratic, and participative forms of authority. WPL embraces the peer principle (see *Chapter 6: Whole Person Learning in a Peer Paradigm*) and thus becomes a laboratory for new forms of power sharing to be applied in a meaningful way, for decisions to be made jointly, for differences to be embraced creatively and for healthy controversy to reign.

It is one thing to remove confidence in external authority and it is quite another to live out of a self-chosen form of inner authority. As people lose confidence in something that appeared unassailable and find that it isn't, it brings a complex form of ambivalence along with it. On the one hand, it brings a restless rush of freedom to take power to themselves and, on the other, the deep insecurity of not knowing the best way to proceed.

The collapse of external authority does not match the pace at which individuals can take up their internal authority. The psyche has spent many centuries under the sway of kings, leaders, priests and others who exercised undisputed *power over* and it is not going to be an easy transition to remove the internal authority figures carried in our heads. Nor is it going to be straightforward to separate the genuine exercise of internal authority from the distorted expression of long-repressed desires to manipulate or make others do my bidding. All of us are contaminated by the distorted expression of abusive forms of authority.

Internal authority, matched by a will to demonstrate my personal power suitably and appropriately, is therefore not something any of us can claim to know much about yet! We do know that it will lead to very different forms of expression and much more human ways of being together than those that have been traditional for centuries, and which have been used by societies world-wide throughout those centuries to curb the freedom of the majority of their citizens. In the end, traditional forms of authority are sustained by those in authority believing others (those who do not have authority) cannot be trusted with 'it', whereas those who do hold it can be trusted. We who hold it must strenuously ensure we (and others like us) maintain it in order that the less fortunate, who could not begin to understand the weighty responsibilities that go with carrying authority, remain untroubled by such serious concerns! A caricature, but not such a great one and one based on a patronising form of assurance that 'all is as it needs to be'.

Personal Empowerment

A fundamental aspect of promoting a whole person approach with individuals is to encourage them to develop a trust in their own experience, to enable them to develop a way of:

1. 'Sensing' the ways they have of making 'sense' of what is taking place and the effect it is having upon them and others.

2. Refraining from leaping to obvious interpretative conclusions that may only 'make sense' because they fit into their particular categories of idiosyncratic past experience.

3. Remaining open to the unusual, the particular and the specific about this experience in order to allow its distinct contribution to 'appear'.

In his book *Focussing*, Gendlin talks of 'bracketing off' – a term he borrowed from some of the early phenomenologists. The concept of 'bracketing off' is to 'act as if…' it is possible to put markers around aspects or elements of our experience in order to explore them more carefully. 'Bracketing off' a part of an experience allows us to examine more carefully what took place, how it is composed and how we respond to it. In 'focusing' work, Gendlin taught people a very simple technique for recognising their 'felt' sense of things in order to guide their response and he placed great emphasis upon self-directed learning.

In other words, we become able to separate *this* experience from the rest of what is going on along with our responses to it; separating it enough to enter into it with greater attention and therefore gain greater awareness of what is at play. It can be seen as a form of *mindfulness practice* in which we become healthily and naïvely open to our experience once again. This is in contrast to understanding our experience on the basis of our acquired, conventional understanding.

Since cognitive skills are granted such an overwhelming priority in our culture, the idea that someone who is conventionally well-educated, thoughtful and successful should have much to learn about their own experience is one of those challenges that makes WPL the radical endeavour it is.

How do you help someone who already has a view about what is happening suspend their belief for long enough to look again and find more? This is a hard bargain to sell. Most people, when it comes to bringing this kind of attention to their experience and the meaning they make of it, have a surfeit of meanings and don't want anyone else's – not even one more of their own. Responses range from suggestions of 'navel gazing', 'it's a luxury', 'it's point-less' to 'not having the time' and so on, yet when someone does take the opportunity seriously the rewards are tremendous – greater awareness, greater self-esteem, greater presence (as the poem that concludes the prelude reveals).

Suggestions that the 'affective dimension'[23] may be a more influential force upon what is taking place is not going to be received with joy or even pleasure by someone who has placed all their future hopes and past education on the acquisition of cognitive information. Uncertainty and change are not often faced with eagerness and anticipation! It is a new realm and one that holds many pitfalls and possibilities for rendering the very basis upon which the individual 'codes' their reality inadequate, at best, and inoperable, at worst.

WPL has this effect and has it early, because you cannot invite individuals to be open to their experience without them encountering the fact that the *reality* they believe they know so well is largely composed of previous experiences and long-ago acquired beliefs about themselves, others and situations of this kind.

Most of us place a great deal of our personal identity and individual security in the convincing explanations we have for what is taking place. Surrendering that to explore alternatives is highly threatening.

Most people, therefore, have insufficient warrant for trusting their experience about a good deal that goes on in groups and in WPL events. This renders them novices when they may otherwise be regarded within their own world as experts. The resulting gap that opens up may be uncomfortably wide. This in turn may release further reactions to the

---

[23] The affective dimension refers to those areas which are largely ignored in many traditional learning situations i.e. our feeling life, our emotions and interrelationship of our mind/body/spirit components.

experience they are having which prevent them from developing a clearer view both with and of the instrument they are using – namely themselves.

Trusting one's experience is therefore a voyage of epic proportions.

Challenging though all might sound, and it is, there are tremendous benefits for undertaking a WPL process. Greater awareness of how you make choices, what influences those choices, how power is manifested in your life – or not, and how you respond, say, to the way power is used by those whom you meet, will all contribute to living more fully, being more alive and being a more self-generating individual. From this point, then, the following chapter takes us into the realm of the Person, Personhood and the conceptual framework underlying WPL.

CHAPTER FOUR

What Kind of Person?

The person playing the role has a 'self' or I should say he is a self. All too often the roles that a person plays do not do justice to all of his self. In fact, there may be nowhere that he may be himself. Even more, a person may not know his self. He may be self-alienated. His real self becomes a feared and distrusted stranger. Sidney Jourard, 1971: 30.

In this chapter, we explore the numerous arenas in which an individual both has an influence and is, in turn, influenced. The commonly-held notion that we can operate in isolation is countered by the strengthening realisation of the inter-connection of all beings and the links between different systems and bodies that can only be ignored at our peril. The link between individual actions and their impact on the planet can no longer be avoided. It is essential we take note and respond accordingly before it is too late for our planet and ourselves. Here, we focus on the importance of relationship and how we might transcend the traditional and 'conventional' ways of relating and responding to all that is around us.

The Human Being and an Interconnecting Web of Relationships

The human being exists in a network of relationships, interconnecting arrangements and interdependent systems. We are born incomplete and unfinished. The human individual is unique and unrepeatable: a cosmic one-off. We are also interdependent beings. I need you in order that I can become me. I also need you to become you in order for me to also become me. We need each other if we are to become more than we currently are.

> … 'dependency' or 'aggressiveness' or 'pride', and so on. All such words have their roots in what happens between persons, not in something-or-other inside a person. (…) I will get nowhere by explaining prideful behaviour, for example by referring to an individual's 'pride'. Nor can you explain aggression by referring to instinctive (or even learned) 'aggressiveness'. Such an explanation, which shifts attention from the interpersonal field to a factitious inner tendency, principle, instinct or whatnot, is, I suggest, very great nonsense which only hides the real questions.
>
> Gregory Bateson, 2006.

Sydney Jourard, writing at the same time as Carl Rogers, was someone else who was intrigued by the emerging possibilities for the human story. He was similarly engaged in describing the main essentials of what we would now recognise as a 'person centred' approach. In the course of his two most well-known books, *The Transparent Self* and *Disclosing Man to Himself*, Jourard identified four characteristics that he repeatedly refers to as distinguishing features of the person:

1. The search for purpose.
2. The need to seek meaning.
3. The expression of values through choice.
4. The commitment the individual demonstrates to making something of himself, i.e. the expression of the first three aspects of the human condition via the idea of *projects* – activities that give meaning and that express both value and purpose.

Persons are persons only in so far as they are *persons in relationship*. Without the other there is no I. Lost in the other, there also is no I. I and the other have to recognise ourselves as distinct and yet not separate; connected but not so enmeshed that we become indistinguishable. Only then can we become engaged on the task of assisting one another to move beyond who we currently are. Only then can we make more of a contribution as the distinct individuals we have the potential to become.[24]

> In systems thinking, a whole person is to be defined not simply in terms of the integration of all internal parts, but also in terms of the integration with wider wholes of which the person is her or himself part. In other words a whole person is to be defined in terms of both internal and external relationships. The inner nexus and the outer nexus are interdependent in a total web of relations.   John Heron, 1999: 310.

We are connected to those around us through our inheritance and our initial family circumstances, social group, locality and nation state, and ultimately to the wider human family. We are a living part of the arrangements of social structures and institutional arrangements. Our lives are directed by political systems, economic structures and the increasing forces of globalisation. We are also shaped and influenced in part by our

---

[24] If holistic learning of a subject raises issues of what a whole person is, learning how to be a whole person does so even more. General systems theory, increasingly evoked as a post-positivist paradigm (Bateson, 1979; Capra, 1983; de Vries, 1981; Jantsch, 1980; Koestler, 1964, 1978; Laszlo, 1972), commends itself as a framework for thinking about personhood; as noted by John Heron in the *Complete Facilitator's Handbook*, 1999.

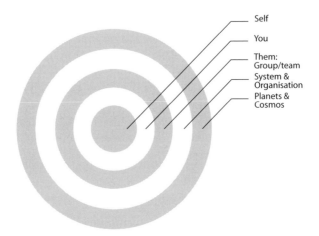

Figure 1 ◆ Interrelated Fields of Influence

surrounding world, landforms, climate, and the abundance of the natural world, the hardships of nature, the planetary system and cosmic forces.

As we become ever more aware of our interconnectedness and our interdependence as one human family, which shares a common destiny on a spinning globe out in the cosmos, so we are ever more aware of that globe getting smaller and our destinies becoming ever more intertwined.

Considering the implications of this interconnectedness and interdependence for educational practice and social organisation, Heron makes the following observations:

> What this model brings out for the definition of a whole person is that to be one involves the complete web. A whole person means someone who is in a set of whole interpersonal relations in a whole culture in a whole planetary environment integrated with its transplanetary field. In each case here, whole means developing in orchestrated harmony. Since the web is not in this state, but is torn and damaged, such a definition is about the end-state of human development. As a definition for today, it is unrealistic and inapplicable. So we have to choose one that is more workable.
>
> The next closest definition, it would seem, is that whole persons are those who have exercised their relative autonomy to integrate their intrapersonal life – so far as this is possible within a total web that is limited – and who are involved in a combined interpersonal, cultural (socio-structural), ecological and transplanetary change programme of activities and commitments. In other words since they cannot now be in a whole and healed web, they are seeking to bring one about. Whole persons are internally together change-agents of a rather comprehensive kind. They are defined in terms both

of relative psychological integration and of holistic initiatives in the other four interdependent spheres. Whole personhood is faced with a paradox. Until all spheres are healed and hale it cannot be achieved, and it can only be achieved by making them so.

What is clear on a systems view is that the purely individualistic account of personhood is at an end. A person is a vast web of inner and outer relations, and all our respective webs overlap and interweave. And the outer relations beyond the intrapersonal are multi-dimensional. As well as culture, nature and cosmos, they include the psychic or subtle and the spiritual. John Heron, 1999: 312-313.

Ego Consciousness and Society

All societies prepare their members to take up a part in the social order. In order to take up a place we have to be identifiable and have an identity. In short, we have to become a *somebody*, which in turn requires that we have an ego and that we work with ego consciousness. Ego consciousness is far from the only form of consciousness, though by its nature it is limited, narrowly focused and self-centred, often identifying what it believes is in its own best interests, even when those interests may be self-defeating. Ego consciousness quickly develops patterned ways of thinking, feeling and believing about 'reality'.[25]

Ego consciousness is the dominant mode of operating in Western culture and the 'developed' world. Ego consciousness reinforces and is reinforced by the idea of ownership, separation, accumulation of wealth and status as a means of shoring up its latent insecurities. We take these aspects of the world around and within us so much for granted that we regard it as the natural order, forgetting that it is a product of thought, convention and social agreement.

There is nothing intrinsically permanent, right or unalterable about this state of affairs. It is predominantly a product of a way of thinking about ourselves and the world around us and it has brought about some lasting and beneficial changes to human affairs. Ego consciousness is a stage in the evolution of humanity; it is not the end product. So whilst it has enabled us to develop our understanding and influence over the natural world, if ego consciousness is left to its own devices we stand in danger of it bringing about inestimable harm to our long-term future. We are so caught up in the world of ego consciousness that we can scarcely conceive of an alternative form of consciousness except in rare moments of imagination.

---

[25] 'Reality' is a social convention dependent on a sustained agreed consensus that things will mean what we agree they shall mean.

> A good deal of our contemporary economics is centred on the manufacture
> and then the satisfying of what might be termed artificial desires. Indeed, the
> 'health' of the economy depends upon this destructive cycle. Modern
> commercial culture thrives upon the continuous invention of 'needs' in order
> to create an insatiable demand for products to satisfy the need that has thus
> been manufactured. As Lao Tzu put it: 'No sin can exceed (the) incitement to
> envy, no calamity's worse than to be discontented'.   L.G. Boldt, 1999: 60.

Ego desires have been around throughout history, but it is only in the
present era that we have developed a culture that sustains itself by
mobilising their discontent and creating a seemingly insatiable desire for
more. The narrow little ego is triumphant like the infant running the
household. The satisfaction of artificial desires via the twin demons of
consumption and accumulation requires enormous amounts of effort and
resources.[26]

It is not that we should stop material prosperity expanding further across
the globe. But when such prosperity comes at the expense of the real needs
to support life that are so desperately needed, our long-term future is put in
jeopardy. Public health measures, good water, clean environments, suitable
housing, social justice: these are not luxuries, but they are not yet a reality for
many in the world.

> Ethics is born of physical life, out of the linking of life with life. It is
> therefore the result of our recognising the solidarity of life which nature
> gives us. And as it grows more profound, it teaches us sympathy with all
> of life... This material born ethic becomes engraved upon our hearts and
> culminates in spiritual union and harmony with the creative Will which is
> in and through all.   Albert Schweitzer in L.G. Boldt, 1999: xxxvi.

Individuals do not operate in a vacuum. The values and organisation of the
wider society shape their range of choices if not their ultimate expression.
The expanding encouragement for citizens to become increasingly identified
with consumption has replaced our participation in the affairs of their
communities and local affairs.

Ego Consciousness

> 'Once upon a time' is really 'Once beyond time' and the tale which follows is
> of a world which temporarily suspends space and time, where play rules

---

[26] In 1990, global expenditure on advertising was estimated at $256 billion; more than the GNP of
India in the same year (quoted by Boldt). Currently, US consumption would require 6 planets, and UK
consumption 4 planets, to satisfy the demand if projected onto a world-wide scale. That such
consumption is unsustainable is a truism but it still remains a catastrophic situation.

supreme and anything is possible. And in as much as the real world is no-boundary, the language and the imagery of mythology is really much closer to that reality than is linear and abstract thinking. Mythology begins to transcend boundaries – boundaries of space and time and opposites in general – and for that reason alone mythological awareness is one step closer to the real world of suchness. Ken Wilber, 1979: 126.

We have moved out of the land of story and myth, at some cost as well as some benefit to ourselves. We live, to draw on Ken Wilber's work, in a world of boundaries. The ego works with 'this/not this' distinctions.

It is easy to confuse the person with their individuality and to regard that individuality as tied together with the narrow concerns of their ego consciousness. And it is this confusion of the person with their personality that helps give rise to and reinforce the economic conditions that are a threat both to the planet itself and to our sustainable survival. It includes a narrowing of focus that brings everything down to the bottom line of desire. Attention is focussed upon the relentless pursuit of narrowly interpreted self-interest – so often at odds with the deeper interests and wholeness of the person.

The experience of separation arises out of the formation of the ego with its capacities to discriminate and distinguish all that is 'I' from all that is not 'I'. In a theoretical sense, we may understand that we live in a world of no boundaries, no separation and interdependent unity. However, in our daily lives the limits of our physical senses and the social conventions through which we process the 'information' that comes to us gives us the experience of a world that has some very sharp edges and some very demarcated boundaries.

For all our theoretical acceptance of the above paragraph, we nevertheless get very offended when the door resists our wish to pass through it because it has the effrontery to open the opposite direction to the one we expect! In numerous encounters in our daily life, we so easily forget the inter-connectedness of all things in favour of being reminded that we are very separate indeed. We are very capable of getting our self-image dented and our self-esteem reduced by some experiences that are remarkably insignificant in the grand scheme of things, but which, nevertheless, we allow to 'get to us'. Learning how to develop a measure of watchfulness and lack of pre-occupation with the ego is the aim and object of almost all spiritual traditions.

The structure of the ego relies on maintaining a concrete and limited sense of time and space. The dominant mode of the ego in action is comparison – this against that; here against there; mine versus yours; ours against theirs. Its function is to engage in constant calculation to maximise what it regards as it own advantage (understood in the narrowest of terms). It is constantly attempting to reduce what it regards as the ever-present threats to its fragile sense of security and permanence. Ego consciousness fails to sense the continuity and presentness of actual experience, and can find little peace or rest as it shunts back and forth between dwelling on the past and obsessing about the future.

The restless, anxious ego constricts consciousness and fuels a runaway culture of materialism. It also takes its own survival as the final arbiter of worth, and the satisfaction of its own desires as the ultimate pursuit of existence. Since it is self-referential, it either 'reads' all contrary explanations and suggestions in its own image, incorporating them as sub-texts to its own greater glory, or discounts or distorts contending explanations of the value of the person. It supports and sustains the dominant paradigm; a paradigm that an increasing number of thinkers and activists from all disciplines and areas of social life recognise threatens to engulf us in disaster. It is in the nature of ego consciousness to operate on an unexamined and barely reflective norm that leads to very real threats to our planetary future.

Ego consciousness cannot bear to acknowledge anything beyond itself – especially the possibilities of transcendence. It refuses to accept its biological source, the unity of all life. It cannot give up its relentless campaign of self-justification without feeling diminished in the process. Although ego consciousness is a social requirement and an important stage of development on the road to personhood, it always runs the danger of affirming its own supremacy. It depends upon the 'fact' of separation of subject and object, self and world, in a way that ensures it is at permanent war with itself – via the 'shadow' that increasingly seeks expression the more it is fiercely denied or discounted.

The shadow is a term first coined by Jung to account for all the unowned, unacknowledged aspects of the person's psychological makeup, not yet incorporated into the ego consciousness. The shadow is not negative; it is simply that which is not yet known. What is not known is not recognised as belonging to the subject of which it is a part. As aspects of the unknown (shadow) appear they have to be refused – denial being one of the commonest mechanisms for displacing away from oneself aspects which one disapproves of and does not want to acknowledge. These fragmentary 'parts' then express their independence in unaccountable and often self-destructive or damaging ways in the form of projections and distortions, which are then explained away or simply denied when brought to attention.

Almost any form of development that aspires to assist the growth of the person to some functioning sense of personhood needs to engage with the shadow aspect. Since amongst the contents of the shadow are all those unwanted and unowned aspects that we would rather believe are not truly an aspect of ourselves, owning them is a journey of painful self-revelation that requires courage and trust. But if we are to gain the value that accompanies what we deny and displace, and make use of it for our potential growth, we have to be willing to be open to the resources that lie in the shadow area. This effort to integrate, and bring into some form of relationship, internal aspects of the 'self' is an important stage in developing the ego consciousness to something approaching maturity on the way to personhood. As Ken Wilber expressed it so well in his book *No Boundary*:

> … Thus, to give just a few very brief and general examples, the aim of psychoanalysis and most forms of conventional psychology is to heal the radical split between conscious and unconscious aspects of the psyche so that a person is put in touch with 'all of his mind'. These therapies aim at recruiting the persona and shadow so as to create a strong and healthy ego, which is to say, an accurate and acceptable self-image. In other words, they are all oriented toward the ego level. They seek to help an individual living as person to remap his soul as ego.
>
> …. In extending the person's identity from just his mind or ego to his entire organism – as-a-whole – the vast potentials of the total organism are liberated and put at the individual's disposal.   Ken Wilber, 1979: 12.

As the growth of personhood evolves and the individual incorporates more of all that they are into their available sense of themselves, then they are able to be at ease with themselves internally. They are more likely to be open to possibilities rather than insisting upon their own way. Including the good and bad alike (terms that begin to mean little as we move beyond the narrow 'right'/'wrong' view of life and events that so dominates the ego consciousness), the individual is less and less judgemental and narrowly 'selfish', and much more a functioning whole. Rather than being at sea, adrift upon a tide of conflicting ideas, aspirations and contradictory emotions, the emerging person has a steadiness of purpose and an internal centre of action.

Breakthrough to Mindfulness

Behold the clarity of nothingness. Emma [27]

---

[27] Emma was a participant on a co-operative inquiry researching 'Transforming the World through Transforming the Self' supported by the Blaker foundation of the Scientific and Medical Network, and facilitated by the author and a colleague, Joan Walton. The initial length of this inquiry was over two years (2001-2003) and the participants continued to meet for a further two years. Even now, some of the inquiry members continue to meet.

There are many accounts of the formation of the ego consciousness from psychological and cultural observers and social scientists. The account offered here is a working framework and, for the interested reader, other accounts can be found that are much more detailed.[28] The framework included here is chosen because it emerged from an eighteen-month co-operative inquiry into the terms 'integrated practice and holistic (whole person) learning', initially facilitated by John Heron in San Cipriano, Italy in 1998. These stages seemed to many of us to express something of the nature of the learning we had achieved; supported by accounts of other researchers of course, but it was ours.

1. **Pre-ego:** undiscriminating field of awareness. The infant without language.

   Consciousness at this stage is undifferentiated and almost exclusively identified with needs satisfaction.

2. **Ego formation:** congealing consciousness into an emergent sense of self whilst open to ineffable experience simultaneously. The child grows into a sense of itself. 'Look at me!'

   As the emerging person travels through the experiences that are associated with infancy, encounters 'others' as distinct from the 'self' and begins to learn 'who they are' and who they are expected to be, then we see the first stages of ego-formation. In other words, becoming someone recognisable to themselves and others.

3. **A) The Sub-Conventional or Wounded ego:** over-identified attachment to threatening sources of experience from the past. 'I am both without needs and at the same time I am deeply in need of special attention.' There is ambivalence and sudden shifts of position, and a narrow field of identified awareness. 'My personality is me. I am separate from all.'

   Somewhere in late teens and early adulthood we have a sense of who we are, and who we are not; those things we belong to and those we reject. Our identity is something that we know has continuity over time (or so we believe). We have also begun to acquire that shadow-side and we denounce those things in others that we don't like in ourselves, or excuse those things in ourselves for which we would rather not be accountable.

---

[28] Humanistic Psychology has a number of accounts that are both readable and accessible. Gestalt and Transactional Analysis, perhaps two of the most well known, are practically useful and can be appreciated using whole person methods.

There is a healthy aspect to the functioning ego and there are also parts of that functioning ego that can become problematic and dysfunctional, given sufficient 'pressure', stress or reminders of previous traumatic experiences.

Almost without exception, each individual experiences some highly charged and seriously threatening experiences before they reach adulthood. These may take the form of experiences from abusive others, from natural events, from illness and so on. The consequence of such traumatic encounters is to reduce the functioning ego from clarity about what is happening, replacing it with strong over-reactions that are related to the accumulated and un-discharged distress of the past.

The age at which these 'traumatic' experiences occur and the type of experiences they are – how prolonged, how they are dealt with by those taking care of us and so on – all determine the degree of dysfunction and the range of 'trigger' experiences they bring into play in our day-to-day life. They also influence how far we are aware of their impact or not.

Once these reactions are underway, it is very difficult for the individual exhibiting them to have any objective insight into how 'taken-over' they are by the reactions they are displaying. Of course there are some people whose personal history is so compromised that they are operating at this sub-conventional level a great deal of the time – irrespective of whatever social position they might hold on to.

B) The Conventional or Self-managing ego is exemplified by the person who can work within the restraints of the conventional world; can sustain a role and manage their responsibilities with a degree of ease; can recognise they are self-accountable and self-responsible – though not necessarily all the time.

The self-managed ego is expressed through the capable individual that we all would like to think we are the whole of the time. Usually, we aren't. The self-managed ego is then a construct that helps identify how we would like to be and how we often are, but which from time to time we 'leave'. We 'leave' because some emotional association takes us back into past experiences or we get caught up in anxieties and concerns that take us away from the steadiness of 'here and now awareness' out of which real choice derives.

Most accounts of learning assume adults are in this state during the learning process, when they are applying their learning and when they are being examined or assessed. But, as we know only too well, this is anything but the case!

Only with some degree of emotional awareness, via opportunities to develop emotional competence and insight into how emotional dynamics influence one's 'performance', can someone begin to claim they are working with something approaching a self-managed ego. Even then, it is not a permanent feature of life. The recognition that comes with this stage of development is that we have an increased level of awareness but that it is tentative; that it is available more than it was and that there are still areas of functioning that will benefit from further emotional development.

Commitment to develop this degree of personal autonomy is a prerequisite for WPL. Taking responsibility for one's own emotional difficulties when they occur; dealing with them responsibly rather than 'projecting' them on to others or denying them, and being open to skilled facilitation to minimise their impact are part and parcel of what goes with WPL.

4. **The Semi-autonomous or Self-creative Person or Open ego:** relaxed field of open awareness. 'I am present to my experience.'

With appropriate support and assistance as I grow into adulthood, there are large areas of my functioning awareness that remain uncontaminated by any of these past hurts and difficulties. I am operating freely and with a contemporary awareness. I am neither importing judgments nor fears from the past, nor anticipating concerns and anxieties about the future. I can appraise the situation, the responses others make and the needs of the circumstances with a degree of equanimity. I can make choices based on information and preference rather than out of defence or insecurity.

My attachment to a role or a position is reduced and my 'identity' is as much related to my inner relationship as any outward connections. Ambitions, aspirations, challenges and all life's turbulences have a real and deep impact, but I am not attempting to force life away nor cling to desires that are a form of protection. I am much more able to create lasting commitments yet not get so invested that I lose myself in regrets or self-satisfaction. I can take life with a degree of equanimity. I am on my way to richer states of personhood. I may not be a self-transfiguring person[29] but I am more and more a self-creative person able to set about my own projects, act autonomously, rejoice in my contribution and accept my limitations with a good deal of compassion.

---

[29] John Heron outlines his own range of personhood states in some detail both in *Helping the Client* and in *Feeling and Personhood*.

5. **The Self-transfiguring Person or Minimum ego Identification:** reflecting in action; able to be with themselves and be in touch with their own process. 'I am present to myself and that which is before and outside me. I am distinct but not separate.'

    With some considerable commitment to development and inner work, the person begins to emerge and flourish; is able to spend greater and greater amounts of time with no strong ego attachment. They, of course, know how to play the role expected without being overly invested in it. More and more of their activities are generated from their inner appreciation of what it means to be an emerging person relating to all that is around from a position of unity and connection. They move away from the stance of being one thing relating to other things, taking what it seeks by virtue of its 'power over'. As Thomas Berry expresses it, 'we are no longer amongst a collection of objects but part of a communion of subjects'.

The table overleaf gives a more detailed breakdown of the above ego states three, four and five i.e. the conventional and sub-conventional ego, the self-managed ego and the minimum ego identification, and relates them to another, business-related in this instance, framework – The Seven Modes of Being.[30] This tool was devised to help managers understand the way in which they need to manage both themselves and especially their staff in relation to where they function in the table. In both views, there is a major point of transition from operating within relatively adapted behaviours to a much more autonomous way of behaving.

    Getting this point across is far from easy, not least because no one operates within just one category; we move between them. Moving to more sophisticated levels of responsiveness and working from a more relational perspective allows greater flexibility of contribution and greater openness to working with difference and challenge – all of which require an ability to manage oneself in increasingly challenging situations through the use of negotiation.[31] Generally speaking, the more mature the individual in their emotional development, the more they are able to tolerate higher levels of uncertainty and ambiguity without resorting to frustrated appeals or rigidly enforced rules.

---

[30] The full title of the publication is *Levels of Management Performance Learning and Development* by Leary, Boydell, Van Boeschoten and Carlisle. Sheffield City Polytechnic and the Manpower Services Commission, UK Government (MSC), 1985.

[31] Both *The Evolving Self* and *In Over Our Heads* by Robert Kegan are useful texts for those involved in understanding stages and phases of adult development, and the fact that none of us remains permanently in any single stage but move between several according to the circumstances and life issues with which we are dealing.

Mode of Being	Comparable Ego State	Features
Mode 7 Dedicating	5 Minimum ego Identification	Having a sense of the task (of the times) in front of me – and my part in it. Being able to see through things to the essentials – to sum this up in a word or an idea. Having a deep sense of purpose. Finding meaning in what I am doing and the way it is done.
Mode 6 Connecting	4 Open Ego Self-creating person	Realising that things are somehow connected, are interdependent. Seeking wider overviews; bringing things together. Widening my outlook, my perspective, looking at the consequences and implications. Being able to work across a whole field of activity.
Mode 5 Experimenting	3B Conventional Self-managing ego	Needing to find out things, experiment and try out. Taking active steps to discover more to increase my understanding. Planning how to carry out experiments. Having a deep urge to discover, seeking, striving. Developing new ways of doing things – for myself and others.
Mode 4 Experiencing		Learning from experiences – and using this as a basis for action. Noticing what is going on and how I am affecting it – and how it affects me. Having my own ideas and theories, which work for me. Being independent and working things out for myself. Doing things 'my way' – expressing myself through what I do.
Mode 3 Relating		Being sensitive, aware and in tune with what is happening. Understanding at a deeper level what is going on and be able to explain this to others, in terms of established ideas and theories. Having a 'feel' for the situation, relating to it in an appropriate manner – as defined by the norms, customs and practice. Tuning in to the situation and responding in a skilled and effective way.
Mode 2 Adapting	3A Sub Conventional	Responding to variations from the routine by adapting the way I operate. Recognising patterns of information and noticing the effects of changes. Desiring to make procedures work well, making modifications to bring things back into control. Putting together a series of skills and behaviours, making slight modifications to the way I have been taught.
Mode 1 Adhering	Wounded Ego	Working to set standards or ways of operating that have been previously set down by others. Operating from memory, thinking in terms of rules, checklists and set procedures. Feeling insecure if there is no 'correct' answer provided for me. Carrying out prescribed routines, implementing them 'to the letter'.

Table 2 ◆ **Modes of Being and Ego States**

WPL can only begin when individuals can accept a degree of personal responsibility for their own actions and choices. The author takes the view that higher and higher orders of functions, inter-dependence and collaboration will be required over time because social change will increasingly demand it.

Becoming a 'Person' and the Role of Education

Any educational system can make the claim that it helps individuals to 'become persons'. At the same time, every system will encourage them to become certain kinds of persons. Everyone grows up to be an individual but not everyone grows up with the sense of being a person – with a clear sense of what rights attach to their personhood. How we conceive of ourselves as a person, with what rights, obligations and potentials is, in part, a result of what is suggested, promoted, advanced and approved by our culture. The person who we become is, in part, a result of the filtering process to which our experience is subjected. Those filters include the cultural and social expectations that come our way as we grow up in our particular culture and have few alternative models to set against the one we are absorbing on a daily basis (though the internet and global media are changing that a good deal).

If we take the view that persons are devious, hypocritical, self-serving and exploitative of one another then the educational system we devise will, in part, have to contend with those features of human nature. It will also have to ensure that there are strong prohibitions to act as a deterrent and that limitations are put upon demonstrations of aggressive self-expansion. Transgression will have to be met with firm restraint. Persons in such a system will need to learn that the untrammelled expression of their own self-interest has to be tempered with conformity to following the prescribed norms.

If, however, you take a different view of human nature and the purpose of human activity, then educational systems would reflect those differences – you would hope. If people are capable of working things out together, can collaborate together and realise themselves most fully as persons in some sort of open and self-disclosing relationship with others, then the system within which those attributes will flourish will be very different from that outlined above. Rather than curbing wilfulness and self-aggrandisement, such a system will encourage creativity and give opportunity for self-expression. Rather than requiring people to submit to externally imposed norms of social appearance, there will be strong encouragement for individuals to find their own internal commitments to their personal values.

They will recognise that the pursuit of personal values is essential if they are to meet others *authentically* i.e. with an inner and outer consistency. If I am to meet you in some way other than as a social construction, a socially adapted individual, I have to know who I am: not simply who the world has determined I *should* be, who my parents expect me to be and who my friends *encourage* me to be.

It is not that these aspects of our social identity are not important: they are enormously important to the development of our sense of self. But they are not the whole story of who we are either. Sadly, for many of us, we oscillate between these kinds of influences rather than transcend them. In the past, these major forms of socialising an individual into society, along with providing them with an identity, was done unawarely. In our own times the choices of identity, the range of possibilities, the shifting patterns of friendship and connection all make it no simple matter to become a person.

The idea that individuals are simply that – isolated social atoms without any necessary connection to anyone else – is patently absurd. It may be a useful device for social scientists of a past era to identify trends and calculate data to regard people in this way, but it bears no living relationship to the human journey anywhere on the planet.

> To an existential phenomenologist, a person is that which makes a specific view of the world, time, and space come into being. A person is an origin for action, which changes the world for himself and for others, for weal or woe. Further, a person is a situated being who embodies projects – plans, interventions, creations – that in time will be disclosed to the world. Projects are vows, commitments to transform self and world in some way that first exists as imagination, like a work of art. When consummated they become perceptible to others and to the person who first invented them.
>
> Sidney Jourard, 1971: 50.

Educating people as persons would be a vital ingredient in any movement to enhance personhood. It is not only in what we are educated, as we have seen, but vitally how we are educated, that persons come to value themselves or not, come to trust in themselves or not, come to affirm their capacity for self-responsibility or not. An educational system that is at odds with the project of personhood is not going to foster the qualities that personhood embraces. It therefore makes the task of gaining a sense of personhood all the more difficult after formal education is completed. If one of the primary means of developing a sense of personhood is the exercise of choice, then our children are given very little opportunity in their educational lives to exercise and develop those powers.

We have a long way to go yet before we have an educational system that will foster a notion of reciprocal personhood and where we consider ourself as a person in relation to other persons sharing a joint project on a fragile planet in danger of collapse. There is increasing pressure applied at ever earlier ages for pupils to aim for ever higher grades. This is in obvious contradiction to the desire to provide nourishment for the whole child. The preoccupation that amounts to an obsession with attainment tests, for example, serves to do no more than exile any real interest or encouragement in personhood from appearing, except as a marginal activity that flutters around the edges of school life.

Personhood in Relationship

Discussions, assessments, reviews and reaffirmations of our growing sense of personhood 'for us together now' 'in this or that endeavour' are an essential part of being a planetary citizen. As Bishop David Jenkins expressed it so splendidly and so simply some years ago: 'Men and women are what their relationships allow them to become'. When we begin to inquire into what makes us the person we are and what constitutes being the person we are, we are already engaged in a process of change. We are inviting a level of awareness to enter into our experience to which we do not pay attention ordinarily.

If I need others in order to evolve into the person I might be, then how far I regard others as persons like me will be deeply important. I cannot demean you and gain. I cannot make use of you for my ends without at the same time reducing my own intentions and undermining the social trust upon which we all depend. Every time I exploit you in the name of my personhood, I am actually undercutting the very endeavour I am claiming requires me to 'subjugate' you. I cannot reduce you without at the same time reducing myself. Together as persons we can enlarge the field of possibilities. Alone we can make little progress and even that would be sadly self-referential.

The rights that attend upon being a person are therefore 'givens' to all persons, including children. None are exempt. And persons are what we are, at least by the time we arrive on the planet and, depending on your belief structure, even before it.[32] This does not make all persons socially

---

[32] When an embryo becomes a person with rights is a matter of deep ethical consideration. From the time of birth onwards, however, the person is there, a unique presence upon the planet and with all the rights and protections that are to be attached to personhood.

indistinguishable, nor does it make different talents and possibilities of no account. Instead, *a priori* of those endowments and attributes, *we share in personhood together.* How those attributes are fostered, socially encouraged, subsidised by the community or ignored are in part how the community of persons evaluates the worth (at 'this time' in 'this moment' of its development) of these gifts. No community of persons is likely to be able to have the resources to develop the talents of all its members indiscriminately (and who would want it?) but *persons in relation* together have to assess the priorities that are to be given attention. This means *social* priorities, *cultural* priorities, *economic* priorities and *spiritual* priorities are determined by *persons in relation* as self-directing individuals capable of decision-making and collaborating, able to come to some form of agreement about these things.[33]

Of course, our world is not organised in these ways or for these purposes and is not likely to be in the foreseeable future, and this is hardly the point. Having an outline of what *persons in relation* might strive for helps give a sense of the direction to what it means to become a person. It is not a prescription for what *should* happen. How could one person unilaterally give a direction to be imposed on all others about what they should do? They can only put out a call inviting others as persons to come together to inquire into the possibilities that may exist if they…

All cultures, it can be argued, take the raw material of the human and shape it into some form of civilised regime in order for the social world to reproduce itself. All forms of social life require adaptation to social norms. What is important here, however, is the degree of awareness of those norms. (To move beyond the conventional ego structures to a more internally developed and individually held autonomous ego or self-creating ego.) A degree of discernment in the expression of feelings, for example, is not the same thing as manufacturing social hypocrisy on a grand scale; just as trusting the expression of personal feelings is not to be equated with inviting an outbreak of violent lawlessness.

Social conformity may make people socially adaptable and able to do unpleasant things without even realising it (unless they are on the receiving end), all in the name of the 'job' or the 'needs of the situation'. It is a sure way of creating a person alienated from their own inner life of feeling to some degree or another.

---

[33] What is hinted at in this description are the elements that would be found in *a self-generating culture* (see pp. 316-319 in John Heron's *The Complete Facilitator's Handbook,* Kogan Page, 1999), i.e. a culture of freely associating individuals who are choosing how to make the sum total of arrangements for living a communal life together an intentional project. This would go all the way from choosing what work is required, to what type of relationships; from what forms of sacred expression to their collective acknowledgement of their planetary position and cosmic setting.

Personhood and Freedom

Self-management and self-regulation are mythic terms in the absence of real opportunities to learn how to choose and how to develop a link between choice, action and consequence. Freedom takes a lifetime of learning to handle – real freedom, that is. It requires ample opportunities for testing out the implications of choice, action and consequence and sufficient trust in those who share the inquiry.

Who would not wish for self-management? But once obtained, who would want to impose it upon themselves? After a lifetime of subjection to other people's orders and commands, who would know how to exercise such self-management? Who would not be terrified at the very prospect of taking *that* degree of responsibility for *everything* that occurs? A necessary outburst of licence and excess is guaranteed and certainly to be expected once the fetters are removed. And this is what keeps the fetters in place. You are only free when ... you have forgotten what it might be like to have it and have 'bought into' so many of the kinds of restraints (material commitments, for example). You may be safely self-regulating, but from a suppressed position rather than from a consciously, internally committed way. You are no threat or challenge to yourself or the world in which you have placed yourself.

It is a difficult, painful and risky business dismantling the social inhibitions that have been put there and reinforced over a lifetime. It is also lonely and very disturbing. Taking out what you do not need, stripping away the more absurd ideas seems like a good idea until you begin. You soon realise that some of those limitations that you have hated all this time, whilst of no real use to a person, have, nevertheless, kept at bay the much more painful and difficult question of, 'What else instead?' Personhood as a project for living brings anyone trying it face to face with the fact that there are so many socially internalised rules that it is difficult to know which are the authentic expressions of you as a person – or what else might be an improvement. However exciting, it is also emotionally gruelling.

Our emotional life is rarely included for exploration either in our culture or our educational system. Self-restraint, suppression of emotion, repression of difficult feelings that may arise, let alone some of the darker aspects of exploitation and abuse, all ensure that emotional freedom is a very uncertain prospect. Learning to lock away 'secrets', painful memories and events about which the person has inherited some sense of failure, shame or worse, all contribute to making the search for personhood a quest that will open the Pandora's box of emotional suppression. Emotional skills are in short supply and mature development of them is not encouraged in the way our social and educational life is organised.

The current popularity of developments like 'emotional intelligence' and 'spiritual intelligence' (and all the other many contemporary expressions for personal development that are now available) calls attention to the increasing and widespread interest of people wanting to develop more of the person that they are and they are greatly to be welcomed. Whilst these innovations most certainly move towards WPL, there is always the risk that deep and fundamental aspects[34] of what it means to be a human being – a person – stand in danger of being isolated, 'commodified' and sold on to give some people the edge over others in the market place of opportunity.

WPL has the potential for enabling individuals to be more 'whole'; to integrate their emotional self, their cognitive self, their spiritual self, their physical self and how they relate to the world around them in a more coherent and aware manner.

---

[34] Clearly, anyone able to manage themselves better is a gain; however, if it is taught as a skill, without exploring underlying relationships, and if it arises out of an attempt to simply get an advantage over others, then it is fundamentally flawed and misses the whole concept of personhood and being in relationship with others.

CHAPTER FIVE

The Emergence of
Whole Person Learning

Independent learning entails the experience of fascination. Fascination is a response to an invitation or challenge disclosed by the world.
Sidney Jourard, 1968: 120.

In this chapter, we begin with an overview of the major learning approaches before focussing more specifically on the background, emergence and principles of WPL.

A Spectrum of Learning Approaches

There is a spectrum of forms and styles of learning which can be related to the degree of participation and involvement of those taking part, as illustrated over the page.

Transactional/traditional forms of learning are generally content-based. Little attention is paid to engaging learners in the selection, design, management and assessment of their own learning process. Such an approach to learning is about the transmission of knowledge and the accumulation of understanding. The relationship is one largely centred on passing knowledge from the teacher to the students.

The next level along the spectrum, *participative* learning, goes some way towards acknowledging a greater degree of connection between those teaching and those learning, but the power and control in all significant areas of the process still remains with the staff as representatives of the institution. Those taking part may be offered some measure of contribution, albeit restricted, into some aspects usually of the content or the sequence of the learning tasks. An example might be, 'Today we are going to examine methods of population control and we can begin in one of three ways. They are 1,2,3 – which would you prefer to begin with?'

Students may have opportunities work out 'how' they will do something, but not 'what' they will do. Neither will they influence the standards against which they will be assessed. Participative learning enhances the experience, but it does not change the very nature of the enterprise. Such a modification to the traditional model does not require

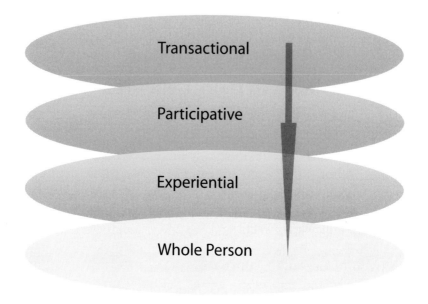

Figure 2 ◆ **Spectrum of Learning Styles**

either teachers or students to embrace a different educational philosophy or stance towards the educational venture. The aim remains primarily one of being taught a predetermined content that the student is 'choosing' to learn.

The familiar phrase, 'learning from experience' often indicates 'learning on the job' i.e. a period of training in situ. It is used in occupations such as nursing and teaching, for example, and the use of internships or work placements in other occupations and professions. Although this method can be useful in discovering what a particular job might entail, it is usually only one element of a larger scheme of learning. The rest of the provision is likely to be based on a traditional model and the overall 'experience' is, therefore, not one that would qualify as an experiential learning programme in the way the term is used here.

Learning by experience and *experiential* learning are very distinct. Experiential learning, as used throughout this work, involves participants more in working out what they will examine (content) and how they will fulfil it (sequence and process). It also involves all those taking part in reflecting together on the success of the enterprise or not, since they are jointly responsible for the whole event. In all experiential work, therefore, feelings are regarded as just as important a source of information as the cognitive dimension of the learning.

If members are to share experiences, give and receive feedback about behaviour and engage in exploring their emotional responses to what they do, then the relationships between group members must be as open and authentic as it is possible to make them. Greater depth in participation and exploration of the affective dimension begins to reach the point where new skills need to be developed by both facilitators and participants. Experiential learning is the approach that underpins qualitative research in its many forms, and it is a forerunner of WPL.

Qualitative Research

WPL can trace links to qualitative research approaches such as action inquiry, participatory inquiry and cooperative inquiry (see below). In qualitative methods, the degree of process engagement between those involved in the researching may be a good deal less emphasised than would be the case in a WPL event. Both, however, represent the increasing trend towards personal engagement in learning and research and the willingness of those involved to put themselves forward to be scrutinised as *one with others*. There are several points that distinguish qualitative research themes and models and which are closely allied with whole person approaches to learning. In his book, *Phenomenological Research* (1994), Moustakas outlines them as:

1. **Recognising the value of qualitative designs and methodologies**, especially in studies of human experiences that are not approachable through quantitative approaches.

2. **Focusing on the wholeness of experience** rather then solely on its objects or parts.

3. **Searching for meanings** and essences of experience rather than measurements and explanations.

4. **Obtaining descriptions of experience** through first-person accounts in informal and formal conversations and interviews.

5. **Regarding the data of experience as imperative** in understanding human behaviour and as evidence for scientific investigations.

6. **Formulating questions and problems** that reflect the interest, involvement, and personal commitment of the researcher.

7. **Viewing experience and behaviour as an integrated and inseparable relationship** of subject and object and of parts and whole.

And again, in a recent book on the subject of Action Inquiry, the influential thinker on the subject, Bill Torbert, writes:

> Action inquiry is a way of simultaneously conducting action and inquiry as a disciplined leadership practice that increases the wider effectiveness of our actions. Such action helps individuals, teams and organisations, and still larger institutions, become more capable of self-transformation and thus more creative, more aware, more just, and more sustainable.
>
> Surprisingly, action inquiry is a virtually unknown process, perhaps because learning how to practice it from moment-to-moment is no easy trick. For action inquiry is not a set of prescriptions for behaviour that, when followed, invariably manipulate situations as we initially wish and yields the success we dreamed of. Action inquiry is not a process that can be followed in an imitative, mechanical way, learning a few ideas and imagining that parroting them back to others occasionally means we are doing action inquiry. Action inquiry is a way of learning anew, in the vividness of each moment, how to act now. The course of both its difficulty and potential is that action inquiry requires making ourselves, not just others, vulnerable to inquiry and to transformation.
>
> William R Torbert et al, 2004: 2.

Torbert has long advocated personal action inquiry as a means of 'creating communities of inquiry within communities of social practice'. It exhibits transforming power which operates through 'peer cultures, liberating structures and timely actions'. Cultures are truly peer-like, structures are liberating, and actions are timely, if they simultaneously promote widening inquiry about what is the appropriate mission, strategy, and practice for the given person or organisation or nation.

Further, as Reason and Bradbury (2001) say, participatory inquiry (another form of qualitative research) holds to the following values:

> Participative forms of inquiry start with concerns for power and powerlessness, and aim to confront the way in which the established and power-holding elements of societies world-wide are favoured because they hold a monopoly on the definition and employment of knowledge.
>
> This political form of participation affirms people's right and ability to have a say in decisions which affect them and which claim to generate knowledge about them. It asserts the importance of liberating the muted voices of those held down by class structures and neo-colonialism, by poverty, sexism, racism, and homophobia.   P Reason and H Bradbury (eds), 2001: 10.

In this way, learning as inquiry is dynamic and adaptable to the discoveries of the members of the enterprise as it progresses. Certain elements, however, need to be held consciously if the process is to develop both the rigour to delve beyond the superficial and the safety to enable participants to risk more than their usual self-image. There is the need for:

- **Creative management.** The underlying purpose is to 'generate transformative action for...' The more members remind themselves of the potential for the work to have transformative effects, the less likely they are to get 'hung up' on procedural mechanics
- **A balance between reflection and action**
- **Encouragement to develop 'reflection in action'** as well as to evolve creative and authentic accounts of the learning gained
- **Developing a working model of managing emotional distress** (a working concept and skills in releasing cathartic tensions)
- **Developing affective skills,** including those that recognise, interrupt and discharge the dysfunctional appearance of past distress-laden responses and reactions.

The Experiential Learning Cycle

The experiential learning cycle described here is based upon the work of Johnson and Johnson[35] (2002, 7th edition) and the influence of other writers in the field, such as Kolb. It is a model that is both simple and well-recognised and useful in beginning to understand the movements of the learning process the more the person is involved in its design, management, assessment and evaluation. Heron has developed his own account of the process considerably further and it is his account that needs to be examined in more detail for anyone wishing to take WPL further (see below).

As 'active learning' methods evolved and descriptions developed, we have become familiar with the idea of the learning cycle of *action, reflection, learning* and other descriptions. The terms may vary, but they illustrate the interrelationship between five essential elements:

1. **Concrete learning experiences** are offered and followed by
2. **Observations** of responses and reactions, which lead to
3. **Reflection** upon what took place, which leads to
4. **Learning:** the formation of tentative connections, generalisations, modifications of view and so on, which lead to

---

[35] Their book, *Joining Together: Group Theory and Group Skills,* is an excellent and outstanding introduction to the value and use of group learning methods.

5. **Longer-term influences:** new ideas or connections, which form the basis of new responses to be tested out in future actions and in new experiences.

For many years, Kolb's description has been one that has had wide currency in the world of business and management – often linked to the idea of individual learning styles – which reflect individual preferences for different stages of the cycle: there being those who enjoy the reflection phase, others who prefer the action stage and so on.

This recognition, that a link exists between how people like to learn and their overall stance to their experience ('temperament' is the word we would use in Oasis), has been influential in widening the appreciation that facilitators and trainers need to have for those whose learning approach differs from their own. The initial model has been greatly expanded by different commentators, thinkers and facilitators, but there is something fundamental and useful about the simple cycle. *Think, plan, do, review* is another simple version of what we know to be a highly complex interaction of elements.

The Whole Person Primary Cycle

The model developed by Kolb, Johnson and Johnson, and others, has since been developed into more sophisticated models, particularly John Heron's outline in *Feeling and Personhood* and *The Complete Facilitator's Handbook*. He identifies four dimensions that will enhance the possibilities for learning and for integrating that learning; they each need to be present in a learning experience for that experience to be a whole person approach. They are:

1. Feeling and emotion.
2. Intuition and imagery (including perception, memory & imagination).
3. Reflection and discrimination.
4. Intention and action.

These can then each be connected with Heron's description of an 'up-hierarchy' in holistic learning:

> …practical (intention and action) is grounded on the conceptual (reflection and discrimination), which is grounded on the imaginal[36] (intuition and imagery), which in turn is grounded on the affective (feeling and emotion)…

---

[36] See John Heron's, *Feeling and Personhood* and John Gray's, *A Tour of John Heron's 'Feeling and Personhood'* for more on this aspect of the cycle.

A good example of this at work, illustrated below, is in one-to-one facilitation or counsellor training, where the trainee (female) is practising counselling skills with another trainee (male) who is being a real client. The four modes – affective, imaginal, conceptual and practical – are shown as circles generating motion in each other in that order.

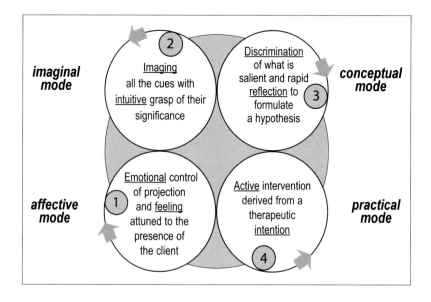

Figure 3 ⬥ **The Whole Person Primary Cycle**

Stage 1. Affective. The trainee feels empathically the presence of the client, while attending to and managing her own emotions.

Stage 2. Imaginal. The trainee notices the whole pattern of the client's behaviour, both what he is saying and all the nonverbal cues, intuitively divining its meaning as a whole.

Stage 3. Conceptual. The trainee discriminates selectively among all this data, rapidly classifying it, and with quicksilver reflection evolves a hypothesis about the client's process.

Stage 4. Practice. She converts her hypothesis into a practical intervention based on an underlying therapeutic purpose. She is using intention and action.   John Heron, in D. Boud and N. Miller (eds), 1996: 85-86.

Whole Person Learning

A new form of consciousness is beginning to emerge in a small slice of contemporary Homo Sapiens... we are astounded by the new awareness, and when we go to speak of it, we discover that we have no easy or efficient way of transmitting this mode of consciousness.   Brian Swimme, 1996: 6.

In WPL the range, depth and level of what takes place in the group all change. It takes the concept of the individual being responsible for their own learning and their capacity to direct and shape the learning still further. Learning about one's self and about how the individual operates and relates to others is central to the endeavour and is always peer-based in its approach. In this way WPL is applied learning; the person is practising their personhood in the very act of developing it further. In WPL the teacher (who moves into an even stronger facilitator role) increasingly makes it apparent from the outset that power is to be shared with participants (rather than students[37]).

The crucial differences as we move towards WPL thus include:

- There is **increasing involvement** by participants in all aspects of the learning process
- There is an increasing expectation of the **level of engagement** expected from those taking part
- There is an **increasing degree of collaboration** between participants and facilitators in all decision-making processes about all aspects of the time they spend together – power-sharing, in short
- There is a **greater range** of matters with which the group is dealing
- There is **greater depth** of the matters with which the group is dealing
- The **interpersonal and group processes** that emerge are increasingly seen as equally legitimate areas of exploration and consideration as the content undertaken
- **Facilitators need considerably more skills** the further along the spectrum towards WPL they are operating.

Issues of gender, power and authority are not only acknowledged and open for discussion and/or negotiation in WPL, they are actively pursued. Any aspect of the work to be done or the process to be undertaken is open to challenge so long as it falls within the terms of the contract[38] set up at the beginning of the meeting or programme. This form of learning draws individuals who want to become more self-initiating, self-directing and self-generating. In addition, in a fully developed WPL enterprise these principles

---

[37] In traditional education institutions, those involved are usually 'staff' and 'students' rather than 'facilitator' and 'participant' – a reflection of the power differential and role separation. As events move more towards WPL role separation goes and facilitator and participant become more appropriate terms.

[38] Learning contracts in WPL events are explored in *Chapter 9: Living the Learning Transition: Facilitating Whole Person Learning.*

are all carried forward into self and peer assessment and accreditation.

There is an explicit commitment from all participants to work with their own process, with the interpersonal and even transpersonal dimensions as integral areas of the learning. There is considerable emphasis placed upon the need for *processing skills* of a high order – skills to manage the way events happen, skills to assist participants to identify and articulate the responses they have to what happens to them and ways of managing conflict and difference, for example. This represents a considerable shift on the part of staff and the abilities they need.

WPL is a method that is consistent with a way of viewing relationship as a *collaborative endeavour*; an endeavour that regards people as capable of making decisions about matters which affect them and sees them as having a rightful place in assessing the value of any learning they have acquired.

The more self-initiated and self-generated it is, and the more issues of authority, role, gender, power, influence, status and levels of collaboration are all open for examination and discussion, the more the event is likely to be a WPL event. The more the facilitator embraces the concepts of the person and personhood (in the sense they are used in this book) and the more they incorporate the practical, affective and imaginal dimensions, as well as the cognitive, that enrich and deepen the possibilities for what can take place, the more the event will be WPL.

Affective Competence in Whole Person Learning

In a WPL approach, facilitators need to bear in mind strongly that the *imaginal* realm and the *feeling* realm are vitally influential elements to the whole process. It is not simply a matter of thinking; it is much more a matter of being open to one's own wider processes that influence how 'thinking' gets to be the result. In the same way, it is not simply a matter of 'doing' once the experience has been identified, but that the feeling dimension is a fundamentally important element in the whole rationale and purpose of WPL.

Enabling someone to become more in tune with their own feeling life, and able to draw upon it sensibly and sensitively is an underlying dimension to WPL. Equally, if parts of the person that have been injured or damaged in the past resurface as a result of the influence of contemporary events, the conditions need to be such that promote the space, care and attention within which to release the distress. If this part of the process does not take place, for whatever reason, it will continue to act as an obstacle to the individual being able to deepen their own connection and relationship with themselves and others.

Main Features of Affective Competence

1. An event can give rise to either positive or distress-laden emotions for the person at the centre of that event.

2. Not everyone will have the same response to the same event. The response is determined by the individual's own internal processing.

3. *Catharsis* and the release of distress emotion are evidence of self-healing, not evidence of breakdown. Such release can enable people to be more present. It might, too, be the first time such a release has been accepted and honoured.

4. Enjoying and expressing positive emotions, as well as noticing when these are clouded by distress to such an extent that we need to take time-out to release them.

Affective competence lies at the root of much of the change that is needed to create the kinds of conditions for us all to flourish – rather than for some to live at the expense of others. Of the distress condition of humans on the planet, John Heron (1992) writes:

> This is a vast social pathology, a vast malaise. It cannot be regarded as a therapeutic problem, other than in the short-term individual case. It is an educational issue. We need concepts of child-raising and of education at all levels that foster the progressive development of emotional competence, in the same way that at present we foster the development of intellectual competence.   1992:133.

Affective competence begins with the capacity of the individual to be able to identify, take responsibility for and accept emotions of all kinds, along with the accompanying ability to switch and redirect emotional states with some elegance and awareness. At an everyday level, being affectively competent means, firstly, being able to spot the restimulation of old emotional pain and, secondly, to interrupt its displacement before it is let loose into forms of distorted behaviour that is then acted out upon others or internalised upon oneself. Such 'pattern interruption' begins to remove old hurt-laden agendas so they are no longer 'projected' out onto others, nor are they 'transferred' onto current situations inappropriately. Such a view is based on the general insight that early traumatic experiences have a major influence on adult behaviour.

So, for example, when an individual expresses a distress-laden response, they may well be able to manage themselves as an effective participant until later, when they may seek some support and some assistance. However, it is still acknowledged *within* the group. It is not something to be hidden by the participant, disapproved of by the group or something to alarm the facilitator. Similarly, if there is a conflict or distress-laden response expressed so strongly that it interferes with the capacity of those involved to continue, then the process of learning about the content is set aside to work with the process issues. Open and conscious decisions need to be made as to whether the situation is sufficiently dysfunctional to demand immediate attention or whether it is possible to carry on working with the content.

This shift into the overtly affective domain, for example, involves a good deal more risk since it reveals so much more of the person. The more people are invited to disclose aspects of their 'inner' self to others, the more an event will be moving towards WPL. The key points for those facilitating such learning events are that:

1. They do not ask people to do what they themselves have not done (or would not do with the present group.)

2. They do not create an atmosphere of 'pressure' that makes the choice of withdrawing no longer a realistic possibility.

3. They err on the side of the safety of participants without keeping them in cotton wool or being overly protective.

The implications of developing an emotionally competent culture would go a long way beyond the claims made for most forms of affective management or self-control in the way they are increasingly popularised. It would mean being able to spot institutionalised and professionalised forms of displacement used to avoid taking on notions of mutuality and collaboration more fully. It would mean finding other, more participative ways of managing long-held traditions and strategies that have served to defend institutional interests in favour of looking at the underlying influences and seeking to resolve them by finding more rational, flexible behaviours.

> This is a crying need in all the helping professions. So the doctor abandons the repeat prescriptions of psychotropic drugs and cultivates an ability to handle psychosocial disorders. The academic relinquishes sixty-minute lectures and develops more skill in facilitating self-directed learning. The priest stops preaching sin and acquires competence in enhancing spiritual self-esteem.

> It means being able supportively to confront other people who are unawarely acting out their denied distress in negative and disruptive forms of behaviour.

> The confrontation does not shirk the behavioural issue: it deals with it straight and true. At the same time it does not attack, invalidate or abuse the person who is being confronted about the issue. The uncompromising feedback is fundamentally respectful.   J. Heron, 1992: 134.

Affective competence means many things and is, in the author's view, a richer concept than that of 'emotional intelligence' which suggests that emotions have an intelligence rather than that persons have intelligent ways of managing their feeling life and that 'emoting' is only one way of expressing feeling.

Engagement and Whole Person Learning

Since WPL seeks to gain the engagement of participants in their own learning process and since they relate to one another as peers engaged upon a co-operative learning endeavour in which all contributions have potentially equal weight, the twin principles of equality of consideration and equality of opportunity are crucial.

> **Equality of consideration**. The needs, interests, skills and resources of those entering a course are equally worthy of consideration. In other words, if people are invited to explore some aspect of behaviour, some element of the human condition, then all have a right to consideration of their contribution and the right to comment upon the programme as it develops. Not all contributions will be equally valuable and relevant, but it is equally important that they are all heard.

> **Equality of opportunity**. Anyone can contribute or intervene in the course process in any way judged to be relevant and appropriate. Again, this should not be taken to imply that all contributions are of equal value in fulfilling the objectives of the course, nor that the skills and resources of individual participants are equally pertinent in respect of meeting the course objectives. Some will have more or less experience, more or less skill to offer and it is important that these differences are not only recognised but used creatively.

These two principles mean that **equal attention** must be given to a consideration of what different individuals require from their participation upon a programme, and that equal opportunity is available to enable them to make their needs known, to exercise their judgement upon events, and to influence the process and direction of the course by using the skills and talents they already possess.

When implemented, these principles inevitably lead to the shift in perspective regarding those important concepts of power, status and role separation. The traditional distinctions between staff and students are not obliterated as may be supposed but the balance changes; each has different needs, skills and resources:

> ....the discovery of these differences is essential to the vitality of the course.   John Heron, 1974: 3.

Process Aims of Whole Person Learning

Specific topics and themes pursued in a WPL event will require aims and methods specific to the given content; however, there will also be a number of wider aims that are broadly applicable to the *process* of WPL, irrespective of the content. These include:

- An increase in insight and awareness about the impact of an individual's typical behaviours and how these are viewed by others

- An awareness of the range of perceptions which an experience or event may generate in a group

- An increase in sensitivity to the behaviour of others by becoming more familiar with a wider range of stimuli – both non-verbal and verbal

- An increase in the ability to diagnose accurately how others are feeling and responding, and an increase in the range of personal responses available in others

- An increase in awareness and understanding of the interactive processes that can facilitate or inhibit individual or group relationships

- Extending existing behavioural skills to increase the choice of response over a wider field of situations and experiences

- Enabling individuals to match their behaviour to their intentions and to achieve their goals

- Encouraging the spirit of inquiry into personal behavioural style

- Increasing individual awareness of the opportunities for change in order to gain more productive relationships and results

- Increasing understanding of internal needs, values, perceptions, resources and reactions

- Promoting individuals to take charge of their own learning and their own life.

A primary source of learning in such a model is the process that takes place *between* people as distinct from the task upon which they are engaged. Not only is the 'what' important in such learning, but the 'how' by which that is achieved is equally important. Recognition of the importance of the process, alongside the content of the course, needs to be brought to the awareness of all the participants since they can expect to be engaged in reflection upon and clarification of the processes.

It becomes apparent through this emphasis upon the process – the 'how' – of WPL that acceptance of self and of others helps clear the way to more direct and open communication. Openness is encouraged; though it is not a fixed quality, but a relative one. (Some groups are more open than others; some individuals are more freely self-disclosing than others.) In addition, using group behaviour to promote effective learning assists those involved realise their roles as people who can also contribute to the learning of others, whether as colleagues, peers, friends, parents or children.

Evaluating Whole Person Learning

The evaluation of WPL involves both the *process and content elements*, though most participants will rightly be more interested in how far the course has had an impact upon their ability to influence their lives across a wider range of circumstances. They will not, primarily, be interested in evaluating the course as an example of WPL. A facilitator, on the other hand, in their assessment of the overall success of the course, will pay considerable attention to the way the process issues emerged and were handled.

Evaluation Issues Relevant to both Participant and Facilitator

- The ability to transfer learning
- The ability to contribute and influence the programme appropriately
- The appropriateness of the model offered
- Knowledge gained and the potential for it to be applied
- A balance between personal needs and task focus

For the programme or event to continue with a WPL perspective, participants need to be involved in appraisal and evaluation processes. Participants can be involved through periodic course reviews and planning meetings, in order to determine the future direction of the course in the light of accumulating information and experience. 'Before' and 'after' responses to parts of the programme could also provide useful methods for generating information. Facilitators and participants are also engaged in the process of evolving methods whereby individuals can systematically monitor their own performance in their own areas of professional competence and provide evidence of self-monitoring and self-evaluation of their own individual programme.

WPL is peer learning in its radical and most collaborative form. Since a WPL event is determined largely by its greater depth, range and level of involvement, power-sharing, and openness to the process, it will be evident that not all peer-based events are necessarily WPL events. The next chapter explores the spectrum of peer-based approaches, the importance of the peer principle and how all this relates to the world in which we live.

CHAPTER SIX

Whole Person Learning
in a Peer Paradigm

The individual carries within themselves the impulse to realise their own potential, to contribute to the development of those around them and to make a contribution to the life and quality of the groups to which they become attached.

Beware the man who works hard to learn something, learns it, and finds himself no wiser than before. He is full of murderous resentment of people who are ignorant without having come by their ignorance the hard way.
Kurt Vonnegut, 1998.

The shift to forms of WPL is a radical and fundamental one. How we meet and relate to one another, how we manage arenas where difference and conflict are embraced rather than denied or avoided, and the degree of involvement in our own learning are all key aspects of the peer paradigm that are explored in this chapter. In addition, further aspects of the peer paradigm are highlighted:

- The relationship between personhood and WPL
- Open-ended learning
- Aspects of WPL
- The education of 'Whole Persons'
- How the peer principle impacts upon the world of expertise, the professional and the 'expert'
- The peer paradigm spectrum
- Co-operative inquiry
- A WPL Community in practice.

Personhood in Whole Person Learning

Personhood as a concept is fundamentally about the quality of human meeting – meeting as peers. It is about regarding those with whom we share our learning as co-creators in the making of that learning – whatever temporary or transient roles they occupy. Our peers act with us as co-authors in the venture in which we all share. Persons have a right to play a part in and have an influence upon the decisions that affect them. It also means that they have a right to contribute to the ways in which power is ordered, distributed and exercised; how influence is exercised and how authority is expressed across the spectrum of activities in which they are engaged.

Meeting as peers engaged together upon the *learning enterprise* means our personhood is not some fixed quantity but a potential that we strive to realise in company together. It is a quality that emerges out of the depth of our encounter and our shared willingness to bring more of ourselves forth in the meeting that takes place. Learning then is inescapable. This ensures that the *process* is every bit as important as the *task*: the process may or may not be designed to facilitate the acquisition of the information that forms the content, but it will *always* affect us as persons. It will always have the potential to contribute to deepening our ability to become more of who we are together, or not. It will always be part of the inquiry and not something ever to be taken for granted.

One of the contradictions about learning through relationship is the notion that there is some previously identified and agreed way relationship 'should' unfold; that there are those who already know; others who can, in their turn, come to know, and all of it contained within the confines of a curriculum. In reality, working with relationship is too varied and complex to be capable of such a reductionist approach – one reason why there are so many competing views on the nature of what it means to be human.

The stance we take to how we regard who we are as persons is the bedrock of our joint efforts together, and who we are as persons is revealed in the process of our coming together, the work we do, the learning we undertake. Developing the habit of critical evaluation, self-scrutiny, clear and mutually respecting feedback, sharing ideas, notions and half-formed ideas all play their part in *uncovering the process*. A large part of the *transition* we are in is to develop increasing intentionality[39] about how we go about what we do and to make ourselves more conscious of the way we come to be as we are. And there are many, many, many potential sources of reflection.

---

[39] See the work of John Cowan. He is a University teacher who has strenuously promoted many of the ideas contained here. Co-counselling has an abundance of techniques for bringing forth the half-conscious and even some unconscious processes. In the safe space of the other's undivided and uncritical attention, I can begin to surface some of the restrictions, limitations and unprocessed features of my inner experience. Out of it we can, together, sift out and winnow away the detritus of redundant ramblings to find the nuggets of supressed thought, withheld longings, unclaimed potentials and more intentionality can be the prize.

The more I know about how I learn and that I can learn in *that way that is particular to me*, the more I will learn and the more *I will value not only my own learning but, increasingly, value myself in a healthy and non-obsessive or narcissistic way*. Perhaps there is no more fundamental a feature of WPL amongst persons than the right of the person *to learn* in their own way and to have it validated, because such a form of learning is about the whole person and it is the whole person that is validated. Academic ability alone is not what counts, skills by themselves are not what matters; it is the degree to which the individual risks their wholeness and attempts to bring it present before others is what is of most value. Those other things listed above come afterwards.

Accounts drawn from almost any creative artist describing how their creative process unfolds combines many, if not all, of these elements. Learning of this kind is essentially a creative enterprise. It trusts people will identify valuable questions, pursue lines of inquiry that will add meaning to their 'projects' and purposes; increase their intentional capacities to act consciously and accountably. And, through such creativity, enable people to enjoy much more meaningful and creative versions of their lives far more than a curriculum-based approach is likely to do.

Holistic Whole Person Learning

WPL is, then, not simply a holistic approach to learning a subject. This is a distinction that needs to be made clear. 'Holistic learning of a subject' is the phrase used to describe the situation where those involved find ways to enlarge the range of influences that are drawn upon to make the subject matter more accessible and contextually related. It may well encourage wider modes of learning or greater areas of experience (and may have aspects of a whole person dimension).

> What is holistic or whole person learning? The answer depends on what you think a whole person is and how you believe such a being functions. So we are into personality theory: the structure and dynamics of the person.
>
> John Heron, 1999: 37.

The impact of involving more of the person in their learning has taken on many forms. We can see its expression in the movement to develop more reflective practitioners – where reflection soon opens up the inquirer into the more troubling terrain when the attitudes, beliefs and values of the inquirer begin to have an impact on the matter being reflected upon, along with the somatic content that goes with it.

We can see it in the ready interest of organisational members to gain insights from approaches such as those of NLP (and its variations). On the one hand there are, today, no shortages of training programmes that involve the person *more*, often a great deal more, in their learning without necessarily embracing a whole person approach. There are far fewer opportunities, however, that are based upon an intentionally peer-based model and which therefore set out to investigate the complexities that such an approach opens out.

To involve more of the person in their learning is clearly (in this paradigm) something to be welcomed. As a result of increasing familiarity with the techniques and methods of experiential approaches in mainstream provision, its impact has clearly been felt in many ways.

It is rare to attend a meeting these days, for example, without some form of introductions of a participative kind. And, thankfully, it is increasingly common for someone 'facilitating'[40] to have the confidence to outline the purpose of the gathering, check people's understanding and potential contributions, in order to ensure that there is an agreed understanding about the work to be done – small details that originate from the days of the Human Potential Movement.

Increased involvement, however, as we have shown, is not the same thing as adopting either a whole person approach or a holistic view of the work to be done. It is at the point at which we adopt the peer principle and its application that WPL really comes into its own and the full implications can be recognised. It is an approach that seeks to bring together:

1. The **context** (place) with an understanding of the **nature of personhood** (presence).

2. Learning tasks that are selected and chosen in **collaboration** with the learner (participant) to enhance their functioning toward the **goal** of more complete personhood (purpose).

3. The practice of a more **responsible engagement and effective participation** in the human order and the planetary sphere (process).

These five elements – the place, presence, person, purpose and process – of the education of whole persons are inextricably linked and influential upon each other, as the diagram overleaf demonstrates.

---

[40] There are any number of people in some sort of educational or training role who are given the title 'facilitator' when in reality they are managing a process that is clearly well orchestrated (and needs to be). They are doing an important job in stage-managing a process to ensure that people have an opportunity to take part effectively within the confines of a relatively well-understood approach of small and large group discussion. They are not, though, facilitating in the way we have been using the term throughout this book.

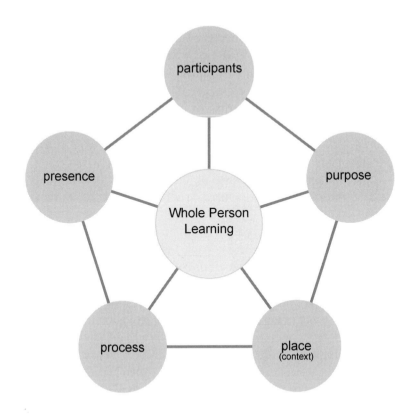

Figure 4 ⬦ **Elements in Holistic and Whole Person Learning**

All the above elements will become increasingly important in WPL and each has to be considered in conjunction with the others and how they interconnect. WPL does more than 'open up the ego' while the learning takes place or simply for the purposes of learning. WPL opens the ego up so that it will remain open in the hope that the learning attained will inform one's future way of being in the world. It also recognises that whole chunks of the ego may be permanently dissolved as the individual revises not only their conceptual map of the world but their stance to their experience of the world. The learner may well be dealing with:

> ... old emotional fixations developing integrated functions in interpersonal behaviour and in promoting cultural and ecological change, and acquiring a psychic, subtle and spiritual perspective – which begins the process of self-transfiguration.   John Heron, 1999: 310.

Open-Ended Learning

Fundamental to this concept is that *the person learning is learning to become the person they are!* Of course 'who they are' at the point in question is only a *provisional* who they are. They are in the process of becoming who they are throughout time. Becoming who you are is a ceaseless process and who you are at any moment is only a snapshot taken on the day.

This implies that individuals will learn different things at different rates in different ways even from the same broad experience. It also means that there is no simple instrumental end point to the learning. WPL does not have to have a direct vocational end (though it can also be used as a primary vehicle for vocational preparation); individuals might simply be learning more about their personhood and how they function in the world in a wide sense.

WPL can have a strongly vocational element and be primarily about enabling individuals to become integrated in their practice of any number of vocational tasks, from engineering to counselling and psychotherapy, but the means by which they gain such accomplishment has wider values and larger aims. Of course, getting a job needs attention, but a WPL programme is not predicated on preparing persons for … some end that those who design the system decide is an appropriate point for others to reach. It is designed to enable those involved to create together the profile of the practice they are all, in their unique and personal ways, intending to perform.

It therefore requires those involved in facilitating such a process to exercise their power and authority with great lightness of touch and deftness of manner when it comes to creating forms of educational experience that others will undertake. Further, there is a need to be uninvested in uniform outcomes. All participants may be aiming to improve their leadership potential and decision-making skills, for example, and they may all experience the same activities as part of the programme, yet they will not all learn the same things. In this way, they begin to develop their own individual profile. It may well be that all concerned have a desire to perform to some agreed standard (see the later chapters on assessment and accreditation) but they will not go about it in the same way. The enjoyment of WPL is working with the diversity of learning styles, approaches, methods and expressions of learning that individuals, when given the freedom to experiment, can come up with.

Similarly, experiences will not be organised to shield people from the economic realities, just as they will not be based around ensuring the economic system reproduces itself as it is. Depending on how those engaged in the project of WPL conceive their venture, it will include or exclude ('bracket off') those areas of experience deemed by them as not sufficiently relevant to assist the focus of their inquiry. Clearly, if peers working in this way never considered thinking about the real world, then social collapse – at least for those involved in the enterprise – would fast arrive.

The diagram below is an illustration of how WPL might operate within one particular context – human relations in this instance. Naturally, the specifics in engineering, say, would be different, as they would be for nursing, yet there are many commonalities too.

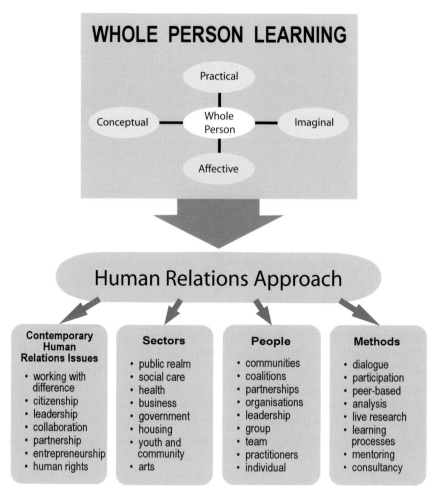

Figure 5
The Context of Whole Person Approaches in Human Relations Enterprises

Currently, WPL is almost certain to be tentative and experimental, a prototype idea, as those involved begin to map out the possibilities for such an enterprise.[41] They will undertake exploration of certain aspects of experience, practice, or understanding, formulate their programme together and undertake the learning. All this will be provisional. It is not being suggested here that WPL could be introduced like the National Curriculum by fiat, by decree. Even if this was thought desirable, it would not be possible because it requires *persons to be in relation together to work out the nature of their project*. It is about dismantling the way matters currently are conceived, prescribed and managed at the pace those who take part can manage. These remarks are made to suggest possibilities and offer guidance, not to exhort people to fling away all concern for current external realities.

What makes a more radical future possible is the fact that many forms of employment will continue to change and some will disappear. This offers the opportunity to revise our views of what education must do and how it must do it. Preparing people to become part of their social world and not just the economic order will become ever more important given the increasing malaise that accompanies consumer-based individualism, the fragmentation of social relations and so on.

Without practice in how to be together, resolve differences and share resources, there is little hope for progress in society, developed or undeveloped. The social order and the learning enterprise reflect each other. *Persons in relation* who are undertaking a whole person educational enterprise would increasingly attend to all aspects of that endeavour. This would ensure that it is rooted in reality. Of course, to get the whole enterprise underway there can be all manner of varieties and styles of experiment.

The Peer Principle

The *peer principle*, and its implications, is, I believe, the foundation of all real human meeting and it lies at the heart of the radical WPL paradigm. It is the essence of significant development. It is the basis of the recognition and value of human worth. It describes how persons stand in relation to one another. It is the foundation of the human order where people meet as persons, relate as persons and act together as persons-in-relation – irrespective of whatever distinctions or differences they also have to acknowledge.

---

[41] There are some illustrations of WPL activities in which Oasis and colleagues have been involved at the end of this book in *Whole Person Learning: The Way Ahead.*

> The human order is nothing other than this world we build together. That we build it together does not mean that we have to conform. On the contrary, one must stand one's ground and make one's unique contribution. This not a matter of the individual versus the society, for we are all part of the common order together.   Maurice Friedman, 1992: 94.

WPL is the application of the peer principle in any learning situation. If we relate in free and equal association with one another, as in the peer principle and WPL, then the whole notion of hierarchy, power and control has to be re-examined.

In common usage, the word 'peer' suggests a group of people who share a sense of commonality that equalises them. For example, members of the House of Lords are 'peers' because they are equal to one another; they are also equal in their supposed superiority over the rest of us! What is understood by the phrase 'a group of peers' is, therefore, that they are people who stand roughly on equal terms with one another in the matter at hand. It does not, however, extend beyond that area. First grade piano students, for example, may not be peers in any other area of their lives. In this way, general usage of 'peer' often leaves the boundary of peerdom implied and always limited to the activity of the people in question. In contrast, *the peer principle is the educational expression of the universal principle of equality: that all beings are unique and have an equal right to their own destiny with and through their fruitful association with others.*

To be a true peer I must wear my expertise lightly and enter into the fullness of human meeting on each occasion. I must beware of arriving 'knowing' what is needed or required and remember that 'we make our reality together'. To be sure, we each contribute something particular and distinctive; this is what makes it unique and unrepeatable. We must always remember that we cannot go back and do it again: it stands for all time. There is only *this* time and it is only *this* way, yet this is simply something to remember rather than be chained by. Each meeting is unique. However hard we try to make it the same and however much we make meeting a habit and our relationship a predictable pattern, if we are to meet as persons we have to be open to the unique, the particular, the uncertain and the unknown. This is an uncomfortable commitment.

The peer principle works at the heart of the issue of 'professionalisation' and the potential misuse of expertise to mystify and maintain a position of power *over the other* rather than share *power with*. Working from a peer perspective, one would look to find ways to unlock power so that expertise becomes a means of giving 'power to', of *empowering* – not an easy commitment for those professionals who find security and kudos in their power and status. Concepts of service and humility are important, too, and they, in turn, raise the issues of motivation and intention.

Many perceptive thinkers, particularly Donald Schon, John Heron and Edmund O'Sullivan, have pointed out that professionalisation can lead to much restrictive practice. In addition, much contemporary social change is at odds with an expert-driven model of development, since the spirit of the times is moving in an inexorable direction towards people working things out together, promoting forms of increased participation and greater involvement.[42]

Upton Sinclair once observed, "It is difficult to get a man to understand something when his salary depends upon his not understanding it."[43] Clearly, the distribution of functions and specialist skills will always be part of a rational ordering of society. A profession that wanted to reduce the hierarchical dependence of those it serves (i.e. to de-professionalise) could teach others to take over more of the functions that once only the expert could do. It would thus begin the process of empowering its clients to become more involved and help them to understand what is often kept as a mystery in traditional hierarchical models.

In this way they become useful social agents encouraging self-determining, self-help initiatives in the more intellectually and technically accessible areas of professional practice. The professional, in other words, does not seek to create a form of redundant dependency in the public. They seek a healthy balance between 'I'll do it for you' and 'Do it yourself'. The educational system is a very clear example of all these contradictions. Knowledge and how it is acquired is as much about perpetuating a socially divisive society as it is about the acquisition of both knowledge and skills to enable the individual to make a contribution to their own life and those around them.

Unless I accord the other the full dignity and worth that I would hope to find offered to myself, I in my expert role am likely to cast around for some suitably plausible authoritarian justification for taking over the other, in 'their best interests' of course. I do it in order to give them the benefit of what *I* know *they* need. My expertise then becomes the warrant for bending the other to my purposes. The temptation to take over is an ever-present danger of the professional in their desire to help unless they are willing to enter into the fullness of relationship with the other and

---

42 We clearly need experts, and never more than we do now. It is how we expect and allow them to express their expertise and what power we confer upon them for that expertise that is being called to attention here.

43 Quoted in *An Inconvenient Truth: The Planetary Emergency of Global Warming and What We Can Do About It* by Al Gore. Rodale Books, 2006.

attempt to create a partnership and a joint endeavour out of the meeting.

Efforts to introduce a greater level of participant involvement clearly have implications for the underlying values and methods that the facilitator or trainer draws upon. One of the themes throughout this book is that WPL can be adopted and employed in many valuable forms to increase participant involvement without the necessity of adopting a new paradigm. However, if an educator is to promote coherence of practice and congruence between theory and practice, then the more the facilitator moves toward a peer paradigm (in our view, the inevitable long-term necessity), the more the facilitator will be faced with some challenging decisions about the point at which the old paradigm of 'power over' – the expression of hierarchical authority in relation to knowledge – will come under review and require revision.

The more the facilitator or participant embraces WPL principles and practices, the greater the challenge to any remaining loyalty to the existing paradigm. WPL, as practised through a peer paradigm, demands an internal coherence in all aspects of life, including how we bring ourselves into encountering the wider world, those who share in it with us and the planet's biosphere. The implications of living out of a peer principle go deep and are far-reaching and the author recognises that not everyone will want or be able to take them on wholesale. But the reader should be aware of the extent of those implications and work out how far they will go in meeting them – especially if they are promoting them for others to adopt.

Key Elements of the Peer Principle

Self-direction. A cornerstone of peer working is trust in the person to work things out; to take an increasing measure of responsibility for themselves and to 'opt in' as an adult. I may not always know what is in my best interests (it's called 'making mistakes'), but I will never learn if there is always someone else to decide on my behalf until they decide I am now ready. Self-determination and self-direction offer individuals a chance, in a relatively risk-free setting, to try out actions and ideas that they have never previously felt able to do. They have a chance to review the consequences and decide if they want to continue. Self-direction can only be respected if the contract is truly voluntary and the individual knows they have the right to withdraw at any time they choose.

Immediacy and a willingness to work. The stress on immediacy, on the 'here and now', on the doing it sooner rather than later and on the capacity of those involved to work it out, all further emphasise the importance of those involved as the guides and arbiters of its value. Reports of what went on and descriptions after the event are all important, but they are not 'it'. 'It' is what we make of it, all of us who are party to 'it', not just the facilitator, or the awkward individual who got in the way, but all of us who are creating the event together. This is the 'community' dimension that is, perhaps, one of the least developed elements of the original radical impulse of the Human Potential Movement

Removal of third parties and intermediaries. WPL places those acting together as the source of authority and not some third party or some regulatory body elsewhere. There is a positive recognition that only we who are working in this way can assess the appropriate forms of accountability about both the what and the how of practice – and mostly it is a shared responsibility if we are learning together. Third parties may be used as validating yardsticks but they are not to be placed in the role of deciding what those yardsticks are to be, how they are to be imposed, assessing and judging 'results', or of being placed in authority 'over' the participants. Third parties may be useful for facilitating difficult situations, but not as 'experts' brought in to give explanations or provide solutions.

Peer accountability. Peer accountability is the willingness to place myself before my peers, both those with whom I am working and other groups of peers who are involved in similar work. It is a form of review and monitoring; a way of minimising the potential for personal delusion, collusion and illusion. Without some form of peer accountability much of the rest is dubious because it largely rests on my description of my experience with no check from anywhere or anyone – and there is nothing radical or innovative in that.

Consistency of event: contract, content, method and review. Since the intention is to offer a radical style of approach, course material, the course contract, the process and the style of programme all need to be explicated for the benefit of those considering entering into such a programme.

Content and process. Similarly, the content is no longer so much the unambiguous focus of the learning. It is essential as a means by which individuals are comparing and contrasting, evaluating and discriminating their own views and responses. Process and content become interrelated in a fundamental way. Learning gained from what happened, rather than from the information about the topic itself, may be much more important. However, the content must still relate to the needs of those signing up for the event.

The prerequisite of participant involvement. Such an approach puts the learner at the heart of the enterprise. The individual's involvement and participation, not simply through attendance, but by engagement with the programme and its themes, the other participants and with the atmosphere the group evolves, all influence the involvement of everyone taking part. Working with such multi-level awareness is demanding, tiring and potentially risky for all concerned.

Decreasing role of authorities. The peer approach to learning is at odds with reliance upon external authorities to validate the experience, to set the agenda, to determine the programme. Shared responsibility and peer moderation are much more congruent approaches to the question of quality assurance. (See the assessment and accreditation chapters.)

Whole Person Learning: A Radical Paradigm

Tough, open, honest confrontation is the norm to be aimed at in WPL and when it doesn't work out as politely or as naïvely as those involved might hope, they need to be willing to keep on working at it to improve. Ways are not to be found to avoid challenging one another by developing a set of bogus 'rights' and 'privileges' that exempt individuals from being able to be met and challenged by anyone else. An atmosphere in which mistakes are OK and somewhat to be expected at some point from everyone is encouraged.

There are no right and wrongs – only consequences[44] and, providing you are prepared to meet whatever they might be, just about anything is permissible within the ground rules you together have agreed to abide by. That way, people do learn what works, what doesn't and why it doesn't, not according to someone's theory, but according to what it is like to have to live it.

There is no confusion between development and training. Training is something many of us are aiming to get away from. Most people on WPL events have 'trained' to death in a set of procedures and skills that rely upon a paradigm of power and authority that is almost never made visible and never inquired into. In contrast, WPL methods are a matter of building a personally owned way of operating, through practice, reflection and

---

[44] The aphorism comes from Sheldon Kopp's wonderful account of this kind of learning in life: *If You Meet the Buddha on the Road, Kill Him!*.

challenge. This means that power structures are relatively transparent, since they are established by those taking part within a framework that is outlined at the beginning of the event, or via the publicity material that is circulated.

Central to all this, as must be clear by now, is the primacy of the individual and their experience. Subjective reality is the keystone and starting point for any individual inquiry and was something that so much intrigued and fascinated those involved in the Human Potential Movement. Paradoxically, however, the individual soon realises that 'my experience is only valuable in relation to the discoveries of others'.

In order to get the most out of experiential work, I need to check my findings against those of others, not to see if I got the answer 'right' (i.e. the one they got) but to discover the subtleties and nuances of interest and meaning that we find appearing when discussing our responses and tentative musings. *Conjoint inquiry, mutuality, interdependence*, these are all terms to describe this essential, shared element to working with individual potential and human experience.

The contributions of those with an educational or developmental role must increasingly recognise that it is not methods or techniques that are required to enable men and women to better influence the world in which they find themselves. We need to provide opportunities for people to understand how they make sense of their experience; to provide forms and frameworks for understanding that encourage meaning-making collaboratively and in a way that is experienced as safe enough to explore with freedom and imagination.

WPL recognises that the individual creates from their experience those things of most value to themselves, but this does not give licence for individual predilections and fancies. Neither is the objective content disavowed or made nothing more than a stimulus for internal play without responsibility: rather, it is to be engaged with and internalised in personal ways.

In the end, all knowledge of this kind is personal: to be owned and then used. Knowledge is much more dynamic and alive than the simple accumulation of information. Such knowledge is based upon interaction both with the world 'out there' and with the 'self'. Education is not a neutral process, as we have maintained throughout this book, but has social and political implications both for the way in which it is conducted and for the purposes to which it is put.

At a time when traditional understanding is breaking down in many fields of knowledge and inquiry, application and activity, a WPL learning approach offers a new paradigm for the demands of the future. Learning how to participate in a WPLC,[45] whilst developing not only a better way of understanding the subject matter, but also of my 'self', and myself in relation to others and their relations with one another, creates a dynamic field of action. It enables the learning achieved to be set continuously against the issues of the wider world.

A WPL approach may draw upon a wide range of other contributing influences. When linked to a developmental perspective, for example, it is possible to explore the opportunities for change by challenging rigidities in thinking and practice which so often act as obstacles to progress. WPL and a developmental approach arise as responses to the increasing interrelatedness of *personal, social and wider planetary concerns* that express themselves in a variety of ways at an *individual, collective, and global level*.

To work in this way is essentially an educational activity. It raises questions of values, purpose, identity and commitment. If we are to create a way of learning and a way of developing that begins to meet the issues of the times in which we live, individuals not only need to 'know' more, they also need to have the potential for implementing that understanding in useful action in the world. The three underlying assumptions inherent in this approach are:

1. Development is possible in all situations.

2. The potential for change requires those involved to engage with themselves, those around them and the circumstances in which they find themselves at all levels – cognitively, affectively, somatically as well as spiritually.

3. This is essentially an educational activity. It raises questions of values, purpose, identity and commitment.

The Peer Spectrum: How Peer is Peer?

As we have seen briefly in the previous chapter, there is a continuum of involvement and participation within peer-based programmes. A two-day content-based programme on a specific topic, for example, does not have the same opportunities for involvement and peer decision-making as a two-year open-ended experiential inquiry.

The structure to hold a two-day programme together may give little room for any real peer work beyond the sharing that takes place in skills-based sessions. It may be little more than participative in what it asks by way of commitment from those involved. The structure may be

---

[45] See later for a fuller discussion of the implications of participating in a WPLC.

very tight, the content in the hands of the facilitator and negotiation over the programme minimal. This doesn't violate the peer principle; it is a restricted version of a peer-based approach and it is chosen on rationally understood grounds. These would go something like:

- A short event, with inexperienced participants meeting for the first time, is already laden with many concerns for most of the people without adding further uncertainty to it by making the whole thing openly negotiable

- The peer learning paradigm requires individuals to develop their experience of increased learner autonomy within clear boundaries

- This enables them to surface frustrations and tensions at a manageable level. This is far more productive and educational than immersing them in the full-blown anxieties of uncertainty that co-operative inquiry,[46] for example, necessarily involves.

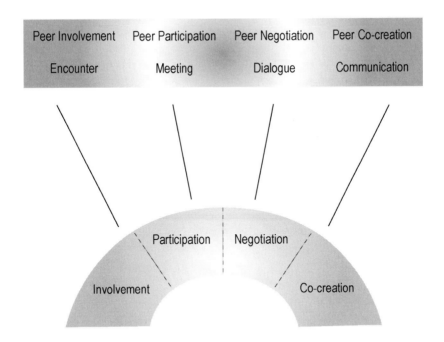

Figure 6 • The Peer Paradigm Spectrum

---

[46] We have included an example of co-operative inquiry as an example of WPL because we believe it has immense potential for future learning – especially for matters involving whole persons and which require deep immersion and reflection.

Nancy Peden, who offers a contemporary example of taking WPL into the challenging environment of educational establishments in the USA, writes:

> According to Temple Grandin, and many of the philosophers in the new field of participatory research, all knowledge is created in relationship. This form of knowledge and meaning creation might even be called 'associative' as Grandin wrote. Simply put: the participatory research paradigm suggests that we meet and we engage with our environment, and we express and co-create reality.
>
> Research into the human condition can then be seen as art and practical problem solving rather than unethical, systematic objectification for the benefit of those outside the research, powerful academics or corporations. A research method becomes a useful process available to communities rather than just an occult tool of scholars in universities (quoted from the website December 2006: http//lived learning).
>
> Lived Learning is interested in promoting skilful, effective collaboration that shifts power relations and that as a process allows participants to become their own authorities. While there are many wonderful methods available, we have found Co-operative Inquiry designed by John Heron (1996) and practiced with Peter Reason to be one of the most complete methods available.   Nancy Peden, 2004.

A great mistake, in my view, of much participative training and development is that it confuses participation with *power sharing*, and involvement with *learner autonomy*.

It may make good sense to involve people in what they are learning, but this is a long way from working within a peer-based model. Parents, for example, will involve their children in all kinds of learning experiences, but there is no suggestion that they are in a peer relationship. Involvement with an activity to promote learning seems a useful approach, no matter what the underlying principles of the pedagogy. The degree to which power lies with the educator/facilitator or with the individual within the group is linked very clearly to the level of peer involvement in their learning, as is illustrated in the following table.

WPL is neither the same thing as unstructured learning nor the same thing as an *autonomy lab* where people make use of the invitation that is offered to work things out in relation to a topic in hand. Nor is it a version of Open Space Technology, another educational innovation that frees people more than traditional methods. It is not a version of World Café learning either, though all these recent innovations share an encouragement to greater forms of participation and involvement of the learner and, in that sense, all share a broad interest in encouraging wider participation in learning events and foster learning that engages and involves more of the whole person.

Involvement	Facilitators make visible their suggestions, with participants able to negotiate in regard to their specific requirements.	
	Facilitators determine what are the givens and learners are able to negotiate around everything else.	
	Assessment is developed through joint decision making and is in the hands of the learner as far as they can develop a mutually agreed process with others.	Power moves to Educators
Participative	Facilitators make the key decisions and may consult about what is wanted.	
	This level requires the learners to be actively involved in the learning activities.	
	In regard to assessment, staff take behaviour and evidence into account and give feedback about decisions and actions taken by the learner.	
Negotiation	Increasing amounts of freedom are provided within the structure for learners to participate in their own learning agenda.	
	There are opportunities provided where participants can design specific aspects of the learning methods.	
	Assessment is based on a framework developed by the facilitators with opportunity for learners to create their own approach within the parameters.	Power moves to Peers
Co-creation **Whole Person Learning**	Learners and facilitators share responsibility for the content of the learning.	
	The design aspect of the programme is an act of co-creation.	
	In assessment, deciding the criteria is a process for which all are individually and mutually accountable and responsible.	

Table 3 ◆ Four Levels of the Peer Learning Spectrum

All this is not to hide or evade the confusion and uncertainty that can enter the room at any time when people take up the offer to share their views; it is to promote the idea that we need to know how far we are inviting people to opt into the process, on what grounds and over what issues. People can contribute to:

1. **Structure**: they can decide what is done when.
2. **Content**: they can decide what topics are covered.
3. **Process**: they can decide how far they engage in determining how the process unfolds.

The levels of involvement can be identified by and linked to the kind of peer event or programme:

1. Participants may contribute by deciding from within a given range of options – with facilitators holding the overall contract about the nature of the programme, duration, etc. We could term this a **'limited negotiated learning contract'**.
2. A contract is developed which enables participants to create ground rules and conditions for their programme or event, if the time is available for this process to take place effectively and successfully: **a facilitator initiated, group led approach**.
3. Participants may be given a programme outline that forms the basis of what they design together with facilitator involvement in offering structuring and process involvement. We could term such a programme **'a facilitator initiated highly collaborative peer approach'**.
4. Potential participants may be offered an invitation from a committed individual to explore the option of entering into something. This committed individual then may or may not facilitate the initial process to get the thing underway or to find out if there is the degree of commitment required and the interpersonal skills necessary. We could term this an **'unstructured peer group'**.

Co-operative Inquiry

Co-operative inquiry is an example of WPL at the most radical end of the levels of participant involvement. It appears to be unstructured but the methodology of repeated reflection-action cycles is what gives it structure, rather than there being any pre-ordained curriculum, content or topic decided by external authorities. A call goes out and people respond out of their internal commitment. It is, therefore, a collaborative and co-creative way of working together as a group. It is a method of investigating the world as a way of learning about it and doing this with others. It starts from the working assumption that much of the personal world we live in overlaps with the social world that shapes and forms us. These two worlds are not separate in experience. According to John Heron, the defining features of co-operative inquiry include:

- All the subjects are as fully involved as possible as co-researchers in all decisions – about both content and method – throughout all phases of the inquiry

- There is intentional interplay between reflection and making sense on the one hand, and experience and action on the other

- There is explicit attention to developing appropriate validity procedures for the inquiry and its findings

- There is a 'radical epistemology for wide-ranging inquiry methods that can be both informative about and transformative of any aspects of the human condition accessible to a transparent body mind; that is one that has an open, unbound awareness'.

There are, as well as validity procedures, a range of special skills suited to such all-purpose experiential inquiry; the level of affective competence of the participants needs to match the rigour of the inquiry itself, for example. All this immediately suggests a number of departures from traditional models of education and learning. Underpinning it all is that it is built around the free association of adults, devising a task, process and method and so on without the aid of so-called professionals.

The first UK co-operative inquiry was in 1978, Hampstead, London. (See John Heron, *Sacred Science: Person-centred Inquiry into the Spiritual and the Subtle*, PCCS Books, 1998.) Its aim was to extend ordinary consciousness beyond its perceptual focus on the here and now, to access our physical world there and then, at points in space and time outside sensory range

The following example of a co-operative inquiry in the US in 2006 was coordinated by the Research Center for Leadership in Action (RCLA) at New York University, and was facilitated by Doug Paxton. The inquiry is a clear indication of the breadth and vision possible in this form of co-creation.

Seven nationally-recognised leaders and activists of colour came together to explore the following question: 'How do we do our work while we navigate the power structures, join with others and nourish our minds, hearts and bodies along the way?'

The group explored a variety of additional questions, including, 'Is there a tool we can create that can help People of Color walk alongside one another, that helps leaders stay in the conversation, get support and keep walking towards their talk? Is there a way that such a tool could support us in launching CI-like groups in our workplaces? What would that look like? How could we de-colonize CI, to tap its indigenous roots and share a more opening frame for such inquiry/support, like soul work or creating a culture of care?'

Five categories of findings seemed to rise to the top, and were themes that were present all along the journey:

1. The challenge and complexity of race and culture.
2. Healing, regeneration and self-care.
3. Navigating the Dance of Power.
4. Elements of sustaining leadership.
5. Building community through soul work.

This is an experiment in *education as liberation*. What co-operative inquiry brings about and what we cannot describe is the highly demanding requirement for people to work at the limits of their emotional competence; to distinguish rational concerns from irrational anxieties; personal requirements from distress-based needs. Further, it requires people to be willing to work with individual interpretations about the very uncertainties that occasionally occur from the fear-laden terrors of archaic psychic material when they are faced with chaos, lack of direction and no parents to make things 'better'.

Such an approach adds up to the recognition that emotional adulthood bears little relationship to chronological age; it is more of a continuous process of engagement with those reactions, fears and behaviours that arise from distress-based experiences of earlier life.

Interpersonal Skills and Managing Conflict

What is worth noting is that the more peer the invitation to those involved, the clearer the initial contract needs to be and that higher levels of interpersonal skills will be required on behalf of those taking part, including the following:

- Immediacy of response
- Attentiveness to the other

- Capacity for self-management (affective competence)
- Openness to new experiences
- Openness to the other.

Voluntary attendance and commitment is almost a prerequisite for the establishment of any collaborative endeavour. However, it does need to be recognised that there are degrees of voluntariness because people attend for a variety of reasons, which influences how far they are genuinely committed to the event. If the programme offers qualifications or is seen as a route to a form of accreditation that an individual regards as valuable, they may enter with a much more instrumental commitment than those who may be strongly motivated to both the principle and the outcome of the programme. Some people may even be 'directed' to attend, or feel they have little option or choice. These issues need to be raised, examined and 'worked through' before they cause greater difficulties at a later stage of the programme.

Just as individuals bring a range of past experiences with them in relation to both content and process of the programme, so past attendance at other events also influences their expectations. The degree of familiarity with similar subject matter may play a significant part in shaping their style of participation, motivation and expectation. Equally, each will bring a range of interpersonal experience and skills to contribute toward the processes that take place within the overall programme.

A recognition of how the process 'works' must also be linked to encouragement for individuals to develop their skills in facilitating both their own and each others' learning. The level of such skills will play a large part in shaping the atmosphere, both as the event begins and as it develops. The ability, for example, to handle, control, discharge, and transmute feelings plays an important part in the quality of the experience of any group working in a peer-based and WPL model. It may be that the group consciously decides to set aside time to develop these skills overtly in order to improve the level of skills present for managing the interpersonal issues that will necessarily arise.

One reason why so many co-operative endeavours fail, in my view, is that though the aspirations of those involved are high and the ideals they espouse sincere, there is a belief that dealing with conflict is deeply at odds with how co-operative working 'should' happen. Most would-be co-operators have a deep unwillingness to recognise that conflict is a healthy and inevitable part of any group activity. They tend to regard conflict as a sign of people being unhelpful and the 'awkward' member is often scape-goated.[47] Real differences are diluted into collusive pretences and the promotion of phoney compromises is all too common. If this occurs, the group develops a two-tier reality; the one everyone pretends is operating and the one that actually runs the show.

The real issue is not to stifle or outlaw conflict, but to promote it positively and learn how to manage it successfully. The lack of personal awareness of how different individuals are 'triggered' at different points in the process of learning how to work together foils most endeavours that aim to involve people in co-operative ways. Facing conflict is far from easy since each of us has a great store of distress around being seen to be different, being 'put down' and so on. All this past history ('baggage') is brought into the room whenever even a participative or experiential endeavour is underway, and especially so when it is a peer-based effort.

It is important to recognise that the desire to work from a peer model is no indication of ability. For many, learning how to do this is considerably more arduous than they had expected. Many people explore peer methods and find them too extreme for their purposes. They may well question the way power works and how institutions operate, but when they work in a peer model of learning the immense responsibility that it demands may prove too much. They may therefore continue to hold to their ideological views of what needs to change in institutions regarding the use of power, but recognise that the peer process is not their chosen means.

Such a view, in the end, may well lead individuals to facing some uncomfortable contradictions about whether it is possible to change anything in order to further the involvement of those taking part if you are unwilling to learn how to take part yourself. You do run the risk of finding yourself caught in the very dilemma you are setting out to overcome – unilateral authoritarian decision-making on behalf of those in need, less fortunate and so on.

TLC: A Whole Person Learning Community in Action

Whole Person Learning in a Whole Person Learning Community is nothing less than the practice of freedom.

The TLC (Transpersonal Learning Community) began life as a year-long Transpersonal Diploma run by Oasis. At the completion of the programme, many of the participants and the facilitator decided to form a WPLC, a self-generating community, to continue exploring issues around

---

[47] A major influence upon the personal stance of the author to WPL and social life generally is the French writer and cultural critic, Rene Girard. His book, *The Scapegoat*, would serve well as an introduction to his thoughts for anyone involved in group dynamics.

the transpersonal. That was almost ten years ago and the group continues to meet for over twenty days in each year. Members have travelled together to varying parts of the world to meet and work with other figures well known in their particular field.

There has been considerable learning for all concerned on a personal level but supremely in how to be together, how to work with difference, how to manage conflict, how to make the transition from traditional approaches to power, authority and gender.

A WPLC operates outside any imposed authority. It operates with complete autonomy and outside traditional educational constraints. In working out what is at stake, the whole person involvement of both the individual in their capacity to act as both facilitator and peer participant is required. Initially there will be an initiating facilitator to inaugurate 'the call' that gathers people together, but the intention is to relieve themselves of that role once the group has taken hold of the procedures they agree will be used to manage the life of the group and the decisions it has to make.

Though in the beginning they each bring different contributions (usually the facilitator will have experience of similar ventures and will have some regard to the continuity of the endeavour), the facilitator does not stand unquestionably in any position of authority over anyone else. The aim is to create a group of collaborative peers in which the participants at the first opportunity are exercising their skills in facilitating both one another and the process. The originating facilitator meanwhile has dissolved the role into the group and an authentic peer experience of collaboration develops.

Such a common endeavour is a form of WPL. It is a holistic enterprise and is only successfully undertaken from a holistic perspective. Recognition of the intensity of the process is important for all concerned.

Over time, it becomes possible to begin to see the qualities and attributes of others who may initially have appeared unappealing if not downright 'difficult'. As a result of surfacing outmoded attitudes, facing concerns and dealing with challenges of varied kinds, the person emerges at the end not simply more 'educated' about something, but a different person. The WPLC is the crucible for a type of personal change that cannot be evaded. This is an essential aspect of its appeal and its value. However, a WPLC is not something realisable in a weekend, though you may get acquainted with some of the major ideas and learn, experientially, how some of those ideas shape and affect your life.

The concept of the WPLC is an integral part of the Advanced Diploma programmes that Oasis has offered for almost twenty years, and of other in-depth courses, also run by Oasis. The evolution of the WPLC, with the necessity for individuals to both manage their own process and contribute to the decision-making of the community as it goes about its tasks, is regarded as essential. It is recognised as an important forum for issues of illusion, collusion and even delusion to be challenged within individual perspectives, pairings and sub-groups and amongst the whole group.

The individual's involvement with the WPLC is a microcosm of the person in their wider community and participation in such a learning community enables the learning achieved to be set against wider issues. Practice and experience in influencing the balance of power, control and individual decision-making are indispensable aspects of programmes. Such an approach is widely applicable both to the conditions of the times in which we live and the search for a more collaborative and engaged response. All the elements of a form of transformative learning are encountered and within this framework there are opportunities for:

- Giving and receiving feedback
- Meeting challenge
- Appropriate self-disclosure
- Identifying and learning how to manage boundaries more effectively.

Individual Experience and the Whole Person Learning Community

An individual's life journey is shaped by a wide range of influences that combine together to create the unique circumstances and challenges that bring about growth, development and the potential for surpassing our conditioned expectations.

Individual experience is itself without meaning; only by, with and through others does the individual take form, acquire a sense of self and find the communion with others that creates the foundations for a secure individual identity. Time and place are the forces that create the environment within which the individual and the group, family, society and culture to which they belong arise. They form the horizon that leads the individual onwards, or the limit that brings all exploration to an end.

The opening round – the coming together of the community at the start of a session – is an example of how the emerging WPLC can encourage *visibility* amongst its members. In this round, the individual has the opportunity to speak at whatever point they choose, say as much or as little as they like, reveal as much or as little of their own process consistent with the overall purpose of 'getting here', all with the clear understanding that they will not be challenged or opposed. It becomes a space of revelation and learning in its own right for a good many participants. Through the use of this space they begin to learn how to hold themselves before others in a way that is centred and grounded.

'New' knowledge is not something that replaces 'old' knowledge: it is always a development and an extension of past knowledge. 'Understanding' is a better term for this process. Understanding grows in depth, in subtlety, and in richness without the understanding itself being experienced as different from what it was in the past.

A Whole Person Learning Community Approach: Summary

1. **It is peer-based**: adults coming together in free association.

2. **It is participative**: those taking part are involved, to a greater or lesser degree, in determining the structure, the form and the content of what is learned (that is consistent with the course programme).

3. **It is collaborative**: those involved share in decision-making over the range of issues that make up the programme.

4. **It is experiential** (wherever possible): those involved are actively engaged in winning the learning to be gained from the experiences that are designed to enable an area of content to be explored. Content and delivery are therefore integrated into a consistent and authentic balance.

5. **Theory and application are vital elements** in validating the learning and in ensuring that learning has a useful role in the world.

6. **There is a process of self and peer assessment** that is rigorously developed and practised as a principle means of learning about power, authority and submission in educational practice.

7. **The learner is seen as standing at the heart of their learning** and the one who takes their learning with them.

8. **A developmental view is taken of the individual in their life journey**, and the groups and organisations in which people find themselves. This vital aspect of peer learning enables the facilitator to moderate their contribution in the light of where people are, that needs they are able to express, and the destination to which they wish their learning to take them.

9. The principles of **equality of consideration and opportunity** are key aspects for embracing a WPL approach. It is particularly so in a WPLC.

When you apply all these elements together you have *dialogue* – at least, you depend upon dialogue for working out all the many implications that arise from such elements. In practice, this means we want people to ask questions about those things that influence the individual, shape their lives and influence the structures within which they have to find their social purpose.

CHAPTER SEVEN

The Group Dimension of Whole Person Learning

The communication of any truth, any lesson, depends upon a certain kind of mutuality between those involved. It is something more than listening or even hearing; it is more like a form of dialogue based on something deeper than respect, something that amounts to a form of love. (Unknown)

The group dimension forms the background to WPL, simply because WPL takes place in relationship with others rather than in isolation. We all exist in groups of some form or another; many of us belong to a number of groups of differing kinds. Having an understanding of the dimensions of group experience is important both for intending facilitators of WPL events and participants. In this chapter, therefore, we explore a number of facets of groups including communication in groups, types of groups and group development.

Learning and Communication

All of us are engaged in acts of communication throughout our daily lives. It is largely our skills as communicators that distinguish us from other creatures. Without opportunities to engage in communication with those around us, we become isolated and our psychological health begins to suffer. It is no accident that solitary confinement, being deprived of all opportunities to communicate, is regarded as amongst the most serious punishments. There are many definitions and explanations of the process of communication, each one focusing attention upon particular aspects of the wide range of elements that form part of even the simplest act of speech.

Whenever communication is initiated to influence an individual or an outcome, then defensiveness on the part of the sender or the receiver is always possible, just as manipulation is open to both parties. Openness in communication, generally speaking, improves the quality of a relationship, and communication itself is never simply about facts; there are always emotions and feelings involved.

We need to be valued as persons before we are willing to contribute, so the more warmth and respect we receive, the stronger and more real the response tends to be. When people are prepared to reveal themselves to themselves and with others, there is something very profound taking place. It may only happen in moments and it may soon be gone, but it is often a reminder that there are times when we are as insubstantial as mist; we touch at the edges and melt into each other.

> Everything and everybody in the world discloses themselves by some means or another as long as they exist. All of a sudden it makes sense for me to say that a tree discloses its 'treeness'. To receive the disclosure of the world becomes another way of defining the term 'perception'. To perceive is to receive the disclosure of something. And I became fascinated with the question 'What disclosure of the world do I receive?'… As soon as you ask this question of yourself or of another person, it appears that some people, bombarded as we all are by disclosure of the world, receive nothing. It is as if they are blind, deaf, and anosmic.   Sidney Jourard, 1971: 19.

It is rare that we can know other people's intentions – though you may well infer them through what you see they do. It is through our behaviour that we disclose things about ourselves; and our behaviour often only discloses those things we share in common with others. Behaviour often manifests our 'persona', whereas real *deeds* are different. Deeds reveal our deeper self – to others as well as ourselves. When we engage fully with our own experience we are more likely to transcend simple behaviour and become more self-directed; responding out of a deeper appreciation of ourselves and the circumstances rather than merely 'behaving' as usual.

Behaviour in and of itself does not lead to experience in any important sense. The experience has to be perceived, construed, interpreted, all according to some criteria explicit or implicit, conscious or acknowledged. Perception involves interpretation. In many ways this can be summarised as the need to put the experience in the form of a question; an inquiry that the person is then able to pursue with greater intentionality not so much to find an answer as to gain greater meaning.

This is a sophisticated idea in a culture that is by and large interested in 'answers' and instant solutions. Realising that we deepen our understanding of ourselves and our world around us by developing the art of questioning is something that takes time to establish. Of course the appeal of answers and solutions is that they seem generated 'out there' and that they have only to be adopted and applied for the results to follow in train.

In learning, it is not solutions, except in a very narrow sense, that matter. It is how a question opens up a line of inquiry, increases sensitivity to the information that is available, suggests lines of connection and helps people establish links that will help them change their circumstances and ultimately their world.

Questions can be thought of as instruments of perception; a way of guiding our interest and shaping our investigation. And the nature of the question – how it is formed and the assumptions which it contains – determines the nature of the answers that it generates. How we observe – perceive – is a function of the symbol system (language being the main one) that we use. The more limited the system, the less we can see and the fewer distinctions we are enabled to make. The more meaning we can find within our experience, the more new meanings we can generate or acquire.

The level of abstraction at which we use language in any given context is an indication of the extent to which we are in touch with what is going on in the world – rather than what we 'think' is going on. It is useful to remember that the higher the level of abstraction, the less we are in touch with the sensory detail of what makes up the 'reality' 'out there'. One way to use language is to escape from the very reality that it sets out to describe. So called 'facts' are statements about the world as we perceive it; they need to be tentative in the way all our judgements need to be tentative.

In WPL work, the structure is simply the formal arrangement. It is all that is going on underneath which matters. The structure is no more than a container. This does not mean it is irrelevant or unimportant or that it can be casually adopted. It does mean that you don't become entranced by the vase and forget to see the flowers. Every bunch of flowers can be enhanced by the 'right' vase.

In this respect, WPL is more like art than anything else. We value art for what it is, not for what it does – it doesn't have to have an instrumental value. That it is what it is is enough. We don't watch a film with the intention of it providing us with a particular skill. No specific changes are likely or predictable from a Beethoven symphony or a Shakespeare sonnet; they are altogether beyond having some 'desired' effect. Art creates its own measures and they change from one person to another and from one occasion to another – that is why we go back to them again and again. How many people want to go back and repeat their training experience because they might be moved by it once again?

The Importance of Groups

> Groups are incalculably important in the life of every human being. Skills in group functioning are vital to all of us.
>
> D W Johnson and F P Johnson, 2002: 575.

It's not surprising, given the experiences many people have, that they are dismissive of groups. 'Nothing gets done in groups', 'Groups are just a waste of time', are common observations. Individuals often make something of an asset of their dismissal of groups or of their recalcitrance when they are in them. Such reactions, whilst common, often belie a painful or unhelpful set of experiences that have occurred elsewhere – very often experiences that have begun in the family group and have later been reinforced in other groups.

Belonging to groups is one of the most important aspects of our lives. The quality of our life, our working relationships and our personal well-being largely depends upon our effectiveness in the groups to which we belong. And in turn, it is how effective those groups are that also enhances our sense of well-being. In other words, being a prominent and regarded figure in a street gang may be much preferred to the alternative of being a social isolate, but not as socially rewarding as being a respected member of a local games club.

Group membership plays a vital contribution towards influencing our sense of personal identity and overall well-being. The role we play in groups has a decisive effect upon how we see ourselves. It is through our socialisation into the family that we first begin to develop the social competence and skills that are so necessary for successful personal development and productive interpersonal relationships.

Industry, business and civic organisations are based upon *working* groups. Similarly, people discussing the weather, the latest news, or what they did last night also employ the methods of the small group. No one can avoid participating in groups and, if for no other reason, this makes the understanding of how small groups work essential.

Our effectiveness in our group relations is largely determined by our personal group skills and our knowledge of group processes. Group membership is pervasive and has, in turn, a pervasive effect upon us. No one interested in human relations can afford to ignore the impact that group influence has upon our actions; we often act as though under the influence of our reference group even when it isn't present. Similarly, the need to belong or be seen to belong to the 'right' group affects individuals enormously at different times in their lives. Feeling the 'odd one out' can have a lasting effect upon an individual's readiness to join in every group they later have to attend.

One of the difficulties people have in making the effort to find groups useful is that they often feel cast into a certain role no matter what they do, or that they find themselves getting into the same situation over and over again. These kinds of reinforced patterns of behaviour are a result not so much of group life, but of *unfacilitated* group life. Most people are hardly aware of how they behave in the groups to which they belong and often do not know clearly how their behaviour affects other people, unless or until it provokes an extreme reaction. Most of the time, they are too busy attempting to get on with what they are doing, or what they are saying, to have time to observe how they actually go about it.

When individuals are given little opportunity to gather insight and understanding about what is happening and how their behaviours encourages certain things to recur, they come to believe that it is 'the group' that is the cause of their difficulties. In fact, it is *their relationship to the group* that produces the phenomena that leads to their difficulties.

Because groups have such influence upon us, an understanding of how they operate, how they come to make decisions and so on, can help individuals make better use of their potential influence and gain the necessary satisfaction to maintain involvement with the activity of the groups to which they belong. This is a fundamental aspect of any whole person approach to learning as a participant and, especially, as a facilitator. Many people are 'blocked' because they find it difficult to understand what might be an appropriate role to take up in small group activities, or, having found one and experienced its limitations, do not know how to begin to go about changing it.

Individuals begin to realise that what they 'see' is as much a result of what they expect and believe – in short, how they filter their experience. For many people, it is a disturbing novelty when they come to realise just how far that what they 'see' and what they decide it means is unique to themselves; little to do with the understanding of the originator of the behaviour and not much aligned to the views of the rest of the group either!

Models of Group Development

Anyone working with a learning approach that involves any degree of engagement from those involved cannot afford to be without a working knowledge of the stages of group life and the way in which group dynamics plays out at different stages of an event. Without some working understanding about not only the stages but the possible challenges and approaches that may be required, the facilitator is likely to find themselves managing a descent into chaos.

Someone who has an interest in WPL would therefore need not only a strong interest in and wide experience of groups and group life but a critical ability to put their learning into practice, demonstrated by their 'presence' (see *Chapter 3: The Power of Choice*) and how they contribute effectively to the life of the group. In so many ways, the art of the facilitator of WPL is to be nothing more and no less than the exemplary group member. There is a wide variety of models of the stages of the life of a group and the purpose here is to point to a number of key features:

1. All groups go through similar processes; the manner and timing may vary.

2. Groups can get stuck at different stages: sometimes not progressing; sometimes oscillating between two phases and not breaking through into a more productive third stage.

3. Conflict is not only inevitable but also desirable and essential to group growth.

The first model below is a commonly understood model using informal terminology that highlights the key issues. It is useful for getting a feel for where you are in a process. The second model, a four-stage model, is much more detailed and descriptive of both the what (task elements) and the how (process elements), and how they are linked at different stages of group life. With this information, it can be used more as a diagnostic tool.

Forming	Coming together Getting started		
Storming	Honeymoon over Interpersonal conflicts Rivalry over power/structure 'Fight; flight'	Power	**PHASE I** Using power, position and role
Norming	Getting down to it Working relationships established Atmosphere clearer Issues dealt with Process and task separated	Relationships	
Performing	Getting on with it Planning targets: met or revised Relationship not a pre-occupation Satisfaction in achievement Process and task separated	Personal	**PHASE II** Meeting as persons in one's own right
Mourning	Closure, loss Flight behaviour by some Minimising achievement Romanticising the past Looking ahead Commitment decline	Relationships	

Table 4 ◈ A Five Stage Model of Group Life

Stage One	
Task Concerns	**Process Concerns**
Orientation to the task Discovering the nature of the task Discovering and setting the boundaries of the task Grumbling about the setting Intellectualising Talking about irrelevant issues Attempts at defining the situation Mutual exchange of information Suspicion Little work	Testing and dependence Testing relationships with leader Testing relationships with each other Dependency on leader Quick attempts to structure the group To join or not to join Hesitant participation Will they let me join?

Stage Two	
Task Concerns	**Process Concerns**
Emotional responses to the task Resisting, challenging validity Resisting the demands of the task Ambivalence to the leader Experiments with hostility and aggressiveness if task requires high personal commitment and/or self-disclosure If the task does not deal with the self, extreme emotionality is not usually displayed.	Intra-group conflict Defensiveness, competition, jealousy Tension, anxiety, rule-breaking Intense, brief and brittle links Argument Cliques and factions form and break-up Active – passive polarisation Disruption and frustration Rebellion and opposition

Stage Three	
Task Concerns	**Process Concerns**
Open exchange of relevant information Probing and revelation in depth of group members Full description of basic problems Ability to express feelings constructively – helping work Asking for opinions/giving opinions Evaluating opinions in relation to the task	Development of group cohesion Group consciousness develops Group boundaries are established and maintained Consensus, co-operation & mutual support Unity and solidarity Conflict reduces – harmony increases Members identify with the group Authority problems resolved. Norms are established

Stage Four	
Task Concerns	**Process Concerns**
Emergence of solutions Asking and giving of suggestions High degree of work-issues are dealt with in a less excited way Insight and understanding Strong drives towards goals Task-oriented activity unfettered by interpersonal difficulties.	Functional role-relatedness Pragmatism in support of the task. Group structuring in terms of problems rather than interpersonal issues. Clear but flexible roles

Table 5 ◆ **A Four Stage Model of Group Life**[48]

Types of Groups

There is any number of ways of characterising a group: by size, by activity, by style of leadership, by task. A useful way of approaching an understanding of most groups is to view them as being one of three types, though some, of course, have elements of each, but one type usually predominates. The following three broad categories are used to illustrate the different levels of skill needed by facilitators and group members/participants.

1. **The learning group**: largely responsible for delivering content. This is the group we know most about and have greatest experience of from our educational past; the classroom group where people are put together to learn a content that is independent of them and managed by someone else. Individuals come to take what they can from what is offered. Personal needs are not encouraged and if they interfere with the task then an individual may be asked to withdraw.

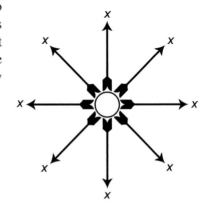

Figure 7 ◆ **Central Provision Group**

---

[48] This model owes a debt to John Rowan.

2. **The work group**: largely responsible for the group delivering a task to an externally agreed standard. This would include Boards, Citizen Action Groups, project teams, office committees. The work group also has a goal outside the member's own individual preferences i.e. to accomplish the organisational task for which they are (usually) paid.

This aspect of work groups is increasingly being seen to have an importance in improving performance.

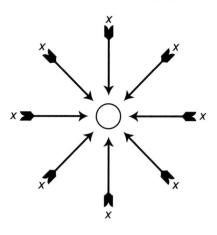

The concentration of the working group is upon the effective use of time and the efficient operation of procedure to ensure the task is accomplished with the minimum expenditure of energy. Personal needs are subsumed under the demands of task accomplishment and may be resented if they surface except in extreme cases, bereavement for example. Individuals in such groups may even believe that liking or not liking one another is irrelevant to the task they are there to accomplish (which it isn't).

Figure 8 ◈ Task Focussed Group

3. **The process group**: efforts focus upon the group's own process and in learning about how that process occurs, who influences it, in what way and so on. Facilitated process groups and interpersonal skills groups would fit into this category and they are in sharp contrast to the previous groups.

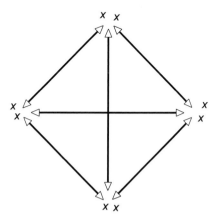

There is often little external content or task; the primary purpose is not to acquire knowledge of a 'content' independent of the process, It is up to the members to generate the experiences from which they can then reflect

Figure 9

Collaborative and Mutual Group

in order to learn how what happens happens in the way that it does. There are no external examinations and success is largely defined by each of the members in their own terms and together collaboratively. Deciding upon the task, allocating 'space' to individuals and allocating time are what has to be managed in the process group.

Interpersonal Groups and Whole Person Learning

Various types of 'leaderless' groups have been tried since T-Groups first began in 1948. They have been successfully used for assisting members to study what happens when people come together and, depending upon the facilitator's skill, interests and development, can encourage members to become aware of their personal style of interaction, group processes, and interpersonal communication.

Below is a table setting out the way a great many interpersonal skills group can be sorted according to type. The growth of such groups over the last twenty-five years has been little short of a revolution, opening up possibilities for individuals to develop aspects of their ways of interacting and understanding a variety of social and relationship issues. In order of focus, groups go from the emphasis being on the individual as individuals attending, to those that look for some stronger interpersonal elements, to those involving the way a person works in and with an issue affecting group life and finally those groups that are based upon recreating scaled-down versions of real life dilemmas.

The WPL group brings features of all of these types into awareness and the facilitator has to learn how to assess the needs of the participant, the needs of the situation and the needs of the organisation (if applicable) in deciding the kinds of interventions they make. So, for example:

1. Do you offer an intervention that moves things on? (Chairperson role.)
2. Do you offer an intervention that outlines more of the content? (Teacher led intervention.)
3. Do you offer an intervention that highlights the dynamics of the group? (Process manager.)
4. Do you deal with the interpersonal, intra-personal, distress-based difficulties of one or more participants? (Group facilitator.)

In addition to all that, the facilitator has to be keenly aware of the level of the development of the group when deciding the strength of any intervention

Focus	Approach	Method
Self/Self	Personal growth	1. Life theme group, e.g. workshop. 2. Via particular orientation, Gestalt, Transactional Analysis (TA), Neuro-Linguistic Programming (NLP) 3. Via interpersonal learning e.g. Sensitivity group, T-group, Encounter group.
Self/Other	Interrelationships	1. Individuals look for personal data and feedback regarding the impact of behaviour upon others and the way in which members deal with one another. 2. Structured situations – designed to highlight or create important and often unresolved issues for individual members via psychodrama, role-play, etc
Self/Group	Group Skills	1. Structured workshop approach to isolate and identify major issues involved in effective group functioning (trust, authority, experience), followed by reflection to secure insight and understanding. 2. Open group: members left to create their own structure and working approach in order to understand the problems and issues in group functioning. 3. Influencing styles of members and the quality and commitment of group membership.
Self/ Organisational Development	Structured	1. To provide participants with simulated conditions reflecting real organisational issues with which they have to contend e.g. competition, conflict. The group processes reactions to an exercise before transferring insights to 'real' situations. 2. Participants engaged in real conflict or difficulty 'contract' to resolve their differences with the help of a skilled facilitator or consultant – with or without an agenda.
Self	Structured Vocational Workshop	1. Structured exercises focus upon aspects of individual job performance and trainees reflect upon performance, identify areas of conflict or tension, and establish action plans for development. 2. Focus upon career development issues (with or without support of host organisation) in order to assess future prospects.

Table 6 · Focus of Interpersonal Groups

they might make. Generally speaking, process interventions can only usefully be made once the group has become more cohesive, whereas content-based interventions help early on in a group to create a sense of safety because they are the kind of interventions that are more familiar to most people from their previous experiences.

It is worth noting that in the UK little formal attention is paid to helping individuals learn how groups operate, how best to participate, what expectations can be predicted and how best to manage to make a useful contribution in a group. Even realising that groups are of different types is a novelty to some people, whose primary experience of a group is 'a bunch of people where things are going to be difficult'. What makes it difficult for many people is that they have never been given a suitable induction into how the particular group operates, what contributions help it progress and what makes it stall, or worse. Having unrealistic or unclear expectations of what the group is able to accomplish is only one of the many ways people find groups 'difficult'.

Comparison of Whole Person and Traditional Methods

With the shifts in expectations and changes in every aspect of modern life, there is a growing recognition that many of the underlying assumptions of a traditional curriculum are simply inadequate or inappropriate to meet these needs and challenges. A caricature of some of those past assumptions, now under challenge, would include:

- There is a given body of knowledge that the student or trainee needs to acquire and the most effective way to attain it is to pass the examinations that demonstrate success: licence to practice mindset

- There is a minimum level of competence for any task or activity which can always be externally verified, via written or practical examinations: anyone can be trained to do this job mindset

- An essential aspect of becoming a craftsman or professional is obedience to the professional body, therefore the form of teaching reflects the unequal power relationship between those who teach and those who learn: the protocols are all mindset

- Only when students have finished learning do they begin to have a right to comment on the body of knowledge they have acquired: by the 'expert' mindset

- By definition, you cannot have a right to a view of what is important until you know what you are talking about: the 'join our club' mindset.

Some of the features that distinguish a WPL from a traditional method of working are set out on the next page. The differences are inevitably stereotypical and are used to sharpen the contrast. In many ways they do not do justice to the work of many inspired, traditional teachers who seek to involve their students actively in their particular field of study. But it is worth noting that, however enthusiastic and inspiring such individual teachers are, they are rarely setting out to encourage students to examine the very basis of the teacher-learner contract, something that a WPL approach does. It is this reason, perhaps more than any other that sets WPL apart from a traditional approach. The way the learning enterprise is itself set up is open for examination, in at least an implicit way, in any participative programme. Most traditional teachers would find this kind of contract such a challenge to their position and authority that they would reject it.

We have a long way to go in our educational thinking and practice before we come close to real student-centred learning. Yet advances have been made. It is no longer the exception for participants, on even short development courses, to have an opportunity to influence the structure of the programme they receive.

Traditional learning expects:	Whole Person Learning encourages:
Acceptance of external decisions	Participant involvement in planning
Respect for those in authority	Participants developing a questioning attitude
Acceptance of predetermined objectives	Participants identifying their own learning objectives
Adherence to aims based on content	Objectives based on participants' needs
Formal procedures and relationships	Individual focus on personal objectives
Focus upon content and presentation	Process: learning how to learn
Pre-determined exercises	Informality and spontaneity
'Right' or 'model' answers	Solving open-ended problems
Competitive and norm referencing	Identifying relevant problems
Authority marking	Self and peer evaluation/co-operation
Classes of 150; 'slots' of one hour	Groups of 20 maximum; sessions that may be 4-6 hours with facilitators present throughout
External validation	Peer accountability for learning
Semesters	One place location
	Self-validation

Table 7 ⬧ Comparing Traditional and Whole Person Learning

CHAPTER EIGHT

Individual Experiences in Whole Person Learning Groups

There is a distinction to make between role relationships – which we all need to fulfil for the show to keep on the road and 'real' relationships. Role relationships depend upon 'a repertoire of behaviour patterns' which must be rattled off in appropriate contexts, and all behaviour irrelevant to the role must be suppressed. Sidney Jourard,1971: 31.

Because WPL takes place in group settings, this chapter introduces some of the forces and influences that affect individuals in groups and the group as a whole. Coming to understand how we behave in groups, how we communicate within them, how we relate to others within them, how we set out to get what we need from them, how we respond and react in ways that seem to prevent us getting what we want are all crucial aspects of discovering more of what it means to be involved in WPL.

Learning and Change

Learning can be thought of simply as 'a relatively permanent change in behaviour', whether this be acquiring information, developing a skill or integrating a new concept. People in general do not like change and they will find elaborate ways to continue responding in the well-tried and tested ways they have acquired over many years. Because change is difficult to accomplish, it is especially important for facilitators to recognise that people are where they are for some very good reasons, however elusive those reasons are. Also, if people say they want to change but 'can't', it's not their 'resistance' to the facilitator's skills and abilities in creating opportunities, it is that the facilitator has not yet found ways to help them.

For change to be lasting and effective, the participants have to see its value and recognise its potential utility within the life they lead. Only when change is chosen, is someone likely to remain committed to carrying it over into other aspects of life. It is important to remember people do not have to change – they have the right to choose, and that means the right to refuse. People change for one of three reasons:

1. They are challenged in their perception of their reality.
2. They are given alternative possibilities that make sense to them.
3. They have tried alternatives and have found enough rewards in those alternatives to have the change reinforced.

Whether people learn or not is only partly something to do with the atmosphere of the group, but when the atmosphere stops people, it can stop them in powerful ways that have lasting effects. Similarly, being in an enjoyable group is no guarantee that a great deal of useful learning is happening – though given how difficult it is for many people to enjoy being in any learning group that may itself be something of an achievement.

People learn in different ways, at different rates and with different levels of motivation. What an individual learns is dependent upon their own style and readiness for learning, and the relationships that exist and develop amongst the participants. There is always more than one way of doing things or finding something out, and the same thing may be discovered in several different ways. WPL approaches need to bear this in mind rather more strongly than traditional approaches, since a de-motivated group creates difficulties that become all too apparent. Creativity in WPL can be encouraged in many ways:

> ...the use of an opening ritual, of an imaginal focus in the middle of the group, of a bell for Tibetan awakening. Other examples which include the whole group are: free form dancing to music, musical improvisation with percussion and other instruments, theatrical improvisation, games, energetic movements, loud noise, time for unfettered reflection, moments of silence and attunement.
>
> John Heron, in D. Boud and N. Miller (eds), 1996: 87.

In WPL groups, individuals are able to gain increased insight into the impact they have upon others, into how this relates to the way they think they are perceived and into how they see themselves. They also gain experience in developing their ability to focus upon the forces which affect the characteristics of the group, and upon the procedures and norms operating upon group members. They gain an increasing awareness of such ideas as cohesion, power, climate and structure and of how they reveal themselves in action.

A WPL group approach requires a commitment by all participants to foster their own and others' personal development and a willingness to use some of the elements of their own behaviour for study. Group skills cannot be taught effectively by conceptual teaching alone, even if it were desirable.

It would be much like learning to swim without going to the pool. I may well know what to do, how to do it, and what should happen, but until I am in the water I can never know if I can swim.

Entering a Group

In the early stages of a group meeting, members will often go to great lengths to seek and find agreement with one another rather than display any sign of difference and disagreement, thereby avoiding conflict and problems of leadership and power. Some members will actively seek to make their influence felt from the beginning and will look for support and recognition from other members of the group. In whatever way, each member will have a style of responding to the problems of helping the group form an identity for itself, because without an identity the group cannot function at all.

In the vacuum of uncertainty, individual members may well attempt to manage their discomfort by attempts to get what they want. They will go a long way, often, to pursue a strategy that they firmly believe will make things 'all right'. Since the energy behind such efforts derives from the anxiety of the situation, their perception is almost always inaccurate and is also at odds with the other, equally powerfully-made claims of other individuals.

Often such *personal needs are clothed in the garb of representing a group need*. One person wants to 'do something' but finds it too confronting to admit such a need as personal and suggests this is a requirement of the group as a whole, and they merely a representative spokesperson. Such efforts are attempts by individuals to seek to impose rigid order upon what is an extremely ambiguous situation. When such efforts fail, as they invariably do, a period of frustration follows.

As we have seen in the previous chapter, there are certain common features to the development of groups. Even a group which has become used to meeting together over a long period can still be observed to pass through a predictable cycle of ritualistic communications before real activity gets underway. This 'warming-up' period of greetings and passing comments to one another *establishes interpersonal contact* between members in preparation for their coming together to get on with their task. If, after making several attempts, contact is not thought to be worthwhile, individuals will tend to avoid one another by mutual agreement (which does not have to be spoken).

There is a whole screen of assumptions, concepts, attitudes and evaluations that each member brings with them about the way groups *should* operate and how people ought to conduct themselves. In experiential and WPL groups, when the usual constraints of having a job to do and someone to organise it are removed, all these assumptions have to be dismantled and reassembled in the light of what takes place. *It is a difficult task for group members to learn to work consciously on the problems of* **group** *and* **member** *maintenance rather than an externally imposed task.* This is likely to raise questions of personal identity, the application of personal power, vocational choice, gender, role and world-view.

Steps on the Way
1. The starting point in any group (and a WPL group particularly) is to learn how best to represent yourself, to know and then to be able to express your own wishes and needs.
2. From that starting point, of learning how to manage *me*, and with the help of facilitation to manage the resulting chaos that sometimes breaks out, I can begin to move on.
3. I begin to learn how to share my needs *with others*.
4. I begin to realise that there comes a point in *our learning together* that unless I help you get what you want, getting what I want is not of much value in itself.
5. If we are in a *real relationship* then we have to work out what *we* are doing.
6. That change – the move from proposing what I want, irrespective of what others want to having an authentic interest in what others may want, whilst expressing my own wants – represents a major shift for most people.
7. There is the realisation that we do not always get *all our needs* met at the same time but most endeavours, when facilitated effectively, can accomplish *a creative way for everyone getting enough of what they want to make the enterprise exciting and a committed endeavour.*

Table 8 ⬧ Steps towards Effective Individual Participation

All group members have some degree of knowledge about what it is they are there to accomplish, though for many this may be unclear and difficult to express. Almost always the purpose of the group will have been made explicit in the literature which has been sent to them – the course description or the job specification – and this certainly focuses people's attention on the nature of the activity they have come together to perform. But it is not the whole story. An individual may join a discussion group out of an interest in the topic, but, as we have seen, they will also use the group to pursue their own interpersonal needs and to help them gain some role in the life of the group. These factors, as much as their interest in the subject and the group, will influence the kind of performance they offer.

Often what appears as a clear and unambiguous aim for the group, such as 'learning how to canoe', involves a whole range of activities, which interested new members may well never have considered. A high level of enthusiasm may quickly begin to wilt, if they are not made aware of the reasons behind much of the preparatory work necessary before they get into their canoe and paddle it. Often they will continue attending, slightly bemused at the relevance of some of the activities.

The Communication 'Game'

In the early days of a group, the flow of communication can appear to follow only a random pattern with individuals making contributions as and when they feel the need. Further study will begin to reveal patterns of communication emerging. People will speak for a variety of motives at different times, but there will be those who tend to seek to impress, to gain support, to show their loyalty to the group image or to the clique within the group, to display their rebellious streak, to gain favour and so on.

In the same way that individuals tend to have particular motivations which influence their individual contributions and which can be observed and identified, the flow of communication between one member and another tends to follow predictable patterns. There are those members who always lend their support to certain other individuals. These (often unconscious) patterns of communication can be positive or negative in their influence upon the group's progress.

Who speaks to whom is very often related to the status differences that individuals believe exist within the group. The result is often that low status individuals make few contributions and await the invitation of higher status individuals before they do. Disagreements tend to follow the pattern that a higher status individual can freely challenge someone of lower status and even interrupt them, but lower status individuals do not challenge higher status members or interrupt them with the same frequency.

One of the many reasons why committee-style meetings are often very frustrating for those who have to attend them is as a result of the status differences between members and the feelings of those with relatively low status that their point of view is undervalued. This leads them to contribute less, to become passively hostile and to feel little commitment to the decisions that are made. It is a prevalent fantasy that decisions by majority vote are somehow 'the best'. Unless people feel they have been allowed to participate in the discussions that lead to the decision, the chances are that they will have little commitment to implementing it once voted upon.

Individuals can 'trigger' each other. Sudden eruptions or predictable challenges can be the result of one member being 'triggered' by another member of the group. 'Triggering' takes place when members consistently make the same kind of response to one another, irrespective of the quality or relevance of the contribution. Sometimes, individuals form alliances with other members in the group which can leave them feeling restricted in their ability to display disagreement out of a feeling of the need to remain loyal to their partner or sub-group. The ability to tolerate and accept differences between members is a significant indicator of the maturity of the group.

Levels of Commitment in Effective Groups

The bond or level of connection that a group needs in order to establish itself can be thought of as the minimum level of commitment required in order for it to function effectively enough to accomplish the tasks that it is set up to do. The bond a group requires, in this sense, is about the willingness of those taking part to stand by the decisions that they take part in without necessarily having to feel that *each of them must uphold all of the decisions.*[49]

All individuals have boundaries and limits which influence and determine their view of things and their willingness to share and work with others. Boundaries can be crossed and changed. But if individuals' boundaries are not respected they are likely to become barriers. Barriers are fixed and they are used to keep people out.

In situations of anxiety, most of us fall back to 'either/or' forms of thinking: it must be this way or that! No creative third alternatives surface. And here is the first appearance of that 'double bind'. The group needs

---

[49] Most people assume that individuals simply decide for themselves, that there must be a majority vote or that some notionally harmonious consensus are the only possibilities for deciding things in a group. The complexities of group decision-making are many, but to assist a group develop the capacity to decide on the basis of, 'We all have declared where we are and no one is vetoing the step' is far from easy, since it appears to give the power to the minority of one. However, rarely does anyone who has been thoroughly listened to and whose objections and reservations have been engaged with sincerely stop a group from progressing when they remain in a minority. It just takes a lot more time to assist people to learn these skills of decision-making than is usually allowed.

enough commitment from everyone to progress and be of a level commensurate to what they are hoping to do. If the commitment required is so low and one which people can choose whether to fulfil or not, it becomes largely tokenistic and is of little value. If, however, the demands are so extreme that they are absurd, individuals will choose to opt out.

> If you are willing to let people drift in and out of sessions as they chose; withdraw from being engaged without requirement to give an account as to why, and generally let a laissez-faire attitude masquerade as a chosen way of facilitating, you might get many groups started but they will make little progress.
>
> If, on the other hand, everyone has to stand on the window ledge 14 floors up and recite their favourite poem backwards before you, as facilitator, believe group members are committed enough to learn with you, then you won't be much in demand as a facilitator.

Allowing individuals to find a sufficient level of commitment and their own ways of expressing that commitment satisfactorily to all concerned is what is required. This is something that a facilitator comes to learn how to judge since a large part of the success of the endeavour lies in this initiating act; something many clubs and organisations have traditionally expected and/or demanded as a way of marking the transition of the newcomer from the status of a nobody to a somebody, so far as the group is concerned.

As the group explores the level of commitment required, they are beginning to resolve their *inclusion* issues. The question here is whether being in the group is worth what they expect to get out of it or whether they would rather spend their time elsewhere.

There is a decisive moment in the formation of a group when, in order to obtain the future benefits of membership, all those involved have to face some concrete and immediate losses of freedom – primarily the freedom to act as they individually wish without reference to its effects upon others. In practice this often means individuals giving up the 'right' to act wilfully; just how fiercely some individuals cling on to this 'right' can be seen when groups are struggling over their criteria for membership.

Those individuals who have difficulty in joining a group often claim that membership really does not, nor should not, require any dramatic acts of allegiance in order for it to work and get on with its mundane job. And yet without some unequivocal demonstration, a group will forever return to inclusion issues on any occasion when it faces a significant challenge to its work or its membership. This is true whether the challenge is based upon decisions which have been arrived at internally (for example, how it should go about a particular task), or whether the challenge comes from outside (facing a withdrawal of resources, for example).

The Need for Security in Groups

We protect ourselves by structures and cultural patterns from fundamental uncertainties and insecurities about human life. Institutions, organisations and groups provide a certain order and purpose in exchange for allegiance and loyalty; outside lies loneliness and instability. It is not surprising then, that in exchange for reassurance, we cease to question assumptions unless challenged to do so. WPL groups provide such challenges forcefully and directly because the situation into which participants are invited contains fewer pre-determined rules and rituals.

Ground rules are a useful example here. Although many people entering a WPL programme have attended events where the expectations and reservations of those attending are considered or where ground rules are outlined, few people recognise their importance or have really engaged with them to the degree needed in a WPL event.

They are not simply blasé repetitions of well-understood conventions to be polite and so on. They need to reflect the gutsy determination of people who intend to engage with the issues and the concerns that they have come to learn about through a WPL experience. Ground rules, therefore, are a critical dimension for building the alternative culture that *this group* agrees to work to, so that when the inevitable breakdowns and mishaps occur (which is what makes the life of WPL so interesting) there is some agreed and acknowledged code by which to explore what happened and how to remedy it in the future.

Through working out the ground rules, people realise very often that the process has served a bigger purpose; it has brought alive the different issues and concerns individuals bring to the event that need to be respected. In addition, it has begun the process of enabling the members to begin becoming 'visible' to one another. The process is instrumental in helping create a climate of greater trust and acceptance; something that merely signing up to exhortations to be 'honest', 'respectful' and so on, simply cannot achieve. In addition, when you work out ground rules for yourself with others, they come to mean something real – for you and for them.

In some cases, the structure of the group may be explicitly counter to the socially acceptable forms of politeness to be found in life outside. When people arrive expecting the methods for settling doubts and arranging the proceedings of this group to be similar to those sanctioned by past experience, only to find this is far from the case, individuals are thrust into a vacuum of insecurity which raises doubts about how matters are to be settled and how the group shall proceed – and often whether the group will survive at all. Individuals are then forced back upon their own resources to legislate and maintain a viable mode of entering into and sustaining their relationships with one another.

This creates a degree of instability that provides the facilitator with their first major task: 'How do you offer a model of personal security in a situation that is fundamentally and genuinely uncertain?' If the facilitator has not already put themselves through some such process, it is difficult to see how they can undertake this role in a WPL event. In other words, previous experience of being in WPL events or WPL communities would seem to be a prerequisite for someone intending to facilitate such groups.

Facilitating WPL groups thus requires the facilitator to have seriously immersed themselves in their own experiences of such learning as a prerequisite. In a fundamental sense, the success of the enterprise rests with the facilitator being able to be at ease with high levels of anxiety being projected their way and a confident (though not arrogant) attitude, providing a strong sense that we can all travel this road together – anxieties and expressions of discontent included.

Our social life is also structured in such a way that little emphasis is placed upon interpersonal and inter-group competition, which leaves many people entering experiential workshops without:

- **An adequate language** to describe what is going on within themselves or of what they see
- **A philosophy**: a ground of ideas and a conceptual framework which would help them make sense of what is happening
- **A reward structure**: a way of pursuing and obtaining personal gratification and enhancing their self-esteem
- **Behavioural skills** to work in collaboration with others and resolve interpersonal difficulties.

The typical background experience and education of most people leaves them sadly under-prepared for working effectively in a collaborative fashion. This in turn leads to some major 'focal issues' that groups necessarily have to confront and deal with if they are to progress.

Social Drives and Interpersonal Needs

A group is influenced by the individual contributions of its members, which in turn reflect the needs they have in becoming members in the first place. These personal needs must achieve sufficient recognition and a minimum level of satisfaction, otherwise their contribution will decrease and their involvement decline to the point where they may well leave the group altogether.

Some may be there to be noticed; some may be there because they want to be leaders; some may be there because they were told to attend; some may be there because they are scared. Some individuals require more interpersonal contact than others. Some people feel the need to gain more attention than others. Some people wish to exercise power and influence rather more than others. Some people are more willing to deal with conflict than others and so on. All these *social drives* come together to produce the starting point for the group to begin working out its own pattern of interaction. This helps explain why different groups possess different characteristics; some being 'cosy', some 'tasky' and others 'prickly'.

It is the result of the mix of personalities and the way the group works in solving its problems that gives a minimum level of satisfaction to those taking part. Each of these social drives is a continuum along which individuals may change their position according to the presence, or absence of a number of factors. These include experience, temporary anxieties, the situation, the role that they are performing and so on. This is a temporary state. In addition, however, they will tend to move within certain broad limits along any particular dimension. For example, it would be unusual to find someone with a high need for dominance continuously acquiescing to other people's decisions. The overall position, which remains fairly stable, is termed the 'trait'.

Some of these social drives include:

Social Drive			
Conflict/Aggression	fight	balance	flight
Dependency	dependent	independent	counter-dependent
Affiliation/Disclosure	under-personal	personal	over-personal
Inclusion	under-social	social	over-social
Power	dominant	shared	submissive
Intimacy	enmeshed	close	distant

Regardless of the length of programme, a sufficient degree of relatedness must be established before the task can be accomplished. How far you balance the emotional needs of the members of the group against the task needs will influence the quality of the group's culture. The nature of the task and the time available will be important factors in determining the level of relatedness appropriate to any group.

In all groups and for all individuals within groups, three crucial interpersonal needs will be present. Facilitators need to have a broad appreciation of the way individuals' interpersonal needs find expression (or are withheld) and have creative ways of influencing the pattern of what takes place. The needs are very closely linked with the stages of the life of the group but can be revisited and recur at any stage. The levels to which these needs are explored, worked with and openly acknowledged are crucial to the effectiveness and cohesion of the group.

The three needs combine to stimulate an individual to relate toward others in order to attain a satisfactory relationship with their *human environment*. As a result of experience and other factors, these needs are not always harmoniously present in individuals or in groups. It is the individual and group balance of each of these needs which gives rise to the particular styles of relationship which develop between people and the particular flavour of the group atmosphere. The balance of these needs within and between people also gives an indication of the way the group will have issues and difficulties to face and resolve. The three needs are **inclusion, control** and **openness**.

1. Inclusion: the need to belong; being in or out. Inclusion, or belonging, is the first major issue that influences the formation and the pattern of communication within a group. It is important to realise some of the implications this has for the future development of the group, since the inclusion patterns of group members have a major influence upon the levels of incident and drama that is manufactured to which the group has to pay attention. Inclusion is repeated throughout group life and may remain unresolved throughout.

At a feeling level, inclusion is defined as the need to establish and maintain a feeling of mutual interest with others. It thus covers things like the need for attention, recognition, status and even fame. Individuality, acknowledgement, commitment and participation are also inclusion needs. Unlike affection, inclusion does not involve strong emotional links and attachments to individual persons, and it is unlike control in that it is more to do with prominence than dominance.

Only as people begin to separate out and become visible to one another does the potential for closer relationships really emerge. Some individuals fear this later stage and are only too happy to keep things chummily superficial.

> *Good interpersonal relationships depend upon the understanding and acceptance of the other as a separate person who is 'operating in terms of his own meanings, based on his own perceptual field'.*
> Carl Rogers (1951) in Maurice Friedman, 1992: 37.

2. Control: the need to establish a satisfactory level of security. Control is concerned with influence and perceived hierarchical positions in the group. Emotionally, this is defined as a need to establish and maintain a feeling of mutual respect for the competence and responsible-ness of others – the sense of trust we hold in relation to others. Control behaviour therefore relates to decision-making and boundary issues in relationships. Power, authority, dominance and rule-making are all part of the control aspect. Rebellion, resistance and submission suggest a lack of sufficient positive influence.

Control is experienced along a continuum that begins with a desire to control others at one end to the desire to be controlled by others at the other – thereby having the authority and responsibility removed from them. A 'control freak' is someone who is most at ease in a known hierarchy, not always someone who is exercising control themselves – though if a vacuum exists for any length of time, their anxiety may surface so strongly that they feel obliged to offer a means for controlling the situation, however inappropriate or unsuitable. There is no necessary relation between an individual's need for control of others and the need for being controlled themselves. For example, many people who are good at exercising authority are often good at receiving and obeying orders. It is not that they always have to be giving them. They simply need to know who is, what they are and what place that leaves them in. This gives the sense of security that they are seeking.

3. Openness/Affection: the need to satisfy the desire for relative closeness toward others unconnected to role and status expectations or demands. The area of openness is focused upon the expression of deeper feelings and highlights the issue of *lovability or lovingness. Emotionally close, liking, personal* and so on are all terms which indicate an openness and/or affection, though the same terms are sometimes used to describe inclusion stages of relationships.

One of the problems people with high openness needs have to face is that *much inclusion behaviour is passed off as openness when it clearly isn't.* Having to wait until the relationship has progressed through the earlier stages into the area of openness makes those with high openness needs often wonder if they will ever get their needs met in groups. A way to avoid meeting the emotional demands of this stage of group development or a relationship is to be equally close to everyone and not make choices. Popularity of this kind may be more an expression of inclusion behaviour. Important connections are more selectively maintained.

A balanced profile is the individual who is capable of relating personally; someone who is comfortable with closeness and with distance as the situation dictates. It is important to be liked, but equally such a person knows it is not realistic to expect to be liked by everyone all the time. Offering and receiving openness is possible and enjoyable, when it is appropriate.

A need may be unable to be met fully or satisfactorily. An individual with a high need (the wanted aspect) of control, for example, may pursue responsibility to the point of over-commitment. They may well find that they cannot manage effectively, but cannot *let go* either. Though the original need for control was to gain security, the way the need is manifested (the expressed aspect) ensures that the individual rarely feels they have the right balance. There can be discrepancies between the amount of any of the three needs that a person offers and the amount they actually wish for or need.

Closure of the group follows a similar process as the formation of the group only in reverse. In other words, there is a phase of leaving the openness behind, the re-emergence of control issues and then the excluding phase as individuals drop out before the end or make great efforts to keep the group alive long after it has completed its work.

Choice, Collaboration and Personal Visibility

A choice that confronts everyone at every moment is this: Shall we permit our fellow to know us as we now are, or shall we remain enigmas, wishing to be seen as persons we are not?   Sidney Jourard, 1971: vii.

Issues of **choice, collaboration and personal visibility** are built-in elements that all participants will inevitably face on a programme or event working within any form of learning that adopts a WPL approach.

Visibility. WPL depends upon individual participation: participation in identifying and expressing one's own learning needs, preferences for what is to be done when, what topics shall be covered, who will be worked with and so on. It puts a high level of commitment upon the individual participating to 'show' themselves to others in a way that is unfamiliar to many.

Individuals first become visible to themselves through others. They must find what it is like to hold their own space, become recognised and acknowledged by their colleagues, as well as become willing to engage in and with the differences that are inevitably revealed.

Choice. *Choice is fundamental to a peer learning process.* Individuals are making choices throughout a programme, about what, when, who. It is through the examination of choices and how they influence one's opportunities that many participants begin to recognise that they only choose at a very rudimentary level. In short, it is a form of sub-autonomous choice. It is based on conventional notions of politeness, expectation and adaptation rather than on surfacing, expressing and negotiating the individual's 'felt needs'.

'Choosing' can be based on a deep recognition of individual needs and preferences, and can be held with an openness and willingness to revise choices in the light of the information that is revealed as others declare their choices. Choosing in this open and dynamic fashion can be a prolonged and existential activity that reveals all kinds of insecurities, fears and distresses. These are frequently based on past rejections, past avoidances and the consequences of having been willing to show oneself and being 'put down', or worse, in the past. Healing such misconceptions, correcting the view that such hurt is inevitable, challenging the notion that choice is somehow not an acceptable activity because their sensitivities might (indeed will) get awakened, is a major issue in the choice of skills groups and other working arrangements.

Collaboration. Collaboration inevitably depends upon the degree to which a person can manage working with the preconditions of *visibility* and *choice*. Unless a peer group actively seeks to examine its own life, it quickly, like any other group, develops recognised formations of pairings and sub-groupings. This results in fore-shortening creativity and experimentation, reducing opportunities for group members to engage with each other and begins to replicate the features of group life in more traditional meetings.

If I am unwilling to make myself visible, will not work with my choices and leave it to others, then collaboration – the dynamic of engagement – is a sham. Collaboration is not the same as majority voting. Usually, the majority is only some cobbled-together collusive assembly of un-worked out preferences that is motivated more with the aim of getting the process over with than in engaging with what results it will bring about.

Collaboration is arduous. It involves surfacing the implications of preferences, checking out the likely results of proposed arrangements, inviting people to reconsider (at the most fundamental level) whether their current position is indeed really expressing a choice. All this is part of collaboration and peers can learn to engage with it strongly and with skill. Collaboration takes time but when people work strongly together, though they do not all get all their needs met all the time, they all know that their needs have been recognised and taken into account in the process that is agreed, and a process is not agreed until it is agreed by all.

It is this combination of *visibility, choice and collaboration* upon which the life of a WPL learning group depends for the degree of challenge and learning that it achieves for its members.

Openness and trust are easy words to write, but they are difficult to live out in the challenging forum of an involved group working with demanding issues.

Group Cohesion

Cohesion exists when people feel that they are together enough not to have to ask the question, 'Am I included?' It occurs when people want to be more 'in' a group than 'out', and feel positive rather than negative when they are attending. In some situations, a form of negative cohesion can operate. An example might be, 'I don't expect a lot to happen here that is of any use, but at least it is better than...'

Cohesion is not stable. It varies according to individual responses at different times and in relation to internal and external preoccupations and is therefore not something to be taken for granted or assumed will continue once it exists. It has to be maintained actively.

Cohesion is indicated in several ways:

- Attendance
- Punctuality

- Trust and support displayed by members to one another
- Tolerance of individual differences (scope to act individually, rather than conformity)
- Ability to have fun together (how far people like one another and the group).

The greater the cohesion, the greater the likelihood that membership will be maintained and more likely the group is to achieve its goals (given any realistic chance to achieve its goals at all). There is likely to be low turnover of membership, low absenteeism, and less disruption if someone happens to leave. Participation is likely to be high and therefore there is a wide range of individual resources available to call on, since one of the by-products of cohesion is high commitment. If important skills are absent, because an individual is not present, they are likely to be searched for amongst those remaining.

A further element of cohesion is willingness for group members to 'own' or take responsibility for the norms of operation and to take responsibility to maintain them. In other words, the group will not only develop its own culture, it will 'own' its own culture and take some measure of responsibility for helping that culture evolve to meet new situations and develop new understandings of the experiences it has as it develops.

Where cohesion is high there is the likelihood of an increase in forms of intimacy, acceptance and understanding of members for one another, and though the expression of hostility and conflict may be open and high, it is more likely to be resolved than be left to work its way through the group in an underground or covert fashion. A further feature of cohesion is that it offers a form of security which reduces anxieties amongst members.

Individual Roles

For a group to progress, members must show a willingness to assume the roles necessary to move towards the group objective. The roles will vary according to the stage of development of the group, the task, and the personalities of the members. In a single session individuals may well switch between several roles; at one moment acting as a *proposer*, then *harmoniser*, and later as *clarifier* of another's position. The greater the flexibility amongst members to perceive the roles appropriate to the situation and to assume them, the more likely the group is to achieve success.

However, the roles many people come to adopt are often restricted and, in part, frustrating. Some people find they tend to take on the same role in every group they join; some find they are coerced into accepting roles they feel do not adequately represent them and may become resentful, thus reducing their commitment. Sometimes membership or attendance at a new group offers an individual the opportunity to attempt a new role.

If groups fail to recognise the roles that exist, and which members play which of them, and if they never talk about it, then some members are likely to feel unfairly restricted. Many individuals feel they get roles they do not like, but find it difficult to know how to change it since everyone has a vested interest in them remaining where and who they are (it makes life predictable). WPL methods encourage individuals to move out of old roles and into new ones by encouraging new responses from them.

Learning is related to motivation and expectation, which is, in turn, influenced by past learning experiences. Some people arrive with unrealistic expectations which the programme is unlikely to meet; they then leave, convinced of one more method that promised everything and did nothing. Some people discover it is not an approach that appeals to them; some discover they are actually antagonistic towards it. Others are able to make the transition and relish the challenge and opportunities for growth and development that are readily apparent.

The amount of change people can make varies considerably, but behaviour established over years is not likely to wither away overnight. Sometimes individuals use excessive expectations as a way of sabotaging themselves. This enables them to have the problem they started out with and saves the bother of having to do anything about it. Enabling people to identify and share expectations in the early stages of a group's life encourages individuals to take responsibility for what happens and to 'own' their learning.

Influences upon Individual Participation

We emphasise the challenges and difficulties that face the facilitator because, typically, most people when they first join a group are:

1. On their best behaviour.
2. Disguising, often from themselves, difficult and damaging experiences from previous groups.

At some point people drop their 'best behaviour' and behave in a more real fashion. As this process takes place, the effects upon them of their past difficulties begin to be demonstrated.

These difficulties and challenges are also emphasised because, in our experience, facilitators are often naïve in the early stages of their career.

They cherish the illusion that everybody will be 'nice' or that conflict will be manageable through the conventions of politeness. If you invite people to be real – which we do in WPL – you will necessarily meet them in some very difficult emotional and psychological places.

As we have already seen, each individual in a group is subject to a wide variety of influences upon conduct and behaviour, just as each member has differing degrees of influence upon other members of the group. Some members are more effective than others at encouraging people to participate, others are better at defining what needs to be done, and so on, but all members come to any new group with a past history of the other groups to which they have belonged.

This, in turn, affects the ways they view *this* particular group and what might happen to them here. Experience in other groups may make some individuals particularly defensive, on the lookout for attacks from others, which may never be intended. For others, having assumed the role of leader in the past is sufficient for them to expect the role will be granted to them, wherever they happen to be. It may be an uncomfortable process for everyone when they have to realise things are otherwise.

The interpersonal skills of members will vary and the balance of such skills and experience contribute to the time it takes for the group to function well. Different members will have differing levels of skill across a wide range of behaviours. Some will have more insight than others about problem solving. Others will show greater awareness of how individuals are responding to the way things are moving. There will be those individuals who can help release the potential of other group members by the way they seek out facts and opinions, and there will be those who bring expertise from activities and interests they have taken part in elsewhere.

In addition to the above factors, people are likely to have concerns, which may be more or less conscious. These insecurities, which are particularly acute at the early stages of the group's life, need working with sensitively and explicitly if they are to be overcome quickly so that they do not interfere with the way the group develops. Helping group members share some of their concerns about why they have come to the group and what they hope to achieve by being there can help put things in perspective. This enables members to realise how much they have in common and how unfounded is the belief that each member is the only one to feel apprehensive, nervous or uncertain. It is quite common for many group members to feel inhibited in their potential to contribute in the early stage. These concerns are linked to the three interpersonal needs already described and play a powerful part in how individuals are able to participate in the event.

Finding acceptance. For a proportion of people entering into experiential work there is a considerable fear that others will not accept them. Usually this fear is accompanied by another myth i.e. that 'If people knew the "real" me, they certainly would not like me'.

Stage-managing the public persona. Individuals often have well-developed social masks and roles they are accustomed to using. In a new situation, they are heavily invested in maintaining a particular view of themselves with which they identify. Together with the fear of not finding acceptance, stage-managing their persona and role-playing combine to produce an artificial and inauthentic presence that the group has to work to overcome if they are to make a working contract with one another.

Avoiding discomfort. Some people have experience of groups (usually hearsay rather than first-hand experience) in which things have gone somehow 'wrong' or in which they experienced discomfort, and look to new situations as potential sources of similar discomfort. A large part of their energy is thus expended in trying to make life safe, predictable and free of conflict. Their response is to wish to avoid issues rather than follow them through.

Being ignored. The feeling of having nothing to offer or nothing to contribute is a fear and a myth that governs some people's every behaviour. They will either discount any experience they have or expect others to know what they know anyway. At the same time as they do little, there is usually an accompanying fear of the group leaving them out: something they actually assist in creating themselves.

Not being influential. Levels of desire to exert power, influence and control vary. Some people have a high need for structure and will want to supply it if any opportunity arises. Others will want to find less overt ways to exert an influence upon the way things develop. Everyone has an investment in pushing things in any given direction, but some fear they will not find ways to exercise it.

Being denied privacy. Some people see groups as claustrophobic gatherings that enmesh all those taking part into over-close and over-intimate contact. To resist this happening, they invest considerable energy in maintaining a suitable distance between themselves and others. Groups can be both over-close and over-intimate, but frequently this is a fantasy which can be confronted.

Group Norms

Over time, all groups develop settled patterns of interacting – group norms. These patterns may be consistent with the agreed ways of conducting its affairs or they may not. The norm is the behaviour that actually takes place, the interaction that actually occurs, rather than what it says in the 'rule book' or what has been agreed already in the ground rules. For example, the group may be timed to begin at 10:00am but if everyone knows it will not start until 10:15 because that's when a key individual, not always the nominated leader, attends, then that is the norm.

These are the internal rules and the modes of conduct, often finely implicit, that are as binding upon members as formal requirements and agreed ground-rules, and which receive equally harsh disapproval if contravened. These norms of behaviour will vary from group to group, and are established as a result of the composition of the group. Some norms may even exist below the level of members' awareness and are only sensed when disregarded. The norms of a group may be so strong that new members coming into the group need to accommodate themselves to the well-established customs and traditions that already exist.

Group norms can be narrow and inhibiting, or they can be flexible and creative, allowing individual members an opportunity to experiment with their role and try out new ways of behaving in a supportive atmosphere. Something as simple as the setting in which the group meets can imply something of the likely norms it will follow; a formal meeting encourages people to adopt a more formal seating position and so on.

Norms stabilise expectations but at the expense of leaving them unstated unless and until someone transgresses them. Norms not only influence individual behaviour but also have a serious influence upon the pattern of interaction because they encourage certain styles of response at the expense of others. In most groups not all norms apply equally to everyone. There are norms for selected group members, norms for all group members and norms that apply only to leaders. There are norms for male and female members. Norms vary in the importance and degree to which they are enforced.

Norms can serve as a substitute for influence because they 'regularise' conduct and they can be appealed to as a form of objective standard. Individuals therefore do not have to risk using or being seen to use their personal power to achieve influence with all the risks that implies. On the other hand, norms may act as a protection against capriciousness and inconsistency. This relates to the central fact about group life: in order for the group to exist, individuals have had to be willing to give up a measure of personal power and autonomy to allow a working structure and norms to develop. Individuals will allow themselves to be influenced by norms in ways that they would never permit themselves to be influenced by others, for norms often take on the characteristics of moral obligations.

Norms can arise by being:

1. **Modelled**: reinforced behaviour of significant members themselves.

2. **Consciously introduced** to promote a particular change or, more likely, overcome a difficulty.

The norm of the group can exert an enormous influence upon the pattern and flow of communication within the group, and rarely are these norms examined. Rarer still does a group set out to change its norms to improve the effectiveness of or the relationships between members. Usually individuals simply go along with whatever the norm happens to be. This does not mean norms necessarily remain static, but change is usually quiet and unobtrusive. Certain questions are really useful in identifying patterns of communication in groups:

- Who reminds the group of its norms when they are broken? How is their contribution received?

- Is conflict always immediately held down?

- What happens if someone wishes to talk about how they feel?

- Do members show signs of accepting norms to control their conduct?

Unhelpful Behaviours

Individuals learn the rules of communicating with other people as they go through life, often absorbing them unconsciously. From the family, through school, friends and other social groups to which they belong, individuals develop and increase their skill and abilities in communicating with others. They also develop some skills, which, rather than promote successful communication in new situations, actually inhibit it. Poor listening abilities, unwillingness to 'see' another's point of view, and inexperience in dealing with a new situation may exaggerate these less effective behaviours and impede the progress of the group.

If the group has too many delinquent members, progress will be held up. Too many over-co-operative members and it can become dull. Agreement reached too easily is suspect and usually suggests individuals have suppressed their real ideas in favour of conforming to what they think is expected.

Many groups function with a number of members who withdraw into passivity or obliging indifference. They put up with a state of affairs which does not really suit them, but which they accept in order to gain whatever it is the group has to offer them. As a consequence, involvement and participation tends to decline, and the group has a tired quality about it. A few 'key' figures attempt to flog people into life. Those 'key' figures can then become the object of hostility and irritation from the rest, who begin to blame them for the way things are – a very convenient way of displacing the blame for what is happening away from themselves onto others.

Examples of negative behaviour sometimes can be useful and necessary, but they can also be damaging. One of the commonest causes for poor group performance is due to members' use, misuse or over use of certain key behaviours, and, frequently, those who make use of them are quite unaware that they do so and have little idea of their effects. Almost everyone has experienced being in a group with people who display the following:

Antagonism: is there open hostility on the part of any member of the group? Does anyone seem to provoke or annoy others?

Withdrawal: does anyone withdraw from the proceedings and stop listening?

Joking: a joke is usually a good release of tension, but is there sarcasm? Is there anyone in the group who makes everything the subject of a joke or a sarcastic remark?

'Blocking': the person who always, no matter what the suggestion, has to object without having any concrete suggestion of their own. Blocking suggestions can inhibit those who are prepared to offer their thoughts and ideas to the group and limit the range of ideas from which the group may choose.

Interrupting others: or shutting them out, ensuring that their contribution is given the least attention. Over-talking, dismissing what has been said, making light of it, exaggerating what has been said to make an idea or the person holding it appear ridiculous, are all methods of shutting a member out and has the effect of reducing trust and openness.

Devaluing contributions via the use of such phrases as, 'With all due respect, I would like to disagree...' or, 'That's all very well, but...' and/or, 'We tried that, but it didn't work'. These are all ways of discounting a suggestion or contribution. They work by appearing to give attention to what has been suggested, yet the use of the word 'but' indicates to everyone listening that what is about to follow is the really important idea.

Disagreement and controversy are important, but how disagreements are stated and how controversy is conducted can be productive or damaging to group performance. It has been said that it takes three members who are willing to encourage and invite others to put forward ideas to undo the damage of one 'Yes but...' member of the group. And 'If you have tried it and it didn't work, then might it not be time to look again and see if it will work now?'

People in groups often attempt to read the intentions behind the other person's contributions and misunderstand what has in fact been said because it does not correspond with the assumptions they expect the person to hold. Similarly, guessing what others mean (rather than checking for clarification) leads to many misunderstandings. When it is coupled with supplying the speaker with reasons for why they have said what they said, it completes the process of total misunderstanding. ('You say you don't like the way we are doing this because you want to do it your way', for example.)

This may in fact be true, but it leaves the individual with little choice other than to start defending and justifying their position so that it appears acceptable. This only takes up time and it is not likely to make the individual change their behaviour constructively and the likely result is that they will withdraw from making further contributions. Supplying other people with reasons for why they do what they do, or 'mind reading', loses valuable energy and generally leads to a reduction in trust between members.

Inter-observer reliability is another issue; 'How do people seeing the same thing, but describing it differently, develop a common language of understanding and how often are they interpreting what they see differently?'

In longer educational programmes, and in interpersonal skills development of almost any kind, for example, individuals can be given opportunities to practise developing just such a common language and understanding. This does not remove all misunderstandings, but it does reduce them and a great deal of learning is gained from the process.

Individuals begin to realise that what they 'see' is as much a result of what they expect and believe – in short, how they filter their experience. For many people, it is a novelty, and a disturbing one, when they come to realise just how far what they 'see' and what they decide it means is unique to themselves, little to do with the understanding of the author of the behaviour and not much aligned to the views of the rest of the group either!

Task and Maintenance Behaviours

Behaviours in groups can be divided between those which are directed towards accomplishing the task and those which are directed towards maintaining the spirit and cohesion of the group. The first are termed *task-related* behaviours and the second *maintenance* behaviours and they are the two major ingredients of all group activity. Most problems encountered by groups fall into the area of maintenance behaviour. It describes such things as:

- Patterns of communication
- Style of leadership
- Methods of decision-making
- Means by which conflict is handled.

For effective group functioning there must be a *positive* social atmosphere. When the group is in progress, it is easy to see that not all contributions are related to the problem under consideration; humour, friendly asides, comments, are all interspersed amongst the general development of the topic and are an important means of keeping members in touch with one another. Men and women are social creatures and they need the positive regard of their peers and a chance to release tension, insecurities and anxieties within the safety of the group. If these needs are 'blocked', a sense of frustration develops. A balance needs to be struck between social or maintenance behaviours and task-directed behaviours. When groups become too socially active, at the expense of the task, they may find they enjoy themselves at the time but on reflection come to feel they have wasted their time. The habit, once established, can be difficult to break.

Task behaviours include:

- **Initiating**: do people ask for or make suggestions as to the best way to proceed or deal with a problem?
- **Seeking information**: discovering facts, views, impressions relevant to the procedure, the content or the method
- **Giving information**: offering facts relevant to the group or the task in hand

- **Orientation**: does anyone summarise what has been covered?
- **Keeping focus**: does anyone keep the group on target or prevent drifting and topic jumping?
- **Clarifying**: do people interpret new ideas, clear up confusion, indicate alternatives, test for agreement?

Maintenance behaviours include:

- **Harmonising**: does anyone attempt to reconcile disagreements or offer compromise?
- **Gatekeeper**: does anyone help others to get into the discussion?
- **Encouraging**: does anyone act in a particularly friendly way and show acceptance of other's contributions (by facial expressions or words)?

Enhancing Group Behaviour

There are a number of simple behaviours which group members can employ to promote better functioning within the group. Perhaps the most important among them is a willingness to share how things are and seem for them personally, and by displaying a corresponding willingness to accept how it is and seems for others. This is much easier said than done, but groups in which members show this skill and willingness tend to function with greater satisfaction for those taking part. Sometimes it takes only one member to actually admit that they feel a particular way about what is happening for others to come forward and share their reactions as well.

It does happen sometimes, and it is important to be aware of it, that someone who is honest and open about the way things are for them is treated badly and comes away from the experience reluctant to try it out again for fear of being put down, ignored, or rejected. Behaviours that encourage a positive, cohesive group include:

Paraphrasing. Before responding to someone else or to what they have said, paraphrasing what you think they mean can help both sides clarify whether what has been heard was what was meant or whether there is confusion in the mind of the speaker, listener, or in the minds of both. Beginning a response with the words, 'Are you saying ..?' or, 'Can I check if ....' can help check out the meaning before you go on to agree or disagree. This is not the same thing as saying, 'So what you really mean is', and isolating the other person's efforts with an interpretation of what they have said in an effort to ridicule it.

Summarising. This is a similar behaviour to paraphrasing but refers to those attempts which try to bring together a range of contributions and restate them in such a way that it helps everyone concerned check if they are in broad agreement about what has been said – though they may not all agree equally about its importance or value. Without frequent summaries, many groups wander rather aimlessly over a whole range of issues without focusing their efforts on what has been accomplished.

Reviewing. Even when things have gone well, few groups ever give attention to reviewing how they succeed in making progress. We are all so well-versed in dissecting how badly things went that we pay very little attention to how things got to be so good – and that is when there are opportunities to gain understanding for future action. Reviewing sessions and enabling members to clarify for themselves and for the benefit of others how they think and feel things progressed encourages skills to develop which can be put into practice in the future and keep members in touch with each other.

Feedback. Gaining from the observations of others is most positively influential when it describes behaviour in personal terms and is given in a supportive non-judgemental way about behaviour that has happened in the present rather than that which is recalled from the past. When comments are made in a general way (e.g. 'You are always being so dominant.') they tend to be received defensively, leaving little opportunity for the individual to know quite how to change, even if they wish to do so. If you say, 'In the last ten minutes you have interrupted John twice, me, three times, and spoken fifteen times', you leave the person free to do something about specific items of their behaviour, yet at the same time you make your point.

Relationships between group members are the most important influence upon how satisfying membership of the group is. Groups with openness and trust toward one another, and with a balance of skill and attention between task and maintenance behaviour, provide members with a feeling of satisfaction and accomplishment, and a feeling that they have something valuable to contribute individually.

In this chapter we have looked at many aspects of belonging to groups and how they can influence how we operate in groups. One key person in group development and group effectiveness is the facilitator and it is to the role of the facilitator that we now turn in the next chapter. We will explore such issues as:

- Managing difference and diversity
- Enabling effective learning to take place
- Setting ground rules
- Power and influence in a WPL group
- Relationships within the group
- Modelling the WPL process.

CHAPTER NINE

Living the Learning Transition: Facilitating Whole Person Learning

I see the facilitator as an educationalist, not as a therapist – whatever the setting. The concept of education is thus extended to include such notions as personal development, interpersonal skills, working with feelings both expressively here and now and cathartically through regression work, transpersonal development, social action skills. John Heron, 1977: 2.

Most facilitation will not enter the realm of great truth or profound instruction much of the time, but it may well have a significant impact upon people in their wider world, so it is wise to remember that the potential for influence of the facilitator role is very large indeed. It is a role to execute responsibly.

As will be clear by now, WPL demands a basic shift in the power and authority relationships between teacher and student (to facilitator and participant) from how it lives in traditional learning situations. The transition to facilitator and enabler requires a willingness on the part of the 'teacher' to let go of a lot of the role-given responsibility and control of a learning situation in favour of 'modelling' how to participate as an expression of their personal power and their ability to participate as a peer; a peer who has distinctive contributions to make that, when offered appropriately, will be adopted by the group or the individual who is addressed.

This is not easy to do. The facilitator is, in a sense, pioneering how to develop a more collaborative leadership style; a style based on mutuality rather than acting from a position of assured authority. In this chapter, we explore how this transition, from the old authority 'out there' to a more democratic, participatory and inner-directed style, can be promoted and undertaken. The areas in which greater collaboration can take place, the importance of the facilitator's role in modelling WPL, levels of decision-making and the importance of group dynamics are amongst the issues explored here.

The Active Learner

Facilitating learning occurs through some form of managed or organised process in a way that is productive for those involved. A spectrum of possibilities is available for the facilitator from the unilateral determination of just about everything – content, method, timing, assessment and award – to a WPLC model in which peers, including the facilitator, determine everything together in a truly collaborative endeavour.

At this end of the spectrum,[50] everyone, participants and facilitators alike, immerses themselves in a learning endeavour that is as much to do with the process of their learning (the 'politics' of decision-making and choice) as the content, and as much to do with discovering what it means to be a person learning as a peer rather than simply taking part in an intellectual inquiry. Affective competence is thus a central, recognised and embraced aspect of such a learning approach. The more a facilitator moves towards peer-based, experiential and negotiated forms of education, the more they move toward the potential for WPL.

Working from the person outwards, the person stands in relation to their learning as an active agent in their own world (see Figure 1: Interrelated Fields of Influence). They are a maker of meaning and an author of their experience – in company with others. The learning that is thus generated is linked to their unfolding being as a person and to the increasing sophistication and complexity of their ability to function as a person – a result of their having integrated their learning within their own being.

Such a view challenges the nature of the usual definitions even of 'integrated practice' and 'holistic learning'. In the first case, 'integrated practice' is often used to mean little more than an individual has done a lot of different things and has somehow 'grafted' them into a seamless robe; on the other hand, it might indicate no more than a collection of expensive rags. In such a view, 'integration' can be seen as something that takes place at the level of practice; practices are integrated, but as they are acquired they do not necessarily make much conscious or intentional difference to:

1. The practitioner themselves.

2. To the practitioner's view of themselves.

3. To the nature of the relationships they promote towards those they serve.

---

50 See *Chapter 6: Whole Person Learning in a Peer Paradigm* for a more detailed exploration of the peer paradigm spectrum.

It is quite possible to be a sophisticated, integrated practitioner and yet operate from a very self-alienated position that regards people generally as untrustworthy, incapable of knowing what is in their own best interests and that puts the practitioner's own integrated expertise far above what the client may know about their own circumstances and condition. Under this view, practice is largely knowledge-based and qualifications-endorsed. A view which has its corollary when continuing professional development (CPD) is looked upon as little more than a matter of 'updating', as though we are deteriorating data banks that have to be kept 'topped up' with the latest knowledge. The model proposed here assumes the learner has both the means and the right to contribute in the construction of the learning that they require and to make fulfilling choices both for themselves and for those involved in the learning experience.

Such a form of holistic learning is *based upon the learner* and not the learning and is akin to that which we observe in an infant who can be enabled and supported to enjoy and flourish without any particular content or subject matter being put in their way. It not only puts the learner at the heart of the learning (and where else could she be?[51]), but the example of the infant is a constant reminder that unless the learner is at the heart of the learning, the learning is not likely to be of any real use at all.

'Real use' here is the key phrase. There is much learning that has utility in the 'real world' of jobs, promotions and careers, and finding a place in society, but this is not learning that people come to value in an ultimate way. It has an instrumental purpose and they know it. It makes them marketable; it gives them a commodity value. This is not holistic learning, however necessary it might be.

Areas of Collaboration

It is the facilitator's own commitment to collaboration that will make this process work – or not. It is important that the facilitator has personal experience of what it is like to operate within a peer-based approach where collaboration is a prerequisite and where traditional power roles are challenged. If they have not experienced the kinds of insecurities that inhibit people from being free and working openly together, then however strongly

---

[51] It is not unusual in a WPL group to support someone in their pregnancy and for the new-born child to be part of the group for a while. In one particular case, it was a privilege to observe how the infant that was the result of this holistic process also turned the term 'holistic learning' into the most natural process in the world. The infant now almost crawls across the carpet, whilst the group goes on around her. She (the infant that is) makes all manner of noises – some of which clearly fascinate and delight her – and she takes an increasing interest in us taking an interest in her. She is mobile, vocal and directional already in her intentionality – none of it, so far, has been prescribed by anyone.

they favour and understand the importance of collaboration, it will fall short of being an effective demonstration of collaboration as espoused by WPL.

Depending upon the group, the course of study, the time available and the staff, the areas of collaboration will vary greatly. They must be identified in advance and dealt with collectively at an early stage of the programme. To leave important aspects of collaborative work aside for too long only generates a focus on the anxieties of the immediate concerns being tackled, which are not necessarily the most important.

As we have already seen in *Chapter 6: Whole Person Learning in a Peer Paradigm*, the degree of involvement can vary within any or all areas of collaboration. As a reminder, there are three main possibilities:

1. A limited negotiated learning contract.
2. A facilitator initiated highly collaborative peer approach.
3. An unstructured peer group.

Possible Areas of Collaboration

Content objective: what is to be done?

Construction of the programme: the broad areas to be tackled.

Methods: the means to cover the content.

Teaching approach: the role and the responsibility of the staff.

Time: allocation of sessions and distribution of content over time.

People issues: the use of other people, groups, group members, staff.

Physical resources: rooms, equipment to be used and so on.

Assessment: methods, preparation for involvement of staff, participants, and outside monitors.

Evaluation: approach, course evaluation, group evaluation, staff evaluation.

Supervision: how and by whom?

Administration: procedures for fees and so on.

Philosophy: the nature of the inquiry to be undertaken and its purpose.

Some of the areas of collaboration are more crucial than others and some will need to be tackled before others. Some may be partially negotiable; some may be non-negotiable. At the outset, members of staff initiating any programme, whether of three days or two years, are undeniably in a more powerful position than the participants since they 'own' the information upon which the programme is founded. Claiming that the 'literature' about the programme is sufficient for all to have a common starting point is to pretend that everyone meets on equal terms, and they don't.

The staff will know the implications of some of the conditions that will not be known to participants. For example, once you have been through one self and peer assessment process you have some idea of the issues involved and have experience that can help manage the anxieties that a first-time participant simply does not have. Additionally, staff are continuing with the course or with the institution, and this gives them a different set of interests to maintain and preserve. Initiating a more collaborative approach does not eradicate power differentials or mean everyone is equally informed; rather, it means that all areas of the programme are regarded as sufficiently important to be raised and investigated with a commitment to ensuring they detract from the activity as little as possible.

Negotiation and Levels of Involvement

As we have already seen, there is scope for great diversity in the degree to which participants are party to their own learning from first becoming aware of the programme/event all the way through to assessment and accreditation processes. The following table outline is a further way to illustrate the opportunities available.

The more negotiation that takes place, the more peer the event will be. It is possible for certain events to have peer elements within them. A student group of young adults, for example, will have the *content*, i.e. the syllabus, *imposed* yet the way in which this is achieved, the *structure* or method, may be *negotiated*. The most radical stance would be to have negotiation within the structure, content and process.

The more the learning methods used approach those of WPL, the greater will be the need to focus on the process that accompanies the activity, because it is in the processes that take place that much of the deeper learning is to be found. Such 'process learning' – for individuals, for small groups and for the whole group – is a rich terrain and helps explain another of the difficulties facing conventional educational institutions in embracing experiential and WPL more wholeheartedly.

	Imposed	Negotiated	Discussed (Tell and Sell)	Peer decided
Structure				
Content				
Process				
Design				
Delivery				
Assessment				
Accreditation				

Table 9 ⬦ Diversity of Participation

Process learning concerns such areas as the dynamics of the group, interpersonal collaboration and the internal challenges and demands that the individual meets throughout a WPL event. The learning to be 'discovered' in these areas cannot be anticipated in advance of the programme taking place. They depend to a large degree on the development of the participants' ability to reflect and review the experiences as they occur – a factor that has major implications for traditional forms of examination and assessment and presents a further obstacle for traditional provision. Yet another lies in the high level of willingness needed from all those involved to negotiate what they do together.

It needs to be recognised that *all* parties must be involved in decision-making throughout the full length of the programme. It is this prerequisite that ensures that the learning attained will demonstrate a different level of engagement and commitment. Needless to say this involvement must be real, just as the learning experiences must be managed rather than being left to 'happen'.

These three conditions, high learner autonomy, the emphasis on process learning and the extent of the negotiation involved, are in contrast to those educational events based on the presentation of a pre-arranged curriculum expected to generate 'deliverable outcomes'. They highlight, therefore, the challenge to traditional models in two major ways:

1. The challenge for the teacher to move towards becoming the facilitator, i.e. power sharing.

2. The challenge for the institution to let go of the need to control and decide in advance what constitutes worthwhile learning.

Furthermore, those initiating the endeavour need to give people the means of understanding how, at the completion of the programme, those having undertaken it will be enabled to live out their practice effectively.[52] These features of power sharing and developing new forms of collaborative assessment have substantial implications for the newly emerging practitioner from a WPL programme and for those who are committed to promoting WPL.

A Learning Contract

A *learning contract*, on which the assessment depends, is the first point in the life of the programme in which they have enrolled that individuals get a chance to see the transparency of the operation. Its preparation comes at an early stage in the life of any WPL programme, at a time when people are less clear than they are once they have a sense of how things operate, so it is crucial that the learning contract is not fixed and immutable. It is possible for a learning contract to appear to offer a good deal more autonomy to the individual than they discover is the case in practice, but anyone seriously committed to WPL methods has nothing to gain by attempting to deceive potential participants about the level of influence they are likely to have.

A Learning Contract:

Is the point where the programme, the individual and the group come together.

Will be too vague if formed too soon; if too late, too much of the programme will have passed.

Helps set the climate.

Illustrates aspects of freedom and responsibility.

Links content/process/experience.

Should be determined by who it is for, its purpose and the nature of the programme.

The preparation of the learning contract involves exploration of a number of key questions, all of which will be crucial when it comes to preparing self-assessment and self-accreditation statements towards the end of the programme. All the following questions would be addressed in a WPL event.

---

[52] The helping world, for example, very quickly betrayed its own initial radical impulse. Emerging collaborative forms of power sharing were very quickly overtaken by traditional forms of institutional authority and hierarchical structures.

What do I want to learn?

In the areas of:

- Knowledge
- Others
- Self
- Skills
- The group
- Experience
- The course

What will I have to do to achieve that?

- What effort will this require?
- What might I have to give up? (Such as the role I play in the group.)
- How will I have to pace myself?
- Is this the time and place to undertake that?

Is that a realistic goal to aim for?

- Given what I know about myself, is this feasible?
- Given my other commitments, is it likely?
- Is it specific?
- Does it avoid 'fluffy' descriptions like 'a better relationship with my boss'?
- Are the goals under my influence and not dependent on others having to change?

What might get in the way?

- What are the unanticipated factors that could influence my expectations?

How will you and I both know when you have succeeded?

- What criteria will demonstrate to me and to others that I have succeeded?
- How specific can I be in my descriptions?
- Can I give examples that could be verified?

How might I sabotage myself?

- What do I always do that helps me to not quite succeed?
- How do I mess things up in the rest of my life that I might do here?
- What ways do I have of getting out of taking responsibility for myself?

The questions can also be followed in a circular form: information from one question can be used to refine responses to an earlier, or later, question.

Negotiation and Levels of Decision-making

Clearly facilitators have power, as we have seen, and at times they may well need to exercise it *relatively* unilaterally. The issue of empowering learners isn't one of facilitators standing back and gently allowing chaos to break out or major conflict to surface without skilled intervention. As Heron makes clear in his work, 'the nature of the power relationship *overall* determines the appropriateness of any specific intervention *now* in *this* particular situation'.

In the early stages of a WPL event, the facilitator is likely to be more overtly powerful and directive using *authoritative* interventions rather than simply *facilitative* ones.[53] This is for two main reasons:

1. The group is still relatively too unformed to manage their own process with intentional awareness.

2. The management of a group of people in the early stages needs to be clear and firm if they are to feel the event is likely to prove ordered enough for them to benefit.

But the aim is to work from an overall position of sharing *power with* rather than holding *power over*.

Once process issues are acknowledged as important, the traditional position staff hold becomes untenable. Once participants are invited to inquire with their wider responses and move outside of the cognitive domain, the power relationship and the teacher as arbiter of conduct has to give way. Activity that involves process elements being acknowledged in an assessment should necessarily involve a realistic self and peer contribution. After all, who else but the individual and their colleagues can better decide the influence the process has had upon what they have learned? Such a move would represent a radical departure from most assessment schemes, even those currently involving some measure of student contribution.

As we have noted above, members of staff always have an advantage because they know the terms and set them, although the institutional or funding agency may well also set some of the terms. A clear recognition

---

[53] Authoritative and facilitative are the two classes of interventions that form the Six Category Intervention System devised by John Heron (see *Helping the Client* and *The Complete Facilitator's Handbook*). This system offers a comprehensive account for identifying, developing and assessing facilitator interventions and is an indispensable tool for all Oasis WPL facilitation.

about the terms and limits within which the programme is pre-set is essential for the success of any negotiated learning enterprise. And if those organising the event have not given it sufficient thought, you can be sure the participants will – at a time when you would least want them to. There are a number of possibilities, as Table 10 indicates.

Level	Style of Programme	Staff	Staff and Students	Students
1	Traditional	All areas	None	None
2	Progressive	Some areas	Some areas	None
3	Participative	Some areas	None	Some areas
4	Experiential	None	Some areas	Some areas
5	Co-creative (co-operative inquiry)	None	All areas	None

Table 10 ◦ A Continuum of Decision-making Distribution

Essentially, any programme that is provided under the auspices of an institution ensures that the institution has to manage the tension between the freedom of the participant to learn what they want to learn and the institution's commitment to the programmes it offers. This dilemma is usually resolved in the recruitment literature, through giving clear and specific information concerning the range and scope of what is given and what can be negotiated.

It is unusual in the twenty-first century for an educational event to be under the sole control of the representatives of the institution. However, we are a long way from the whole person approach and the radical, participative decision-making about content and method of the curriculum that the fifth level in the table describes.

This is the most challenging method for all concerned, if it is to work effectively, since it demands a high level of collaboration between all of the parties involved. It is more likely, therefore, that many events stay working at level 3 where staff can set the terms and participants go off and pursue the interests that emerge from the suggestions – a form of self-directed study rather than WPL. Most institutions find it too anxiety-provoking to be accountable for educational provision and then place the outcome in the hands of those who attend rather than those who provide it.

Finding the optimum is not simply an ideological question, but one related to the pragmatics of the programme, its length, the style and means of assessment. What learning is to be assessed and how it is to be assessed is intimately related to who has been involved in the decisions about what was to be done and how it was to be done.

Balancing the Balance

The facilitator's task is to bring together the external, given subject matter and the unique needs of the learner via the processes of interaction which take place within the group, including themselves: a complex aspect of the facilitator's role.

Since few individuals have any direct experience of openly negotiating learning with peers and with facilitators, it is not unusual for some individuals at the beginning of a programme to become highly focused upon their own personal learning agendas at the expense of the agreed content of the programme. Learning to manage the displaced anxiety that WPL inevitably provokes in the inexperienced – which is more extreme the more advanced the programme – is a major skill of facilitators.

It is the task of the facilitators to use their expertise to promote the strength of the WPL group, to illuminate the process and to 'stage-manage' the various tasks so that individuals gain greater insight and more competence in how to manage:

- Themselves, 'the task' and their contribution
- Their relationship to other group members
- The decision-making process.

Individuals are placing themselves in a particularly demanding position. They have to become wise to the issues, contribute to their evolution, understand and express their own needs, negotiate areas of the programme and learn about the content of the programme *simultaneously*. This is WPL and affective competence of a high order.

Group facilitation combines individual development, group development and the achievement of whatever goals the group is established to accomplish. It promotes the distinct individuality of those involved at the same time as it affirms the value and importance of collaborative endeavour. Such a tension between the individual and the group cannot always find immediate resolution nor can it always be satisfactorily accomplished.

Group members (over time) can come to recognise that 'my learning' is connected to 'your learning', which in turn is related to 'our' learning. In other words, the inevitable frustrations of group process work are a crucible for individuals meeting and facing some of their conditioning around expectations, authority, influence, structure and relatedness. On longer-term programmes, it is common to find individuals coming to value the very attributes in someone that they have wearisomely complained about for months before!

As a person becomes more aware of themselves, more capable of integrating their own awkward and less pleasant aspects, so they become more generous in their appreciation of the work others do to become more fully who they are. The move from 'being here for me (you can help, but I am here for me)', to 'I am here for us (so that we can all get more than we ever expected)' is one that takes a long time to develop.

The facilitator also has professional responsibilities to execute since they are likely to have been the principal architect of the course design and they are, therefore, offering themselves as a model of competence in whatever topic is under review. This places a high order of responsibility upon the facilitator for course design, structure and content as well as skill in facilitating individuals and groups through the processes that arise out of the topics covered through the course. The ability of the facilitator to model the practice successfully and to provide positive 'permission' for others to *identify and discharge, control and handle feelings appropriately* is a primary factor contributing to the depth of involvement achieved by any experiential group.

Even knowing the underlying basis of what is being facilitated and why, still leaves ample room for participant misunderstandings, for individuals to get their 'emotional buttons' pushed, or to get into embarrassing (so far as they are concerned) conflicts and differences with others. Interventions at a therapeutic level may well be called for.

The ability to move between content-based interventions and therapeutic ones is one of the most critical distinctions for the facilitator ambitious to work within a peer model. Enabling a participant to make connections between their personal response to something taking place now and previous experiences, and the encouragement to manage and facilitate affective competence is a key skill. Knowing when to move on, when to 'move in', when to leave well alone and to have a rationale (whether it is required or sought is not important) is a critical feature of facilitator development. This is not, however, to practice therapy by the 'back door', nor to make therapy an end in itself.

> I see human beings, by virtue of certain general features of the human condition, as vulnerable beings who are differentially distressed: some have manageable amounts of distress that coincide with the prevailing behavioural norms in the culture – but all require a mutually supportive education for living which shares skills in relating to feelings and other features of intra-psychic life, in relating to persons and social structures and situations, as well as skills in relating to data and information of all kinds, in relating to objects, things and the natural order. The heavily distressed and disoriented may require specialist remedial education, but to call this education rather than therapy provides a more honest, authentic and promising climate for change.   John Heron, 1977: 2.

No amount of reading about facilitation will, in the end, make a facilitator, but reading does inform practice, just as reflection and discussion will improve it. What makes for the successful facilitator is their ability to engage with the processes WPL liberates in as open and non-defensive a way as possible. It is about being able to attend to and to interrupt their own defensive reactions, discharge their own distress and 'model' to those they serve that it is part of the human condition not to:

- Know everything
- Get everything 'right'

but that it is possible to make sincere mistakes and to learn from them together.

The Self-as-Instrument Concept

WPL places an increasing reliance upon refining individual perception and awareness, responsiveness and ability to act effectively in one's own life. It regards the individual as the instrument through which their lives are lived and evaluated.

This is often termed the *self-as-instrument*[54] concept and it highlights the fact that no amount of learning, theoretical understanding or 'knowledge' is any guarantee of the individual concerned being effective in working with or through the relationship. 'Knowing about' something is not the same thing as being able to do it. It is not academic qualifications that make a good practitioner (however much people can argue about the importance of

---

[54] The Seven Stage Model, created by Oasis, is a very valuable working tool for developing the self-as-instrument via skills practice, theory, experience and reflection. The Model is described in detail in *Working with Others: Helping and Human Relations*, Bryce Taylor, Oasis Press, 2004.

having some theory); it is not time served that necessarily improves skills; it is not the ability to describe what you do that enables others to benefit (though no-one is saying that it is not useful and even important). None of these things is vital.

What is vital is the awareness of how the practitioner uses the self they have and are. Important, too, is the degree to which they are able to offer a reflexive awareness of their own process, and how far they are open to that process being subject to engagement at a level of emotional depth of the kind they all too often, and all too readily, inflict upon others. Developing a reflective practice is a critical feature, whether that be group peer supervision, one-to-one supervision or some other form of reflection.[55]

This concept has far-reaching implications when it comes to working in and through relationship, for we only have (each of us) our own experience to go by. Assessing and sharing what that experience is, testing out alternative understandings and practising new behaviours are all aspects of the self-as-instrument concept – a vital element in any experiential programme. All forms of practice which rely upon the individual creating a relationship with the other in order to offer their service or perform their task must address this in training as well as in the establishment of forms of accountability (see *Chapter 11: Living the Learning Transition: Accountability and Whole Person Learning*).

Working with the Process

A 'process issue' is any interruption that results as a session proceeds and requires some response from the facilitator either to manage or to note. There are process issues that by their very nature cannot be ignored; there are other process issues which are best left observed – when it may be wiser to pay attention to what is going on rather than draw everyone's attention to it.

The choice may be the result of the evaluation the facilitator makes about the level of the issue's intrusion into what is happening or the relationship of the issue to other more important concerns. Sometimes a process issue needs to be 'tracked' and information gathered before either the group or the facilitator can offer any useful response to work with it. Raising an issue because you have noticed it is not sufficient in itself to justify the group being expected to deal with it. The criteria for working with any issue are that *it should be related to the needs of the group and the task they are attempting.*

---

[55] See the forthcoming book by Bryce Taylor, *Reflection as a Radical Technique*, for an in-depth exploration of reflection and reflective practice.

Facilitating WPL means working with issues that are 'live', as well as with the full range of group dynamics issues: power, conflict, the facilitation of group contributions, surfacing issues that are being avoided and so on. In addition to these, there is the need to facilitate personal process issues which may be raised by past association with the content, difficulties with the process, unaware acting-out of distress in relation to authority, for example. Taken together, this makes for a high level of sophistication and one of the principal reasons why WPL has not been widely adopted to date.

It is these last two elements that raise the temperature and radicalise the climate of WPL. If you are inviting people to enter into a whole person way of learning then they will bring with them the parts of themselves that are dysfunctional, distress-laden, half understood, along with their rigidities of behaviour, their fixed and limiting beliefs as well as their general stance towards authority, power and gender relations. This is a powerfully creative mix of forces, influences and dynamics and it all ensures that the facilitators cannot expect to exempt themselves from the learning processes they generate. Indeed, it is the degree of willingness of the facilitators to work with their own processes, albeit appropriately and not always in the group, that is a major influence upon the seriousness with which those participating develop an appreciation for the approach.

There are times when some major upheaval breaks out, a sub-group gets into some tangle or the process begins to unravel. Then, whatever it says on the timetable, we are in the land of the unknown and all of us will be working hard to figure out what is going on and how we can move on creatively. It is important to remember that in a WPL event, progress can sometimes be far from satisfactory to all parties, but enough of a consensus has to emerge in order for things to move on – a process that requires a high level of affective competence.

A skilled facilitator is likely to sense an issue that is gathering pace in the group long before most participants do. Or they are likely to see the group implications of the way an individual is either managing or not managing themselves. This is a very sensitive area of facilitator development and it raises a vital question:

> How does the facilitator raise issues that are bound to be challenging and upon which a participant's self-esteem in the group may well rest, whilst also being aware that they cannot ignore or avoid the issue?

If the facilitator does not address the issue, group members will not tackle it either because they see the one they regard as having the most skill in this area (i.e. the facilitator) being unwilling or unable to do so. Equally, the group is also observing how the facilitator models the intervention itself when they make it; the degree to which they honour the person, regardless of the behaviour; how real they are in how they put the feedback or comment together; how 'caring' (in a real sense – not some professionally required performance) they are of the person in their vulnerability.

Knowing how and when to invite someone to contribute, who so far has made very little apparent effort to belong, is quite a different skill to that of helping someone who is confident of their role, but who has just been taking 'time-out' during the group session. Recognising the difficulties facing the person in the first example and the possible avoidance behaviour of the person in the second is important. How you manage each individual member is going to have consequences, not only for your relationship with that particular member, but potentially for your relationship with all other group members.

Diagnosing emotional blockages, identifying potential conflicts and rivalries that may exist in the group and responding to them constructively, are all aspects of process skills that facilitators can develop. Developing strategies to encourage participants to opt-in without being over-solicitous, challenging individuals in ways they can respond to positively and motivating individuals to take increasing responsibility are important aspects of this very wide area of expertise.

Once a person embarks on the facilitator role seriously, they are strenuously engaging with the question of how to meet others in their full human frailty and vulnerability as an other; an other who has their own pain, difficulties and vulnerabilities. They may not necessarily be on display now or here, but they are there. Hiding behind any facade or pretence at competence that it is not genuine will alienate more than the single individual you are speaking with and will do lasting damage to the reputation of the events you are promoting.

Skilled facilitators will make use of their own difficulties and issues creatively; they do not adapt to functions and positions that compensate or insulate them from their unresolved issues, which is what, of course, many of the participants, in the beginning, habitually do.

In a WPL event, that kind of 'defence' from a participant will not go unnoticed for long. How far the person is willing to unpick it will vary enormously. How willing they may be to release their control over their persona that maintains their internal security is part of the delicacy of the work. No facilitator has the right to demand a participant open themselves to exploring their inner wounds. On the other hand, no facilitator should be willing to allow someone's dysfunctional behaviour to gain an opportunity to oppress others or compromise the event, simply because the participant has found they are in an arena where their usual strategies to dominate or to exploit, to reject or to create unhealthy alliances, is both noticed and challenged.

So much of the potential success or otherwise of WPL depends upon those involved understanding the demands with which they are being invited to work. The critical issue is that those offering the event make clear in the initial contract the degree of challenge the programme is realistically likely to represent. It is unhelpful, for instance, to explore 'gender relations' and not expect there to be some immense issues to work with.

Dialogue, for example, in a WPL event means listening as much to myself as to you. Why? Because I need to listen for how strident and unfree I am in my claims, for example. It means being open to revising how and why I take the stand I do and facing the realisation that the degree of investment I have in my stance to the topic may be out of all proportion to the very reasonableness that I say I hold so dear.

Being a facilitator, if you aren't careful, offers opportunities to exceed the licence of the role and to offer more than is strictly necessary; to take up an issue in which you have more than a healthy investment or to get overtaken by your own self-knowledge. You are not immune to the same temptations that influence others, but hopefully your colleague's comments will help restrain you from some excesses. Important as helping others speak their truth as best they can is, it has to be mirrored in you also speaking your truth at the time and place, and in the way that honours you – when it matters. If the aim is to be real, it will cost the facilitator too at times. And that is often where the learning is; a challenge met and moved beyond is growth for all involved.

When people begin to realise much of their stance to issues is based, not on the cool assessment and appraisal of the facts as they like to think, but are often projections of their own fears, hopes, idealisations or prejudices – in short, that much of our 'understanding' is contaminated with less rational elements and influenced by our more regressive past experiences – then individuals are indeed working more in a whole person way. The anxieties that this brings about have to be managed at a level appropriate to their distress and in keeping with the event.

Facilitators should also model being open to challenges themselves about aspects of the content, method or process. They may or may not explain, but they should be able to respond openly to questions individuals put so that a climate of participation can ensue. All this makes supervision for facilitators essential and opportunities for those involved having support outside the event itself a prerequisite.

The radical implications of this paradigm are gradually opening out in every area of human endeavour. There are implications for science, sacred practices, artistic endeavour, ecological respect, political arrangements, social justice, redistribution of resources and the economic order. No field of activity is spared.[56]

Hidden Agendas

The term 'hidden agenda' refers to the personal, and usually undeclared, aims pursued by individuals, often at the expense of, in spite of, or in conjunction with, the stated purpose of the group. In most social and work groups, hidden agendas are not explicitly raised and are usually dealt with in covert and often unsatisfactory ways, such as rivalry, bickering and similar behaviours.

Sometimes the hidden agenda is a collusive arrangement by the whole, or part of, the group. Many groups, for example, collude with one another around starting times. There is an unspoken rule that it is acceptable for certain individuals to arrive later than others and no comment is made about it. Groups will often have a hidden agenda to keep certain key issues from surfacing, because they threaten the fabric of relationships of those involved, or some other arrangement that exists elsewhere.

There is also a hidden agenda on the part of the facilitator and the institution in traditional systems. Teaching, after all, is one of the most influential means by which society inculcates social rules into its members. In *Teaching as a Subversive Activity,* a book first published in the 1960s, the authors list the hidden agenda of the conventional educational process. It is reproduced here as a comparison to the aims of true experiential learning.

- Passive acceptance is more desirable a response to ideas than active criticism

- Discovering knowledge is beyond the power of students and is, in any case, none of their business

- Recall is the highest form of intellectual achievement and the collection of unrelated 'facts' is the goal of education

---

[56] *Feeling and Personhood: Psychology in a New Key*, by John Heron, is a definitive text in this area. An excellent introduction into it is John Gray's *A Tour of John Heron's 'Feeling and Personhood'* (only available from Oasis Press).

- The voice of authority is to be trusted and valued more than independent judgement
- One's own ideas and those of one's classmates are inconsequential; feelings are irrelevant in education.

The argument goes something like this.

> There is always a single, unambiguous, right answer to any question. English is not history and history is not science, and science is not art and art is not music, and art and music are minor subjects and English, history and science major subjects. A subject is something you 'take' and, when you have 'taken' it, you have 'had' it, and if you have 'had' it you are immune and need not take it again. (This view is commonly known as 'The Vaccination Theory'.)   Neil Postman and Charles Weingartner, 1987: 32.

The importance of dealing with hidden agendas is, in part, to introduce a practical application of *the principle of having open and clear communication between people*. This cannot happen if people are engaged in concealed manoeuvres which are not confronted, or challenged. It is also, in part, to assist people to understand that it is permissible to have personal aims to fulfil, quite at variance with the purpose of the group. *The real question is the manner in which those aims are pursued and what effect it has when that happens.* Some of the most common hidden agendas are:

- The desire to maintain a particular image of oneself
- To conceal potentially damaging information
- To disguise a dislike
- To seek to establish a personal relationship.

Others refer to control and the exercise of power and influence. It often happens that once the hidden agenda has been brought into the open and people have spoken to one another directly about their perception of one another, many of their wishes can be fulfilled at no cost to the progress of the group. Bringing the hidden agenda into the open requires a willingness to enter into the realm of interpersonal skills with commitment and some courage.

'Modelling the Process'

The facilitator's role includes managing and facilitating the unexpected. The situations in which the unexpected appears become more difficult in proportion to the time group members spend in activities outside the main

Aspects of Modelling the Process

Make explicit both rationale and content of any approach. A facilitator should be willing to share what they are doing, why they're doing it and how it appears to fit the needs of the group. This does not mean that they have to, or that they should do, to meet an over-anxious request. They can choose, but they should know.

Be creative and innovative. Exercises designed to meet specific needs help keep a facilitator challenged and involved: course and exercise design are important facilitator skills.

Respect and protect the right of choice. The facilitator is the initiator and the guardian of the individual's right to choose. This does not mean it is up to the facilitator to continually intrude, but that when the principle of the individual's right to make their own choices is under challenge they need to be aware.

Encourage and use feedback skilfully. In their role as a modeller, the facilitator will offer comment and feedback upon behaviour, process, interaction, response and so on. Providing such feedback is a model to the participants of how it can be done.

Validate efforts. 'What you stroke is what you get.' People will begin to perform up to the expectations made of them. Validating their efforts does not mean phoney compliments; it means recognising their best efforts.

Provide conditions in which participants can identify and express their needs. One of the primary tasks of the facilitator is to provide participants with the opportunity of surfacing what they most need to gain from the course or workshop.

Be willing to acknowledge and deal with conflict. (The importance of not ignoring, stifling or 'outlawing' conflict is highlighted in *Chapter 6: Whole Person Learning in a Peer Paradigm*).

Be willing to work with individual distress. Experiential work involves risk. Sometimes individuals recover elements or experiences from their past which have been hurtful or distressing and become 'triggered' into old feelings long since buried. A facilitator needs to be aware of such processes and how they occur and have some skills in helping others in distress.

Have an awareness of their own personal distress. All of us carry around ideas of distress, rigidities in thinking and behaving, blocked-off parts of our feelings; facilitators as well as participants. These too can be triggered by events and a facilitator needs to model the skills of handling and discharging such distress in ways appropriate to the needs of the situation.

Aspects of Modelling the Process continued

Opportunities for a peer relationship with another similar facilitator are one way of working through issues outside the confines of a course.

Continue self-development. A facilitator who isn't learning is a contradiction. Unless someone is actively learning it is very difficult to see how they can encourage others into the process. A committed facilitator will actively pursue their interests, not simply to increase their professional competence but for their own wider personal development.

work room. If groups have gone away together to process some activity or do some small group work, the result can be disturbance or confusion as the small group activity begins to influence the large group when everyone reconvenes. The facilitator, of course, is unlikely to know how or where this has arisen and remains at a disadvantage in being able to work with it effectively.

Similarly, a group will get a good deal more useful learning out of a focused explanation, guided by a few suggested areas to look at, rather than an open-ended topic with little direction about how they might proceed. An example might be: 'Take the next forty minutes in small groups to discuss what you think about leadership' – or sexuality, or...

The facilitator in a WPL group is primarily a *modeller of the processes* of working experientially, even if they are not an expert on the content upon which the group is engaged. To make this point clearer: a facilitator with good *process* skills may facilitate groups and teams on issues about which they have only a rudimentary knowledge, since they are being asked to assist in *illuminating the process* that is taking place. Clearly, recognising the *limits of one's individual competence at a content level* is important. A skilled process facilitator who deludes themselves into a false belief of knowing the implications of unfamiliar content lays the way open to confusion. A whole person approach for facilitating groups makes more explicit this idea of the 'facilitator as modeller'. As we have said repeatedly, it is unlikely anyone would be able to manage a WPL event if they do not first experience this manner of learning and working together for themselves.

Promoting Learning

Promoting learning is the essence of any facilitator's activity; promoting the learning of those involved and having a range of methods and approaches to encourage that to happen. In some ways it can be viewed as the end result of being able to put everything else into practice. It is identified separately here, however, in order to draw attention to the importance of the knowledge and awareness a facilitator needs to acquire which should then inform whatever skills they are applying and whatever style of development they are using. There are three major items under this heading:

1. *Responding* to the needs of the group.
2. Having an ability to *understand and work with group activity*.
3. Possessing *strategies* for enabling participants to take responsibility for their own learning.

1. Responding to the needs of the group. However well-prepared you are as a facilitator, however well-briefed by the organiser of the event and however motivated the people, you still have to shape the content to the mood you find when you begin working. A session mid-morning on the first day of a five-day residential course is a very different prospect from a mid-morning session on a two-year course. It is a different group on a 'good' as compared to a 'bad' day. Groups have moods: even 'well balanced', stable groups can fluctuate in interest and commitment as a result of factors quite outside your control. Being able to respond to the needs of the group means being able to adapt your programme as the need arises; even to put it aside if people simply cannot learn because there is too much else getting in the way.

Some facilitators are very confident in this area and can work with whatever is going on. They seem to have an endless capacity to create suggestions that fit the situation with ease. There are other facilitators who feel very insecure if they step outside the agreed timetable.

Responding to the needs of the group is an important part of being an effective facilitator. The more you know about how far you can respond, when you will not respond, which boundaries are negotiable and which are not, helps to create a clarity to the structure in which participants are being asked to work. However, responding to the needs of the group does not mean being cajoled into going along with pressure from any source, or giving way to those who make most noise. It is the willingness to be clear and to negotiate how you and the group will work together on the content you are there to provide.

2. Group activities. Even in a formal, lecture-style presentation you are still addressing a group of people. They may have little else in common except that they are attending the particular session you are delivering, but even so, being aware of how to make best use of the fact that there is a group gathered together is an important part of facilitating learning. Many people, for example, find speaking in a large gathering quite impossible, or do it with great tension. A facilitator can help individuals to raise questions and comments by having the group split up to discuss in pairs and to ask questions that have arisen from the presentation before taking responses from the floor.

In other group learning activities, the group itself is a very active ingredient in the learning that individuals may or may not achieve. How they feel about other members, whether they feel listened to or respected, will all contribute to the ease they experience. People who are tense and anxious about their role and membership of a group will not learn much and will spend most of their energy attempting to 'manage their discomfort'.

Facilitators need to know something about the roles people play in groups, the phases of group life and the processes that occur,[57] so that they can encourage the learning that people are making as part of the group dynamic. It is not a question of becoming an expert in group dynamics, but of having a sufficient grasp of such issues to work effectively with the groups you train.

3. Strategies to enable participants take responsibility for their own learning. Whether you negotiate the content of sessions with groups before you begin, as some experiential facilitators do, whether you ask people to discuss their expectations and reservations, or get individuals to programme their own learning, the aim is to enable those taking part begin to recognise the importance of their own contribution. Without this commitment to contributing to the process, events may take place, but people are unlikely to learn anything significant.

---

[57] See *Chapter 7: The Group Dimension of Whole Person Learning* and *Chapter 8: Individual Experiences in Whole Person Learning Groups.*

Even in lecture-style presentation sessions, it is advisable to ensure participants understand the role you are expecting them to play and the likely involvement you will require of them, if they are to benefit. Not only are such formal strategies important, but it is equally important to have informal strategies for 'nudging' people along at the right time with a useful question, a challenge, or even the refusal to answer a question to encourage people to learn. Many facilitators, if they are not careful, have a temperamental compulsion to do the learning for the participants.

Leaving people with things to think about or feeling confused, if done with awareness, can be a positive strategy. People do not have to learn it all today, nor do they have to learn all you have acquired over the last two years, six months, or even a lifetime, in one afternoon. Helping group members identify and take the next step in their learning is the important thing.

In addition to these three areas there are a number of other factors for facilitators to be aware of and to consider. The following sections cover these in some detail with a series of checklists and reminders to act as tools for reflection.

Working with Responsibility

Individual members may well seek to shift the responsibility for what is happening and for their own frustration in a group away from themselves and toward the group facilitator, appealing or challenging them to take some action that will 'make things better'.

The response many members have when confronted with a difficult situation is to hope the problem will go away by the next session, or that it will somehow solve itself. At such times, individual members may indicate suppressed hostility, withdrawal, or critical (but often indirect) remarks. Both the facilitator and the group may well respond to such messages by overlooking them in the hope they will go away. By not challenging what is happening, facilitators can tell themselves that there was little point in staging a confrontation so near to the '.... holiday', 'the end of the course', or some other event and find a convenient rationalisation for not doing anything about it.

Confrontation of such a kind can indeed be difficult, and therefore requires courage and an aware use of responsibility. There is often a vested interest in not dealing with such issues when they appear. However, when avoided, such issues have a cumulative effect upon the group in terms of levels of trust, effectiveness and openness. It can happen that the whole group and the facilitator collude together to avoid dealing with a situation or a group member because it is increasingly unpleasant. Motivation declines, attendance may suffer and the quality of group life becomes poor. Avoidance can be a three-way response exercised by individuals, the group and the facilitator. Some of the common strategies are outlined below.

Possible Avoidance Strategies

Withdrawal. Individuals simply refuse to take a fully active part in whatever is on offer. This is a highly effective sabotage because it is difficult to challenge and likely to meet with denial or justification 'I'm here, aren't I?' and the individual is apparently doing nothing inappropriate. It has associations with the notion of 'dumb insolence'.

Pairing. Rather than come together and work through an issue, group members may fragment into 'matey' pairs and sub-groups, dissipating their time together in chatty, conversational interludes. This can last indefinitely, so that the task is never discussed, let alone attempted. Many groups will pass through such a stage and may even take up a whole session strenuously avoiding coming together as a group, despite sporadic individual appeals to 'get on with something'.

Pairing will occur in most groups from time to time, and will not necessarily be dysfunctional to the group. Pairing is a common strategy employed by members to put themselves in touch with each other at the opening of any session. It is when such strategies impede the activity of the group that they require attention.

Criticism of the facilitator. The facilitator is almost certain to come under attack at some stage for having allowed the situation to deteriorate, and for not having 'done something' to stop it. It is difficult to avoid getting caught into making justifications, since they are almost always interpreted as 'parental' put-downs about how naughty the group has been, or are seen as attempts to reinforce the position of facilitator as the all-powerful patriarch/matriarch 'who let the children play for a while and look what a mess they made of it.'

Many members will respond by sitting back and waiting for some masterful assertion of authority, fully believing that the facilitator has engineered the situation for some magical personal purpose soon to be revealed. Once energy is released by attacking the facilitator, the group will often exhibit energetic co-operation and all the differences between members will mysteriously disappear – for a time.

Selective perception. Sometimes members collude to interpret an instruction or an activity in a way other than intended. Such selective perception is the unaware or deliberate mishearing of what is being requested. If a high level of anxiety is involved, then individuals may rather face failing and avoid confronting their fears; conducting themselves with an apparent understanding of what is required, only later to show innocent surprise at having done something else.

Many people in groups do not 'hear' what others have said and at times the misunderstanding between 'in' and 'out' groups and the rivalries that can exist between individual members can take on the proportions of 'wilful misunderstanding'. Often this is caused by underlying issues that neither party will openly declare and attempt to clear out of the way. Statements made by the other party are then misinterpreted and defensiveness increases between those involved.

Rigidity in attending to task. A rebellious, hostile or unco-operative group can easily evade the real task by so rigidly interpreting a request as to make the activity unworkable or a disaster. A frequent accompaniment is to then blame the facilitator for giving ambiguous instructions.

Flight into fun time. Here the group generates a lot of nervous humour to shift attention away from the task at hand.

Delaying. The group enters into prolonged and distracting negotiations with the facilitator, postponing the task at hand on the rational grounds that the conditions are slightly less than ideal. At its extreme, it finds expression in the 'why do we have to do it at all?' attitude that challenges the validity of the suggestion.

Reminiscing. A favourite pastime in some groups to avoid tackling the task at hand is to become involved in interesting distractive 'chat'. Under the guise of interest in the facilitator (or some other nominated stooge) members ask 'interesting', 'provocative' or 'challenging' questions. With skilful contributions from other members, once underway, the topic can last for whole sessions at a time. The danger is that the questions 'hook' the facilitator and the group can get great satisfaction out of this form of manipulation.

Failure to form an effective bond. Many learning groups never establish themselves as an effective force. This may be as a result of reluctance or insecurity on the part of the facilitator to help the group come together. One reason why formal question and answer sessions can be ineffective is that group members do not have sufficient contact with one another to establish the degree of trust necessary to be willing to be seen to 'get it wrong' in front of the group. Everyone waits for everyone else, until someone mounts a 'rescue' operation by stepping in and filling the silence.

When a group or an individual displays signs of avoiding the task in hand, it is important to ask if the task has been set at an appropriate level and *not to assume anything – either way.* If it passes that test, then diagnosis needs to shift to a further level. Do not immediately assume, 'It must be me', or that, 'It couldn't be me'. Groups which meet at different times, in different places and with different facilitators may 'act-out', because of unresolved issues they bring with them from elsewhere. It is important to check for such things before assuming the fault lies with you.

Equally, groups sometimes just behave unpredictably despite the most careful planning on the part of the facilitator and a session may just fall away because the energy in the group is focused elsewhere. Learning to accept such occasions as part of life can be difficult. Sometimes, individuals can find what appears to be a simple, straightforward request highly threatening; make allowances for such reactions and reassess your strategy. They may, too, reassess their commitment and consider leaving a course. This is not necessarily a personal rejection of you, or the subject matter, but an individual exercising their right of choice. Also an individual may arrive at a session with an unexpected personal crisis that diminishes the amount of free attention they can spare for what is going on.

Finding a realistic level of responsibility for what takes place within a group is one of the major issues of a facilitator. Having sufficient realism to recognise your own failings, but not so much as to take responsibility away from the group and its members, is a difficult balance to achieve. Perhaps one key skill lacking in many group members is the willingness to test out their own responses to what is taking place. Encouraging them to *share reactions* is a key facilitator skill.

Communication Skills

The skills a facilitator primarily relies upon to be effective are the skills of communication. Whether giving instructions to group members on how to go about a particular task, inviting participants to discuss an 'issue' or reflect upon a process, or asking a trainee a question, facilitators are employing a wide range of communication skills. Of the communication skills needed, the three most critical are:

1. **Interpersonal skills.** The skills of working with individuals and groups as they go about their work.
2. **Structuring skills.** Providing clear and explicit descriptions to people of what to do and how to go about their work together.
3. **Presentation skills.** The skills involved in scene-setting and giving information in a relatively formal fashion.

1. Interpersonal skills: whilst a field of its own, interpersonal skills are essential for a facilitator. Beginning to understand your strengths and weaknesses in working with other people and, as importantly, understanding what those strengths and weaknesses are based upon is important for facilitators. For example, some facilitators will work better with mixed groups; others with single-sex groups. Some facilitators will respond easily, if challenged, to explain their method; others will become defensive. Some facilitators can cope with relatively open exchanges between group members; others need a more regulated flow.

Interpersonal skills covers a wide range of behaviour and though we often think of aspects such as questioning and clarifying skills, it also includes the way a facilitator manages their own performance. In other words, how they employ their interpersonal skills to their own advantage and in order to maintain a satisfactory climate to work in. It therefore involves skills that make use of power, influence and leadership style. When looking at your interpersonal skills as a facilitator, it is worth including an assessment of how those skills combine together to make up a 'style' of interacting, not only with groups but also with particular group members, some of whom will be easier for you to work with than others.

2. Structuring skills. Getting a group to 'move from A to B', to 'split up into fours for the next half hour', or to 'report back when you have finished the task', are examples of structuring skills. Even with highly developed communication skills, facilitators can go adrift if they do not have effective ways of structuring situations so that participants understand what is expected of them. In this respect, an over-concern to ensure everybody understands can be just as big a handicap. Finding the balance that gives people enough information is more difficult than is often realised. Structuring skills, then, refer to all those instructions and directions that impose some form of boundary upon what is happening in order to enable the group to function.

3. Presentation skills. These are the skills that are the most commonly related to training and development roles. They refer largely to the skills required to organise and present information in a way and at a pace that participants can take in and use. A great deal of instructional development is based upon varieties of presentational format. Even experiential groups will, from time to time, require mini-lectures, short inputs, or brief overviews of theoretical or practical information, if participants are to make sense of what is happening to them.

Preparation is a key element in effective presentation skills; whereas immediacy of response is at the heart of interpersonal skills. This often means that facilitators skilled in one of these aspects of development are often under-developed in the other. Facilitators who like to work in a relatively unstructured group will often resist giving much information via formal or even informal presentation, insisting the group itself will be able to learn what it needs to learn. Good presenters, in contrast, often cannot see the point of letting people roam around the topic, having a desultory discussion when they could tell the group effectively and interestingly what the group need to know.

Achieving a useful and healthy balance between these two sets of skills is a major challenge to a facilitator who wants to develop flexibility and work across a wide range of groups and situations.

Planning and Design

Effective development often relies upon a facilitator's ability to think on their feet and devise something that fits a unique situation. But like so many things that look easy, such skill comes only after long preparation. Ability to improvise is no substitute for thinking about what you are doing or what is needed. The skill to improvise is often based upon long experience in working at good course design in the past.

Planning and design skills, ways of thinking about how to use the time available and the resources to hand in the most effective, efficient way possible, are hard-won skills; skills often gained only after making mistakes or realising you have overlooked something when reviewing a session later. You cannot learn to design and plan effective learning opportunities, especially in areas new to you, without making mistakes.

Ideally, a facilitator needs to feel confident that they have a range of methods and approaches to draw upon and can select the most useful for the particular situation. In many ways a facilitator can only achieve such a breadth of knowledge through experience. However, it is worth remembering that you can easily get into the habit of simply repeating experiences over and over, rather than modifying or developing what you have already done.

Included in planning and design is the ability to relate elements in a programme, not only with one another, but also into an overall coherent whole. This again is something that can only be acquired with experience, but it still has to be learned consciously. Experience of development alone will not guarantee success. Programme design is a highly skilled activity and not something every facilitator can expect to be good at.

The onus is thus on the facilitator to ensure that the experiences offered follow some planned and self-conscious structure that does, indeed, enable people to get to the desired end-result. However casual it may look, WPL requires a very disciplined effort on the part of the facilitator. It may have little structure, but it will always have *a* structure, though on occasions it may not feel like it to those involved. WPL approaches provide opportunities in which an individual may, if they choose, learn something which becomes part of their living reality, rather than something simply remembered and occasionally applied.

The facilitator's task is therefore not simply one of selecting a topic, but involves thinking about how best to introduce it to participants in order to orient them towards the particular area that they wish the group to pay most attention to.

Monitoring and Review

If you don't know where you are going, wherever you end up will only be
somewhere else.   (Anonymous)

Monitoring and reviewing skills are complementary to planning and design skills. If you don't plan what you do, monitoring what happens won't tell you much about what to do differently next time. Planning well and not paying attention to the processes that occur will leave you without much valuable information for future design. The two sets of skills are essentially interrelated. There is a difference, too, between monitoring what is happening in an attentive way and an over-anxious pre-occupation with whether people like what you are doing for them. Facilitators need to develop an awareness of their work that monitors the group, the content, the pace and the processes: not easy to do whilst having responsibility for a session.

In the early days, the skills of reviewing will be an important way of developing such awareness. Reviewing is a form of retrospective monitoring, of going over what happened in order to learn about how it happened. Again, there is a difference in re-running a session through your mind, or with a colleague in order to learn more of how you worked, or how the material you offered was received, or whether the pace was effective, and simply replaying details of a session obsessively in order to justify or explain away some minor imperfection no-one but yourself noticed.

Sessions do not have to be perfect to be effective; they have to be 'good enough'. A good session can teach you as much as one that went badly and a poor session does not always have to be your fault. However, you should sometimes think twice if it's never anything to do with you. As difficult as the skills of monitoring and reviewing are, they are concerned with developing a frame of mind that takes an interested, but not over-invested, view of what you are doing. Learning to talk through sessions with colleagues openly is an important part of learning about the facilitator's role development. Having a supervisor or consultant, who can take you through what you have done, is an essential resource.

There are a number of ways for getting a sense of how an experience left people, what their reactions are or how they view what has taken place. It is important to ask for the impression that you want or you will get anything that individuals bring to mind. This may be no bad thing, but it should be invited rather than a result of your forgetfulness to shape the invitation well. There are:

- 'Quick and dirty' or 'impressionistic assessments' as a way of identifying how a process operated or how an exercise was experienced
- Via a 'spoken telegram'[58] as a way of identifying immediately where participants are
- Through the use of reflective questions which help individuals structure their thoughts and explore them with another colleague. These are chosen by facilitators as a way of helping participants give focus to their discussions and it helps isolate variables.

You can reflect on:

- Content
- Structure
- Process
- Preparation
- Pre-course experience
- Application work/life

The purpose of reflection in designing a development session helps to:

- Modify a session
- To review the response to a programme
- To evaluate the results of the content, the group, the stage of development people have reached.

It can be short, medium or long-term and relate strongly to evaluation that follows. Evaluation would include looking at:

- **Content:** the needs that the group was established to meet
- **Input:** resources and input
- **Process:** methods and styles
- **Outcomes**:
  - Immediate
  - Intermediate
  - Ultimate

---

[58] Each person selects a single word or a phrase, but no more than a sentence, to summarise their impressions about... For example, 'How did you find the day?' or 'What have you noticed about your response to...?'

Assessment and Evaluation

Monitoring and reviewing are the preliminaries to assessing the value and success of any experiential activity and evaluating its contribution against your initial aims and objectives (and the organisation's too, if they are paying you). Assessing a session or programme can be done in many ways; by you, you and the group, the group, individuals alone, in pairs, against a written form, or by generating questions from participants. It can be done quickly, or be thought about carefully. However it is done, it needs to be related to the programme in question. The assessment of a two-year programme should claim more attention than that of a two-hour contribution to someone else's programme.

Assessment of what has happened and what learning has taken place should become an automatic part of a facilitator's way of evolving, just as evaluating the effectiveness of what has been achieved will provide a measure, however tentative, of the results obtained against the expectations with which you set out. Developing the habit and encouraging it in others can help share the learning and foster the practice in participants that you have to literally 'create your own learning'. It does not simply happen. Useful areas to explore include:

- Were individuals able to transfer their learning?
- Were they able to continue learning?
- Was the model used appropriate / useful?
- Was the theoretical contribution useful / appropriate regarding time and level of abstraction?
- Were individuals able to help others to learn?
- Were they able to influence in intended ways and be influenced in intended ways?
- Have any situations changed or are seen differently as a result of the work?

In addition, it is a very useful skill for facilitators to be able to give summaries of what they have observed as way of testing out any agreed understanding of a topic or review of a process. It is a form of 'reality' check which can inform the assessment and evaluation process for both facilitators and participants.

Useful Facilitator Guidelines

Assumptions can land us in deep water, especially in a 'politically correct' culture, but they can be useful if derived from experience and practice. Amongst people entering educational events, adopting politically correct (pc) language and expectations are a signal that you know how to manage and conduct yourself according to a code, rather than a way of behaving which derives from an individual's internal commitment. This is something we meet frequently in WPL events.

People will occasionally object to something taking place on pc grounds without examining their own assumptions, which they regard as relatively blame-free, and make assumptions about the nature of the event. To give just one example, we met visiting assessors who wanted to see curriculum-based evidence of our ability to work with difference and diversity (a pc requirement), when they were in a room where exploring difference and diversity was taking place right in front of them. However, it is important that facilitators are flexible and willing to change their assumptions in the light of what happens. Assumptions and guidelines that can be useful to facilitators include:

- The group is going on without you: before, during and after your appearance
- The group is always taking place: if two or more people gather together or talk on the phone, for example
- You can only work with the bit of the group you are offered
- When faced with having to learn something challenging about their self-image, for example, people's best intentions to learn and change are frequently left by the wayside
- Assume anything you do or say will be reported or interpreted in some way
- Assume people will talk about you unguardedly – but don't slip into the same way of acting
- The safety of the group lies in you at the start; and your safety depends upon your own self-awareness
- How you treat any one person will be generalised
- Give the 'givens': don't pretend to negotiate what is not really on offer

- It's important to give the 'givens' and change them in the light of what happens, rather than pretend there aren't any or that you can function without any structure of any kind
- If you give too many 'givens' people are likely to feel they have little freedom to be themselves
- Enjoy power and influence so that you are not tempted to misuse it
- Many conditions or ground rules are best thought of as positive intentions and not laws that bring punishments when contravened
- People cannot always learn from their experience AND maintain their positive intentions
- Too much anxiety and people freeze; too much security and people flop
- Remember you will want to work where it suits you
- Remember you have a pathology too
- Remember to check your own sense of things: your perception of what needs to happen must always be open to revision
- Reflection and exploration with someone else is crucial
- The freer you are from 'need', the more the group can establish itself, and the more challenging it will be for you.

In addition, remember that it is essential that facilitators know where they are in relation to such issues as:

- Conflict • Violence • Substances • Medication
- People staying in the group when they are 'distressed'.

All these are issues that individual facilitators have 'positions' about, i.e. have a current place from which they are working. For example, I may not handle conflict very well – yet. I know it affects the level of controversy I encourage, and that when a group begins to get a little 'heated', I spend a lot of time being anxious and trying to 'smooth' things over. This facilitator anxiety does not help the climate of the group, but is the best I can currently manage.

Similarly, I may be an experienced facilitator, able to work with fairly high levels of distress when people are triggered into strong emotional reactions as a result of some aspect of their learning. But where do I stand on encouraging people to manage these reactions? Do I raise the matter at the outset of the group and potentially disable some participants who wonder what is in store for them? Do I wait until someone is triggered in this way and then talk through with the group how this is an OK phenomenon. Do I explain then how we can all learn to 'be with' a person in their distress as they manage the upset caused as they develop a new insight into their behaviour?

A Checklist for Facilitators

1. Useful questions for the facilitator to bear in mind.

- What factors are important in structuring a group activity?
- What strategies do groups devise for handing conflict?
- How do you respond and are you satisfied?
- What situations do you find difficult to cope with?
- What boundaries shape and determine a group's life and who provides them in most groups?
- How does the climate affect the task and vice-versa?
- What are the communications patterns in the group?
- What range of interventions and overall style do you have?

2. A facilitator needs to be able to:

- Model a wide range of interpersonal behaviour competently and appropriately
- Identify and create situations, which promote useful learning
- Introduce new values and perceptions to individuals with little threat
- Facilitate the flow of communication
- Participate fully.

3. The facilitator's role in effective WPL is to promote and enable each of the following elements to be present:

- **Voluntarism:** each participant decides whether they get involved and how far they become involved
- **Choosing:** they decide what they want to achieve

- **Explicit:** the facilitator should be willing to account for why they have chosen the structure they propose
- **Open:** individual reaction and responses are encouraged and respected, however unusual. There are no 'right' answers expected
- **Equalitarian:** everybody shares in creating a satisfactory climate of mutual trust to provide the safety, which encourages people to take risks and try things out
- **Cheerful:** WPL can be fun. Not all the time, to be sure, but a vital element in learning is enjoyment and satisfaction
- **Variety:** there may be more ways of finding the same thing out than one, and one may find the same thing out in several ways. This doesn't have to be repetitive or dull, but be a source of interest too
- **Optimism:** people are intrinsically capable of working together and sharing their time in a way that enhances their mutual understanding
- **Plagiarism:** if it works then use it, and if you can adapt it to your purposes, so much the better.

4. The facilitator needs awareness of issues relating to working with groups, as summarised in the table opposite.

1.Background issues	Creating conditions Gaining commitment Managing the key questions: • What type of people? • What type of group? • What type of programme? • What type of structure?
2. Knowing what you are working with	Clarifying the work Identifying roles Identifying the task(s) Identifying the contributions Identifying progress and/or lack of it
3. Reading reality	Who decides what happened? How in touch with me am I when working? (Self-as-instrument) What gets in the way? What do I know I do to 'mess up'? What do I know I avoid? What forces act upon me when I do 'mess up'? • over-anxious concern for them • insecurity I will not get it 'right' • a wish to get too much done in the time available

Table 11 ◈ A Checklist for Working with Groups

CHAPTER TEN

Living the Learning Transition: Assessment in Whole Person Learning

Assessment is the most political of all the educational processes. It is where issues of power are most at stake.

John Heron in D. Boud (ed), 1988: 85.

The importance of continuing the WPL approach into the assessment process of a WPL programme or event cannot be over-emphasised. As we have seen already, it is at the point of assessment that the depth of collaboration becomes clear and it becomes apparent where the power is really held. If throughout a programme, there has been talk of peer-based learning, the peer principle and of collaboration, but come the close everything reverts to traditional assessment by staff and external assessors, then it is a deformation of 'peer' in the way it is used throughout this book.

Oasis has had over 20 years of facilitating programmes that embrace the self and peer assessment process and this chapter highlights those features and elements of assessment that are consistent with and encourage the peer principle, WPL and the issues that are raised by such a power sharing approach to the learning process. It describes the process of self and peer assessment from the learning contract right through to the learning statement, including the role of the individual, other group members, staff and the institution. Awareness of these issues will enable those interested in implementing a WPL event to maintain those principles right through the programme.

Learning and Living

What people do with their learning is, in one sense, their business, but not altogether – especially if others have paid for the individual to enjoy that opportunity and if yet others are to be influenced by the learning that the person has now acquired.

When the individual undertakes learning primarily for their own personal development, what happens to the learning, how it is measured and how it is acknowledged, what warrant it holds and how it is utilised is much less of an issue than the learning that is attained for professional application. Many elements help foster the attentiveness to the inner process of learning including asking such questions as:

- 'What happened?'
- 'What accounts for the responses and reactions I had to what was taking place?'

The inquiry-based approach that WPL fosters is built upon reflection and review. It is a very explorative and tentative process because we often encounter discrepancies between our prior view of things and our experiences through the event. Internal contradictions and conflicts take patience to surface and time to resolve holistically.

A fundamental part of the learning in whole person approaches lies in this opportunity for individuals to revise their fixed beliefs and judgments about themselves, others, the nature of how experience unfolds and the learning their individual experience holds. There are issues here of personal power and influence. For example, 'How far shall I trust the other in their alternative view and explanation of what I believe I am up to or what I believe they are up to?'

Power and Assessment

Initiating a more collaborative approach does not eradicate power differentials or mean everyone is equally informed; rather, it means that these things are regarded as sufficiently important to be raised and investigated with a commitment to making them as transparent as possible and to interfere with the activity as little as possible.

If learners win the learning for themselves in a whole person approach and if learners have a right to contribute to the way the learning is put together,[59] how it is delivered, how it is managed, processed and decided about, but then have little or no effective influence in the assessment process, they are little more than guests at someone else's feast. However much they enjoy the meal, they don't learn how to cook for themselves. Nor do others get to know how come the ingredients are put together in the way they are for the purposes that they are.

Those institutions that have decided to encourage participants to have some measure of involvement in the process, only then to retain to themselves the final say over this question of valuing the learning (what assessment is crucially about) undermine the whole endeavour. The author himself undertook one long-term programme in which the participants came

---

[59] Those areas of a programme in which participants can collaborate and to which they can contribute are described fully in *Chapter 9: Living the Learning Transition: Facilitating Whole Person Learning.*

close to rioting when they discovered the contradiction between the programme they had been on, which they had largely managed themselves, and the imposition of an external examination that was now going to determine their competence to practice!

The institution, the staff and the participants were brought face to face with the illusion under which they had laboured for two years:

1. Participants that they were empowered learners.
2. Staff that this was a radical enterprise.
3. The institution that it was offering a progressive model of education – for which the participants should be grateful!

In the end, the institution dropped the claim that peer assessment was a substantial element of the programme in its future course descriptions in favour of a more conventional approach. Most such efforts share one thing in common:

A lack of reality between the practice of the assessment process and the programme as it has been lived by those involved.

This illustrates a serious unwillingness to live out the assessment process in the unfolding of the course and simply puts something in place at the end. Such provision violates just about every requirement for a self and peer assessment process to have validity and value. A last minute opportunity to give feedback that is then authorised by someone else is not remotely similar to the process outlined here.

This issue of congruence between liberating participants to engage in the design and management of the learning and its assessment is a vital matter that cannot be shirked. If the participants are not to have a full, blown self and peer assessment process, then the process they do have needs outlining and a rationale proposed, well in advance, if those who are in charge of the educational enterprise are to do justice to the educational process.

Allowing participants to manage their own assessments, with help and rigorous challenge from staff, is, in my experience, perhaps the most liberating of all processes. For them to have the opportunity to realise and recognise the learning that is theirs to claim and to 'own', and to have it embedded in the dynamics of the assessment process is to liberate a whole area of new learning that has previously been hidden.

Assessment as a Development Process

The call for more adaptable and self-initiated learners in industry and commerce is, in part, helping to draw attention to peer-based methods. 'Self-directed' individuals working in 'self-managed' teams need some parameters to guide their efforts – a peer-based approach might help. But as we know, whenever any new term is adopted widely, it will inevitably be taken up with a variety of meanings. This is something we see in the use of the word 'peer' in things like 'peer feedback' or where working arrangements are referred to as working with 'one's peers'. Frequently, it implies a degree of collaboration and a degree of goodwill that is unlikely to be found in practice without a good deal of facilitated support to get it off the ground. In these contexts, it is being used in a much less rigorous manner than the way in which it is used in this book.

It often gives little recognition to the fact that peer-based methods require developed emotional skills and the ability to both offer and receive feedback in sophisticated ways. Moreover, it demands a form of maturity and a sense of self that our current educational practice does not set out to achieve. For those who have some deeper experience of WPL in practice, accountability and accreditation based upon a peer approach need a good deal of articulation and consideration if their practice and understanding is not to be confused with these other, less demanding, forms of working to which people are mistakenly applying the term 'peer'.

Most of the key issues outlined in this section arise out of experiences taken from the human relations world, which has been the author's particular background. Though this is only one particular arena, it does have the advantage that many of the issues encountered here transfer to other contexts where peer efforts are undertaken.

The underlying dilemmas are likely to travel to many arenas where there are tensions between a traditional desire for approval and the kind of reassurance that is supposedly offered by external bodies of validation, with a recognition that the speed of change is now too great for traditional methods of professional development to hold for much longer. Professionals in the financial services, law, health care, education – once the citadels of the professionalised view of the world – have all found their positions called into question as a new range of practitioners become licensed to enter and undertake duties that were once solely the prerogative of the highly, often over-qualified, expensively trained 'professional'.

There is a great deal at stake in this discussion. It is much more fundamental than simply needing to find appropriate forms of acknowledgment of the learning that the individual can take into the world; it is also about ensuring that this learning is being taken seriously and treated with due regard.

Given that many people move careers several times, and roles many more, their base-line professional training may have little direct contribution to their current position or future roles. Many organisational positions have no obvious preparation, but can be filled by individuals from many backgrounds who have the aptitude, motivation and application.

Continuing professional development is a prerequisite for anyone wishing to stay in touch with themselves and their working world and it has two main aspects:

1. Staying abreast of developments and remaining competent at the task.

2. Enlarging one's repertoire of interest and responses that can inform how one approaches work.

As many organisations have discovered, enabling people to learn from such things as sports activities, outdoor pursuits, musical interests, acting, clowning, dancing and other non-vocational pursuits, brings tangible benefits both for the individual and the organisation, since these apparently unrelated activities, nevertheless, reinvigorate the person.

Put like this, it begins to illustrate how irrational is our compulsion to have external examinations and external tests at the expense of imaginative forms of learner assessment. And why? Because, as we have seen, once learners begin to realise what is involved in assessing their own learning, the power of the learning itself is enhanced and the right of someone else to contradict or undermine that claim is much reduced. It represents a major requirement for the development of the person in our society to be able to enhance their individual authority and learning capacity.

Areas of Learning

Educational practice, its assessment methods and procedures are almost exclusively centred upon measuring content objectives and their fulfilment. Anything more complex, such as Torbert's four qualities of reality,[60] is unable to be contained within current conventional assessment procedures or examinations. However, content objectives only form a portion of the experience individuals are likely to have (even on a conventional programme) as we have already seen. There are at least three important areas of the

---

[60] The four domains or qualities of reality are described by Torbert as: 1. the outside world; 2. one's own behaviour; 3. one's own and others' thinking and feeling; 4. the dynamics of human attention as it gains and loses, or changes focus and as it narrows or widens the number of qualities of which it is aware. Torbert in Reason and Rowan, 1981.

learning experience to which those involved could pay attention and which would lead them to begin to grapple with the 'politics' of the system in which their learning is held. Once learners are involved in considering these things then they have a right to demand a greater role in the structuring of the learning itself.

Exclusion from anything other than absorbing the content and reproducing it inclines people to have little interest in the way the system in which they are held operates. It is only to be expected that a system giving so little encouragement to those in it to ponder upon it or actively engage with it produces a population whose interest in the process of their working life, social arrangements and political system is declining with every poll that is taken.

The three important areas of information that contribute to the assessment of any learning experience are:

1. Knowing *what* to know: *content*.

2. Knowing *how* to know: *method and process*.

3. Knowing *that* I know: *assessment*.

Individuals can make contributions to all three elements. The more individuals become involved in each of these processes, the more they will begin to assume increased personal responsibility for their overall learning. The more also they will begin to fulfil the description of an educated person. In contrast, the more they are inhibited from exercising influence upon each of these three activities, the less experience they have of working with the issues that are inevitably raised, the more dependent they will remain and the longer they will continue to hold doubts about their own judgements. Not only will they continue to doubt their right to make judgements about aspects of learning, they will also continue to have doubts about their right as individuals to influence the processes which shape their lives, not only in classrooms, but elsewhere.

In a traditional curriculum, *knowing what to know* is the focus of concern. Staff and students are engaged upon the quest of knowledge. How they do it and how it is measured are decided in other places, sometimes by the staff, sometimes by the agencies but almost never by the students. Yet all three elements are required to make up a sound educational venture. If those who are taking part never have this revealed to them, they are denied vital information. If members of staff never explore these issues, their assumptions will simply go unquestioned. The knowledge base may grow, but the power base upon which it is founded will continue to remain unquestioned and rigid.

The Matter of Trust

Trust is the key issue. Can learners be trusted to be 'fair' or 'honest'? Can staff truly let groups decide their own criteria for an effective performance or level of skill? Won't they act irresponsibly? 'Have they got anything like the experience necessary?' It is true you cannot put a group of 20-year-olds together, let them decide what makes a good nurse and then let them loose on a ward, but that is not what is being suggested. Yet the very doubt that people have the capacity to make such judgements or that they would not make them fairly and honestly says something about the view of the person underlying the way our social and human relations are organised.

> A rational person has no interest in deluding himself about his own competence, and he will use the insight of his peers to attain a just self-appraisal.   John Heron, in D. Boud (ed), 1988: 86.

What, in the end, is to be gained by mass deception or by group collusion? How long would such a 'manufacturing of consent' last? In reality, working out realistic standards together and over time is an arduous and demanding challenge. Over twenty-five years I have witnessed that its overwhelming result is to deepen an individual's appreciation of the complexities of practice, making them more conscientious and much more thoughtful about how the present system operates. It has also highlighted just how far an individual has internalised norms required by others and how far they have searched to develop a personal commitment to those they hold for themselves. Once won, such commitment is fiercely defended, because it grows out of the body of understanding and the realities of the practice that have been reflected upon by the budding practitioner, the emergent whole person learner.

An educational process that includes time spent with effective practitioners and which takes place over a realistic period of time would have many implications.

- It could lead participants and staff together to determine effective standards of practice
- It could serve to promote discussion as to why such standards should be as they are
- It could lead participants to devise procedures that effectively test performance and rate such performance
- Further, such a process could come to completion with an active form

of award to the satisfaction of the individuals in the group, the staff involved and, ultimately, the consumer of the service that they may be providing.

Whilst such procedures are more time-consuming than the simple transmission of purely cognitive information and the rate of absorption of such a way of learning is slower, the learning sticks and not only does it stick, it also travels to other situations because it is embodied in the individual who carries it. It 'models the process' by which people have to assume responsibility for themselves, to themselves, to each other and to the community they intend to serve. It enables them to operate more skilfully in life because it validates the process of collaborative effort and negotiated settlement.

To enter into such a process effectively, all need to recognise they must demonstrate a willingness to work with interpersonal skills and affective responses, issues of power, control and decision-making of a high order. Staff must be very clear about the extent of their own boundaries, be willing to enter into the process as fully as everyone else and live with the results like everyone else.

Learning through Assessment

'How I learn' is clearly important in devising an assessment process; no less important is how I provide the evidence to demonstrate my learning. In courses or programmes which rely upon process skills and group work methods, a good deal of the 'evidence' surrounding what I have learned will lie in accounts of changes in understanding or perception that were facilitated by experiences I have received over the duration of the programme and at which other group members were also present. These will have been 'live' experiences rather than responses to 'taught' material. As such, they are considerably more difficult to specify and make concrete to others. I may know 'my sensitivity' to others has increased, but it may not be as apparent to everyone else, but at least you were there when...

Because assessment itself is such a process 'activity', *it is also a further source of learning that should not be underestimated.* The process involves three key steps:

1. Identifying which criteria are suitable to apply to an activity, how to report upon its effective competent and appropriate demonstration.

2. Devising a means to evaluate such performances realistically.

3. Agreeing how to make claims of competence that are rigorous enough and descriptive enough to be understood outside the room in which they have been learned – i.e. to the outside world.

These are all very challenging activities in themselves. Indeed, they are likely to yield as much useful learning as the course that provided the experiences that are being assessed.

As we have already noted, assessment is an important part of learning. The question, 'What did I learn?' can be answered in a variety of ways; through tests, examinations, performance and reflection. In most programmes of learning what is learned is examined according to criteria established by those who provided the course, rather than those who have undertaken it. This at least has the merit of consistency, since those who are examined have rarely been consulted about what it is they should learn in the first place.

The assumption that learners stand in some relationship of inferiority to those providing the learning runs throughout our educational practices, from primary school to professional accreditation. All learning and assessment procedures are based upon a set of assumptions about the nature of learning, the responsibilities of those involved and the means by which it should be conducted.

If we assume individuals possess a potentiality for self-direction and have nothing to lose from a mutually collaborative assessment with their peers, then many of the assumptions about present educational practice require reconsideration.

1. How far do we acknowledge, in practice, the contribution that learners could make to the enterprise in which they are engaged?

2. How far are present practices rationalised to protect the power of accrediting bodies, the status of 'knowledge professionals' or to maintain standards of selection and entry into professional groups at levels that satisfy the professionals themselves?

3. Finally, how far is the whole process a way of providing a measure of protection and security for institutional lethargy?

The Exercise of Power and Authority

Staff can no longer assume the unquestioned acceptance of their suggestions, minor or major ones. They must be willing to explain and put forward a convincing case for the adoption of any course of action they propose. Their perceptions, however accurate, of the 'process' issues affecting the group are as subject to disagreement and rejection as anyone else's. And yet, they do still stand in some special relationship to the course, if it is only that they are paid to guide the activity and if it is only because they are less transient than any particular group.

As mentioned earlier, staff stand in the position of *guardians of the spirit of the course*, able to hold the essential and non-negotiable boundaries. They can refer to the documentation of the course to support them, the prospectus or course contract, and equally be able to model living and working with uncertainty and ambiguity, surrendering more and more of their psychological power as the course proceeds.

In traditional educational institutions, teaching staff are vested with an institutional as well as an educational authority. They represent the values and standards of the organisation itself and maintain codes of behaviour and conduct. This dual role of authority of, on the one hand, having special knowledge or skills to pass on, and, on the other, being vested with the power to insist upon behavioural standards, is so taken for granted that these two aspects are conflated as though they are one and the same thing. However, once a group moves towards some form of WPL model, these become filled with ambiguity and uncertainty.

If staff insist on controlling all the ground rules to the learning process, the participants may cover a great deal of material, but only at the expense of having the responsibility taken away from their developing the skills to direct their own learning. If staff leave all ground rules open to negotiation, they leave the group open to the risk of losing its way in the struggle to design the structure to contain the task upon which they are engaged.

Since facilitators operating in a WPL model are themselves the product of an oppressive authoritarian system, they will be as vulnerable to self-deception, error and illusion as anyone else. There will be times when they will 'get it wrong' because they do not have sufficient insight into the process to do otherwise. There will be times, too, when they will mismanage situations, offering too much freedom inappropriately, or holding a group back unnecessarily, and these may be difficult things to acknowledge.

As members of staff enter into the process they may have to face much that is uncomfortable. They will also have some measure of difficulty in identifying just what they might wish to change or do differently next time, because the group will rarely give feedback unanimously. Sifting and sorting out group comments about one's own style and use of power is no easy matter. Struggling to maintain the right to learn, too, is not a model most participants actually wish to see in practice from those 'in charge', whatever they believe in theory.

When challenging the power and authority of a staff member for the first time, the peer learning dimension of the programme can become little more than a ritualistic muttering about small issues, especially if group members feel themselves to be unready, or if they feel the teacher is unready to deal honestly with the issues concerning them.

There is little worse than teacher-induced feedback sessions which are defensive attempts to give students a chance 'to clear the air' and ventilate their feelings. Individuals not only need to be allowed to speak openly, they need to know that they have been heard and, even more importantly, that they have been listened to. Many teachers at this point fall back on the standard pose of showing no signs of having felt the impact the comments made (though they might well have felt them) and little genuine dialogue results, leaving the student group feeling they have been outmanoeuvred. Developing a WPL group demands the development of wider facilitator skills than most teachers possess. Few participants have the skills of participation and collaboration at their command either in the beginning: hence it is a collaborative endeavour and no one escapes from learning.

Feedback is not Assessment

Something as sophisticated and committed a process as self and peer assessment is, as we have already seen, a very challenging process. The challenges and difficulties are likely to be intensified if the individual has not previously experienced serious and long-term relationships involving significant disclosure and feedback.

Feedback, however valuable (and it is), *is **not*** the same thing as working out a way of evaluating how you are going to respond to a colleague's account of the evolution of their learning in relation to a field of endeavour. All those involved in this form of collaborative endeavour will have had to learn how to both give and receive feedback as an integral and explicit part of the group's process (including written feedback) yet, whilst feedback is essential, assessment is a good deal more sophisticated, if it is to be worthy of the term 'assessment'.

Such an assessment moves quite outside some notional objectivity about how to rate a case study, a written assignment, a segment of video tape, or even a series of tapes. The reluctance to engage with difference and dispute, to face issues of 'failing' (of people not being competent in the claims they are making or to meet the standard they have agreed is required) is deeply distressing and difficult to manage. Peer assessment, when only practised in areas of a programme that are 'safe' and non-controversial in order to give some semblance of involving learners in superficial decisions, does nothing to promote devolving power and responsibility to learners in a substantial way.

The real decision-making about standards and performance, about facing people with difficult information that has been postponed for too long, makes manufactured attempts to use peer feedback into something approaching what is described here, a risky enterprise. The danger is that of people being given, in a 'hit-and-run' fashion, information that could have been offered a good deal earlier and at a time when something might have been able to be done to rectify it. Unless there is a strong working relationship between those involved, there is every likelihood that such efforts will either become ritualised occasions for pleasantries or the unleashing of pent-up resentments that have not been dealt with at the time and place they occurred. Such activities have no place in a real self and peer assessment process.

Issues in Self and Peer Assessment

As we have already seen, one frequently asked question is, 'Can people actually rate a good performance?' The answer is, 'Yes they can, if given the time to consider it, the time to prepare it, and the opportunity to evaluate themselves thoroughly enough'. They require all those things as a prerequisite. This has implications for how much self and peer assessment can be reasonably introduced to shorter programmes of study and how much the learning group has to be given the trust, respect and authority to deal with the question. *This places the learning group as a continuous entity at the heart of the enterprise.*

Open learning, distance learning, and other methods that do not rely upon the continuity of the learning group cannot expect to develop the skills and competencies to achieve what is being advocated here. Group cohesion, trust and experience together are vital ingredients in the process of self and peer assessment. It is important to encourage a sufficient range of skills and experiences for assessment and not rely on a few which are concentrated on a single aspect of performance.

All longer Oasis programmes, for example, are assessed by a process of self, peer and facilitator assessment; a process that most participants are meeting for the first time. It provides a rich and valued source of learning in itself, making the role of assessment quite different from that experienced in traditional learning approaches, ranging from further education to higher degree experiences and across a breadth of vocational and professional backgrounds. It is one of the most challenging aspects of the course, and is designed to enable both the individual and group to manage their own development responsibly.

Additionally, this process encourages the development of self-monitoring skills in relation to personal development, skills practice and the applied work setting. Coaching/mentoring sessions also offer participants the opportunity to receive informal feedback from facilitators; this contributes to the formative assessment process. Much of the skills-development work takes place in triads[61] and the following triangular method of learning is implicit in the assessment process.

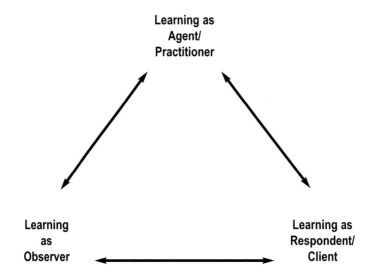

Figure 10 ◆ The Learning 'Triad'

Assessment Criteria

A major challenge in initiating any self and peer assessment process lies in the generation of *useful criteria*. We are so used to other people defining standards of performance on our behalf that most people find the idea of working out what constitutes an effective level or a competent performance of a skill or activity daunting.

'Criteriological' thinking is given low priority in our culture and, as a consequence, individuals may rate themselves effective, or ineffective,

---

[61] Triads: skills practice trios where a listener, a speaker and an observer work together to explore, reflect and debrief aspects of a human relations issue.

without clearly working out the standards they are employing to reach such decisions. Coupled with low self-esteem and a tendency to under-rate themselves, most people, in my experience, are more judgmental of their own performance than they may need to be. This is true both of written work and process skills.

Common criteria are important to groups that accept high levels of accountability to others, including doctors, dentists, counsellors, teachers and so on. In the wider world where an individual has undertaken a self and peer process there is nothing to prevent clinical governance through self and peer assessment. Indeed, Oasis has helped a number of organisations to develop such processes. It is as a counter to the traditional model that makes accountability to one's peers so important.

Autonomous standards set by the individual will be more suitable for interpersonal skills, personal development work, where accountability lies primarily to one's self. However, the contribution of others is likely to be important, so even here a mix of criteria can often be a useful balance to over-rigorous standards of one's own.

On programmes that have a relatively high level of personal development and negotiated content, it is likely that some of the learning achieved is beyond that which an individual expected to learn, i.e. areas in addition to those of the learning intentions of the programme or which did not figure in their learning contract, but which have emerged as the programme unfolds. These may relate strongly to:

- Personal learning

- Applications of learning.

There may well be some things that an individual knows now that *they didn't know they didn't know*. In other words, the range of what it is possible to know may well have increased as a result of development in personal awareness or skills practice. Being aware of such an increase in the potential for learning may be every bit as important as any direct learning that has taken place, since it may be opening up important new directions for the future.

Any programme of study involving behavioural changes, 'live' performances demonstrated in interpersonal skills or other interactive elements, immediately faces difficulties in introducing elements of self and peer assessment into its procedures. The example overpage can highlight the point:

Jane is now 'more able to challenge Peter effectively' as a result of the course. She may think this represents a significant skill acquired and uses it to highlight the changes she made.

But can she challenge others or only Peter? Who has seen her attempt to do this; what did they think? Has she continued to challenge Peter or was this on one occasion and if so, was it a sufficient demonstration of real learning? How far does this ability carry over to other situations and with other people in her outside life?

In many cases, these kinds of questions are crucial. It is not simply sufficient to be assertive on a course; it is important to have the confidence to be assertive where it matters – in life. However, there are few assessors to give feedback when you are challenging a sales person at the checkout on a Friday night! (Though there might be quite an audience!) How others might assess your performance may bear little relation to the very real effort you know you put into the occasion.

In skills learned off the job, but which are related to on-the-job-performance, there are major questions of transferability.

I may, as a colleague, feel you work with me effectively, but I may be a very different person from other people you deal with.

By contrast, I may still think you are far too 'withdrawn as a member of the group', and I may not realise just how mistreated you have been in the past and that being in the group at all may be a major achievement. Such influences are not incidental; they are crucial to the contribution that individuals make.

With interpersonal work of all kinds, some criteria that individuals may want to offer for assessment may only refer to situations in the outside world, whilst other criteria are observable and can be identified from past practice or even offered 'live' before the assessing group. An assessment based entirely on reported performance is likely to be open to challenge in a way that a balance of action and report is not. Participants are not stupid and can see if a colleague is dodging an issue and this, in my view, is why people do not dodge such issues. They acknowledge things that still require further effort to master.

Deciding on a number of criteria is important. If there are too many criteria, people have to say a little about a lot, leaving too little time for real self-exploration. A balance across a range of criteria is important, so that individuals are encouraged to introduce important learning that may appear 'incidental', but which has had crucial effects in all kinds of ways that are now being reported, perhaps for the first time. In addition, generalities need to be balanced with specifics. For example, 'empathy' is important in counselling but difficult to measure, whilst being able to use 'key word reflection' is a specific skill, but not the essence of what makes a good counsellor.

If there is to be a mix between group criteria and individual criteria, again, a balance has to be negotiated and agreed. When the final choice is made as to number and balance between group and individual criteria (staff having contributed as participants throughout), the meaning of the criteria must be made explicit; they should be shared and understandable. The criteria to be used can come from a variety of sources:

1. **Individually**: each person provides their own.
2. **By the group**: via brainstorming, discussion and clarification.
3. **By the staff**: who can offer criteria for adoption or rejection.
4. **By an external group**: which may provide accounts of what it requires or expects.
5. **A combination** of some or all of the above; negotiated with all interested parties concerned.

The assessment is of the individual's progress in relation to the stated purpose of the course. ***It is not an accreditation to do anything.*** *It may well form the basis of an accreditation statement, but that is, in fact, a separate process described in the following chapter.*

The Place of Written Work

It is essential in a true self and peer assessment model that all elements of the course are assessed following the process just described – including written work. If assignments, case studies or projects were to be assessed in the more familiar, traditional way with marks or grades being given by the facilitator (read 'teacher'), it would undermine the whole enterprise and give very confusing and conflicting messages to course participants.

Perhaps, therefore, the dilemmas of peer methods come under challenge most clearly when it comes to this element of peer assessment procedures.

What we come up against here again is a mistrust of the learner; the belief that learners somehow will want to cheat, that they will not have learned enough to measure themselves accurately and that their standards will not be rigorous enough. Collecting in personal journals for marking by a tutor is just one example of such mistrust: either it is a course requirement and not a personal journal, or it is a personal journal and the property of the participant.

There seems to be an overwhelming fear that the whole institutional system of provision will collapse if learners work out together what they mean by 'effective performance' and if they devise ways to measure that performance.

Almost everyone recognises that the capacity to write about something or even talk about it is only tentatively related to the capacity to do it – practice and theory are not much related when it comes to human relations (and just about all other practice-based activities). This is not to suggest that theory is not important, only that it is not the best test of how good a practitioner someone is likely to be. Yet that is what gets the attention; that is what the current system is built around.

Written work is almost always left to the staff to take away, to be digested – or read in haste. This is where the real assessment is made. The written work is there; it can be referred to. It has permanence. It is a form that fits with the traditional measures and it leaves the marker able to make observations that can fail to take into account the cost of the work to the person who has written it.

Traditional reading of another's written work is a solitary experience done by the teacher. Even when assignments are 'double marked' as a verification tool, i.e. by two people, it would be very rare indeed for the author of a piece of work to be directly involved in the assessment process. Writing comments upon it enables the teacher, who has not had to demonstrate their own practice or have it assessed in the way they are about to assess the students' work (let alone their written abilities), to now criticise the theoretical limitations of someone else.

It is a matter of deep personal disappointment to the author that we have an educational system that so successfully strangulates the voice of many of its recipients to the point that they can neither speak confidently for themselves nor write with dignity about themselves. The amount of distress and fear-based anxiety that the term 'written work' generates is hard to imagine until you have a roomful of twenty people all confronting the fact that, although they have been able, skilled and have developed hugely over a period of almost two years (and many of them possess higher degrees already), they are now stricken with terror at the prospect of having their written work 'judged' by anyone.

The fear this generates is a major source of cathartic release and emotional education that arrives just at that point in the life of a programme when it is also dealing with that other great issue we avoid in contemporary life – endings: the death of the course; the parting from those who have been important colleagues and fellow travellers on what has been a life-changing journey.

Participants repeatedly give personal accounts of the way in which teachers have annihilated all interest or self-belief in the individual's capacity to attempt written work with anything other than a painful sense of failure and ignominy. It is a scandalous form of abuse and it is widespread. Participants replay their personal history and often discover they have huge amounts of personal work to do: some are irresistibly punitive of others' written work; others are wounded deeply when they hear any comment at all on their own efforts.

There are few participants who look forward to writing up their biographical history or who take pleasure in their theory piece, and usually they have reached such a place only by overcoming their own history of invalidation somewhere down the line. The idea that the process of discussion that leads to the assessment could be a way of assisting and improving on a piece of written work is little short of revelatory to almost every participant I have ever encountered.

It is not surprising then that all sense of proportion goes when a participant receives a critique of a piece of work into which they have put great effort and commitment (however well-meant the observations). Though it is true that there is always something wrong with a piece of written work, the aim of the exploration in the assessment process is to engage together with the idea or the substance of the work rather than finding ways to demonstrate how far it falls short of the standard of major literary criticism.

Once a piece is done it is easy to see what else might have been included, what else would have been worth looking at, how many other references have been overlooked or not consulted. The questions are, 'Is it enough?' and 'Does it complete the task – adequately?' It appears that most staff find it hard to acknowledge what 'enough' is. Even when praising someone's efforts there is often an implicit, 'How about this?' or, 'Did you think of that?'

When fellow participants enter into this endeavour together, they very quickly develop a real appreciation for what is involved in putting together a useful piece of writing that reflects a real commitment for the person who has done it. When this has taken place over a period of time; when you have seen in depth what this has cost them, because you have been there with them and you too have had similar struggles, the peer assessment process becomes an important and dynamic learning arena in its own right.

Feedback then is much more 'real' and engaged. It will be offered face to face and there may well be revisions and discussions about modifications. Work in progress can be circulated and the whole element of the written work becomes something that lives as a strong and central feature of the programme as a whole, rather than a necessary hoop to jump through in order to gain a diploma.

Preparing for Self and Peer Assessment

An assessment *is not a period of structured feedback*; it is, instead, a rigorous activity in its own right that challenges individuals to lay realistic claims to skills and competencies they have acquired or can use, with evidence and examples to support their claims. Gathering a portfolio is important in self and peer assessment which differs from more traditional portfolios in that the process is undertaken by people together, it will be applied in the real world of practice and it does not need any external verification. Therefore, it requires thought, planning and time to execute. Time alone and time in the group.

Before embarking on a self and peer assessment process, there are three key points to note:

1. Introducing self and peer assessment procedures takes more time to accomplish than anyone can imagine.

2. It will create 'process' decisions that cannot be anticipated in advance and will therefore have to be managed as and when they occur.

3. Not everyone will be able to be involved in everyone's assessment, nor should they expect to be.

In addition to awareness of the above, decisions need to be made about:

1. **What to assess**.

2. **Who shall decide** what we select and what is relevant from all the available elements.

3. **Which criteria shall be employed**. Once we know what to assess, how do we decide the criteria that are important for ourselves, for our profession, those we intend to serve? It may be there are different criteria for different activities or within the same activity. Do individuals decide entirely for themselves, or do the group and staff collaborate?

4. **How to apply the criteria**. Are criteria applied to past performances on the course and/or practical work elsewhere, for example? Shall they apply to work we do outside the course, in our work settings, for example? Shall they apply to a special performance that illustrates our competence, now we've decided on the criteria?

5. **How to go about doing it**. Do we decide it all at once? Is it to be staggered? Does everyone take part all the time in everyone's assessment? Can a small group do it? How shall we go about selection? How much time shall we give it?

6. **Assessing the assessment**. Shall we just forget it now it is over? How well did the process succeed? Did it meet our needs? Can we contribute anything out of our experience to others following behind? What lessons emerge for the staff, the course, the profession, the service users, and us?

Self and peer assessment is an organic, living process. The material for a person's assessment is gathered throughout the length of the programme, involving a continual process of personal review, self-appraisal and possible amendments to learning contracts. Although the formal assessment may take place at a particular time, it is only the manifestation of a continual process of learning and attention to the process. The following sections highlight the sequence and process of implementing a self and peer assessment process.

1. Recording Experience

In courses where a substantial measure of the learning is via participative or experiential methods, citing examples of demonstrated competence might be difficult unless some record has been maintained over the course. Any participant waiting until the closing sessions of a programme to organise their self-assessment is likely to offer patchy evidence for the claims they are making of genuine learning they may well have achieved in the past.

The starting point of the assessment is maintaining and recording progress. A course diary, journal, log, or record is a major device for participants to develop the habit of reflection upon practice that is crucial in retrieving learning from experience. Kept throughout the course in a manner and style suited to themselves, participants enter into a dialogue with themselves that helps the process of self-direction and the development of personal responsibility. (It might not need emphasising here by now but this document is and remains the property of the individual participant, who may or may not disclose the contents to others. It is certainly not the right of any member of staff to expect to examine such a journal without invitation and they never have the right to 'mark' or offer any formal approval of its contents.)

Linked to review elements at the start and close of sessions, individuals and the group as a whole soon begin to recognise the importance of the shared reflection on practice and the value of exploring insights and observations. Experience ceases to be an end in itself, of something good or bad, but becomes the raw material for the individual to 'process' into understanding.

2. The Individual Learning Review

A period of individual reviewing of learning should be an important element in the preparation of any assessment process. Time spent alone to reflect and review where they have been is an essential part of this process. Individuals who enter into the process for the first time can have little clear idea of the many stages and steps involved in what is about to take place, since this is not something that our educational experience, by and large, prepares us for.

It is useful to consider all the major areas of the course and identify major learning gained and challenges encountered within each. Sometimes what is of great value is not the actual learning, but the willingness a person has shown to meet themselves and the challenges of their own development in a new and more honest way. Areas to consider include:

- Those things that I have *integrated* into my learning
- Those things I am presently *consolidating*
- Those things I am *developing* my understanding of more fully
- Those things that are *opening* up to me.

With these elements in mind, there are three central questions that can be the focus for an individual learning review:

i. What learning have I already acquired?

- Those things that I expected to learn
- Those things that perhaps I did not.

ii. Where does that place me?

- What does that indicate about my progress?
- How far does that match what I expected?
- What can I learn about my original learning contract from this?

iii. Where do I need to pay attention from here?

- What priorities does this seem to indicate?
- Are there any outstanding issues?
- Am I concentrating on some aspects as opposed to others?

Many individuals who are for the first time completing a programme that has been strongly peer led will have claims to make relating to their personal development, awareness and insight of self and others that may well be much more ambitious than anything that the programme set out to claim it would achieve.

In addition to the period of review specifically linked to the self-assessment statement, individual review is an on-going process from the programme's inception to its close. This is valuable process for collecting evidence, for ensuring that learning remains relevant and vital throughout the programme, and for enabling the direction of the programme to be amended if appropriate. The learning contract, compiled at the beginning, is an important means by which this on-going review can take place.

3. Mid-programme Review and Feedback

These kinds of sessions, as well as group time, are important opportunities for the processes to emerge to enable people to deal with their feelings about their progress, their achievement, their style of participation and any other aspects of the programme which concerns them.

Depending upon the maturity of the group, feedback may come before a mid-course review, as a way of 'freeing up' the relationships to enable a more challenging climate to operate. Alternatively, a quieter group may begin with a review and use the consolidation of such a process to enter into the riskier arena of more immediate feedback to each other.

4. Preparation for the Assessment

Individuals need time to prepare their self-assessment statement, making notes of their performance in relation to the criteria selected. They need opportunities to consider how best to illustrate their claim to a satisfactory standard. Participants whose ability is otherwise satisfactory can do themselves less than justice if they fail to attend to this stage adequately. Individuals need to work with a partner, from time to time, preparing their assessment and checking-in before the group meets.

One of the difficulties in putting claims together for assessment is often that the individual initially under-represents their learning. Deep personal gains are often regarded as somehow *not relevant* and accomplishments that have had significant effects upon the way an individual manages a wide range of personal or social situations can, at this stage, be overlooked out of a false modesty.

The questions for the participant to ask themselves in this preparation stage include:

1. Is it under-claimed?
2. Is it missing certain elements?
3. Is it overlooking any of the contributions that you have offered?
4. Is it doing justice to the full range of your efforts?

Old restrictions need challenging; it may be safe to under-represent yourself, but it's not a realistic assessment. However, sometimes the assessment claim does need to reflect the ways individuals have failed themselves by not living up to their ambitions. Only by doing so, can they then consider what to do next to change the patterns and limiting beliefs in the future.

> But more important is the affirmation of the learning that has been made, the steps that have been taken and the learning that has been achieved.

The evidence for the claim may come from a number of sources and, by and large, the broader and more comprehensive the range, the more integrated the learning is likely to be. If I have only acted in a particular way on the course that is one thing; if I have tried it out elsewhere, that is another. If I am applying it regularly, then something more is being indicated than simply being able to do it. Evidence may come from:

- The learning contract
- The Journal
- The learning review
- Experience on or off the course, related to the course in some way
- Reports of what has been undertaken elsewhere
- Personal and group reflection
- Observation – what others have seen
- Learning gained in relationship to the content of the course
- Learning gained in relationship to the structure of the course – authority and boundary issues
- Learning in relationship to the pace and sequence of the programme
- Reading and discussion
- Support and supervision
- Actual practice sessions
- Knowledge acquired
- Working with people in a variety of settings and across a range of relationships, which needs to be accurately identified
- Application to work settings and work-based relationships.

The importance of sharing ideas and discussing thoughts with other group members can help to minimise the negative influence and ensure we take a more balanced view of the overall involvement we have had with our programme and the learning obtained. Similarly, discussion with another can start that process of evaluation and assessment, at a verbal level, that will be a beginning for the actual experience in front of a group of selected peers later.

5. Assembling Self and Peer Assessment Groups

If individuals and the group have gone to the kind of trouble required by the process, then the actual assessment ought to reflect that. Selecting the size and membership of the assessment group takes a lot of time to organise. There are issues of membership to be considered: getting a group of peers together that has some balance between those I want, those I would like, those I need and those by whom I am likely to be realistically challenged. Staff forcing the issue at this stage or falling back upon 'pressure of time' and deciding such issues on behalf of the group will undermine the whole process. Everyone has to trust the process will work out – as it invariably does.[62]

Once groups are composed, a running order has to be established. More negotiation is inevitable here, since some people will be asked to be in more than one assessment at any one time. It is essential that individuals make choices and negotiate for what they want. This may well mean that the group has to sit through some painstaking and painful wrestling to get a running order that gives everybody enough of what they want – in terms of the people that they wish to have with them at the time they want to do it.

7. The Role of Other Group Members

Having reflected upon and considered all these elements, questions and criteria, the next step is to spend time in a more focused exploration of learning with two other group members.

- One person would be a talker
- The second a listener
- The third a clarifier who would record the major points.

Time would be divided so that each member of the trio gets an opportunity to work in each role. In the talking period, the speaker should be encouraged to spend some time on the overview before narrowing down to specific aspects of the learning review. Time will also be set aside within each person's speaking session to discuss the implications of what they said with their colleagues before moving on to someone else. Separating the talking time from discussion helps to establish the importance of the speaker exploring their own impressions first, before going on to tease them apart with others. Self-assessment precedes peer assessment; self-review comes before peer review.

The group helps the individual making their claim by:

- Clarifying
- Amplifying

- Extending
- Looking beyond

---

[62] There is no doubt that managing the live processes of group selection, the running order of individual assessment groups and the assessment itself generate high levels of anxiety. This challenges facilitators to manage the resulting anxieties with a rational awareness that if a group is committed to self and peer assessment it will succeed and that it will require creativity as well as openness to the unexpected.

- Challenging
- Verifying
- Enhancing
- Appreciating
- Validating
- Honouring

Such a detailed review as the one just described would hardly be appropriate for a three-day course, for example, but features of this process can be drawn upon at different times for different programmes. Any course that aims to promote in participants a substantial measure of self-direction should provide a similar review period as a means of developing the process skills necessary for the assessment process to make sense and be a worthwhile activity in its own right.

8. The Assessment

Each individual is in charge of their overall assessment period from getting their group together and sorting out how they may wish to record the session (often by tape and usually a scribe to keep track of the key points). Once the self and peer assessment activity is underway, it takes considerable time; 40-50 minutes per person is a usual guide on a longer programme. The assessment has two parts:

1. A self-assessment statement relating to criteria that have already been agreed.

2. Peer assessment based on the self-assessment and any additional remarks that may be requested, offered or negotiated.

Time needs to be allocated to the balance of these two activities so that both self and peer assessment elements are genuinely engaged in as a collaborative activity – no easy matter.

The first time a participant engages in this task they have little to guide them so facilitators need to give careful preparation time. Insecurity about talking about oneself is not uncommon and however well-prepared some people are, they simply ramble for much too long, leaving the peer element with too little time to engage usefully – and hence the whole thing is inconclusive and invalid.

Others say very little and expect their peers to tease out the information. In that way, they abdicate their rightful responsibility for directing what is their own assessment with the assistance of peers.

There are few learning groups that get through the process without major issues of this kind arriving in the assessment process itself. This is something that facilitators have to manage with a minimum of anxiety and a good deal of creativity.

9. The Learning Statement

Whatever criteria have been generated during the course, they need to be addressed in the learning statement. In some programmes, areas for generating criteria may include such topics as:

- Self-development: personal and practitioner
- Self-in-group: participation, relatedness, contribution
- Power and authority: how they have been managed
- Self in society
- Contribution to wider relationships
- Acting as an agent for social change.

The learning statement summarises the principal learning achieved by each individual at the close of the course. This is both a reminder and a record of achievement that clearly illustrates the claims made by the individual participant. In preparing a statement there should be some brief rationale for the method and purpose of those things that are to follow. It should reflect the breadth of the course experience and offer a balanced, realistic account of progress and learning. There should be a match between the statements made, the way they are expressed and an accuracy of description, as well as clarity. Limitations to practice should also be noted, indicating that the individual is aware, not only of what they can do, but also up to what level of skill, experience and expertise they are able to perform.

10. Differences

Differences over assessment ratings may require longer periods to be negotiated at a later time and may involve other group members and/or staff. It can be useful to have an outside figure to appeal to if necessary; to 'moderate the process', not as an authority to decide on the outcome. However, if the process has been done rigorously it is rare for such problems to occur.

In my experience, this has been invoked only once in a period that now extends over more than twenty-five years of involvement. Even where people 'fail' their assessment there is a recognition, often at the time, that they have created their own difficulties and so there is no need to have recourse to outside moderation. That said, it is useful to have some process in place to protect the whole endeavour.

This warning could be usefully extended to the whole effort. The more the process is understood, the more there are fall-back positions in place (like contact with someone who has experience of the process), then the more the inevitable turbulence of this process as it comes to its climax is able to be managed. Those implementing it have to remember they are introducing a novel process at a point in the life of a programme when people are disengaging, when the traditional role of exams masks the separation anxieties of those involved and when the fear of being judged inadequate is still unrealistically high and emotionally prevalent.

The time taken to prepare the process itself encourages people to gain a realistic description of their learning or, if anything, to undervalue it. Indeed, this is one of the issues that self and peer assessment highlights time and time again; the difficulty that people have in laying claim to the skills and competencies they actually do possess.

This whole process of self and peer assessment is concerned with what the individual participant has learned; accreditation concerns the use to which they will put that learning. It is this aspect that the following chapter addresses.

CHAPTER ELEVEN

Living the Learning Transition: Accreditation and Whole Person Learning

To be accredited is to be 'officially recognised' or 'generally accepted'. It is 'having guaranteed qualities'. (Concise Oxford Dictionary)

Not all individuals who undertake a WPL event will feel the need to seek accreditation at its close, yet we do live in times of increasing licensing and demands for certificates and accreditation of all kinds. It is also important to acknowledge that part of the WPL process is the recognition of being part of the wider world, of all the inter-connecting elements around us – and that the learning relates to some context. All this needs to be recognised and it is important, too, to encourage and aid all those who choose to find ways to accredit their work without undermining or diluting the peer approach they espouse thus far. This chapter therefore looks at different forms of accreditation, including self and peer accreditation, and their perceived benefits and limitations.

Value and 'Proof'

People undertaking a programme may well know its value. Final learning statements may give clear descriptions of what they can 'do', to what level and with whom, but anyone providing such programmes must take into account and attend to how well all this lives in the world.

It is essential to give an outline of how it lives, because it is so contrary to traditional models which employ external assessment and follow an imposed curriculum. If this paradigm is to have any influence it has to show how it has a life beyond the WPL programme.

This takes us into the whole question of accreditation. The method of accreditation used by any particular body, group or collection of individuals will also reflect the politics of their endeavour, whether or not they can see or acknowledge it. Here we meet the whole dilemma of a primarily internal source for motivation versus largely externally motivated influences.

A self-directed learner will want to find suitable and appropriate arenas to offer accountability to their peers, if for no other reason than to avoid the delusions that can arise out of individual isolation. In a situation where one person is offering help of some kind to another, for example, a willingness to be personally accountable offers assurance to their peers and to potential clients that the practice is in safe hands. In that sense, every practitioner stands as a representative of the body of practitioners to which they belong.

This realisation – that I am being represented by others, just as I too represent others – creates major anxieties and deep tensions in those conventionally educated and even in some of those emerging from the WPL paradigm.

The Importance of Accreditation

In line with the desire to promote accountability and self-responsibility, those who facilitate longer-term WPL programmes need to give serious consideration to assisting practitioners make the transition into the world that lies beyond the programme, especially the world of employment. They also need to help generate discussion, exploration, experimentation and development of suitable forms of accreditation that align to the world of practice that emerges from WPL learning approaches, those served and the institutional arrangements that have a rightful influence on the practitioner.

Having demonstrated their commitment to undertake a rigorous and congruent process of assessment, the participant is more than ready to take their learning out into the world. WPL is strongly about application – about bringing more of the person we are into action in the world and to take up a more accountable stance for how we offer ourselves. That being so, having some means of proclaiming *it*, having it recognised or acknowledged is not an unimportant or incidental matter.

If a major feature of WPL is a developing idea that individuals can freely stand by their actions and their commitments and have those acknowledged and challenged by like-minded peers, then some form of accreditation is a way of both setting a standard to the outside world and making clear the way in which the practitioner is choosing to be accountable. It offers those they serve the means and the method by which they can act if difficulties arise or if there is dissatisfaction for some reason.

Additionally, if irrational authoritarian forms of regulation are fast coming to an end and peer networks are the way ahead, then peer-based forms of accreditation need speedily to develop rigour and applicability, relevance and appropriateness, if they are to gain the confidence to replace those more outdated forms of regulation. This is particularly so if WPL, as pioneered by the IDHP and as currently operated by Oasis with links to learning endeavours world-wide, is to become global.

Regular self and peer assessment about issues of practice and context need to be part of any accreditation system. So, for example, no applied activity should be without a time limit before the practitioner re-engages with the process of self and peer assessment. A three-year time limit is probably suitable and rigorous enough for most activities. If left longer, people's commitment may well wither and their relationship to the wider community of practice begin to be little other than a token connection. It is important that peer networks are 'alive' and do more than simply offer a place of reference for getting a licence to operate in the world; real progress in this is slow but inexorable.

Just as the assessment process requires the learner to rise to a major new challenge of becoming an adult in relation to their learning and how it is to be collated and presented, so, too, do peers have to begin the arduous task of creating the frameworks within which to manage and govern themselves that are consistent with their values and their practice.

It is the *right and responsibility* of peers who want the practice they respect to survive and flourish to help sustain it practically as well as theoretically. Hence, accreditation processes and ways of bringing this paradigm into the world need due consideration by anyone interested in undertaking WPL in any extensive fashion. An assessment process does not ensure these things and a learning statement, which follows on from it, need not either. An accreditation process is an additional step forward. It may be lengthy or it may be comparatively straightforward, depending on what the WPL event has set out to accomplish and what individuals are using the training to accredit themselves to go on to do.

General Features of Accreditation

Power in any group or organisation of practitioners lies very clearly in the hands of those who can authorise, licence and approve who can do what with what, where, with whom, and for what reward.

Accreditation is the means of controlling the activity, and also of controlling the position the activity holds amongst other activities that are either in competition with or at odds with the one in question. Accreditation also enables those who are included to know they belong to a distinctive body and enables them to proclaim a common form of recognition. They are, as a result of accreditation, able to expect others to know what their status is generally regarded to be worth. Traditional methods of accreditation rely upon the new entrant measuring up to the required standards of those who are already included within the ranks of the practice in question.

Following the satisfactory passing of examinations or tests, traditional rituals, the wearing of special gowns, the transmission of ancient charters and other paraphernalia are developed to indicate the new entrant has now joined the ranks of the membership. Symbolic though they may be, these 'rites of passage' serve several important functions.

1. They announce to the world who is and who isn't approved.

2. They ensure those entering are well-behaved and understand the power of the group to which they are joining.

3. They convey a sense of real or spurious authority over the whole proceedings and, of course, reflect nothing so much as an investiture or some ceremonial religious purpose.

If it is a genuine expression of an authority that reflects the internal commitment of the individual who is being invested, then it is aligned. But many individuals go through accreditation processes with a low level of commitment and are simply seeking an external imprimatur on their right to act as they intend to anyway. The whole thing then becomes a cynical exploitative device in which all parties collude.

By mystifying the joining of a special group in this way, the real economic and market function is disguised. Essentially, such rituals are devised to maintain obstacles at the point of entry that serve to discourage the faint-hearted and to create an aura of exclusivity for those who enter safely inside.[63]

Accreditation in the Modern World:
Statutory and Authority Accreditation

It is from notions such as these that the need for legalistic forms of accreditation derives, and still draws, its strength. At a time when most people will move careers (and maybe even professions) every few years, what value, you might wonder, is there in spending a fortune getting accredited to an activity that may be your livelihood for only a few years?

---

[63] It is interesting to note that most professional accreditation procedures rarely require the person seeking accreditation to demonstrate competence across the range of activities that go to make up the practice, whereas in most trades it is necessary to show you can 'do' what is required and not only 'know' what is required before you join the ranks.

Because it eases the transition from one place to another when you can arrive with a badge of membership to a group that is not dissimilar and that operates in not dissimilar ways to the one you have previously joined.

Where some group has a legal framework established by the state to prescribe its parameters (the **statutory** element), there is likely to be another separate authority actually charged with the regulation of the activity. It is, however, usually given over to a professional body to regulate and licence those who are able to practice, such as the UKCC (United Kingdom Central Council) for nursing or the GMC (General Medical Council) for doctors in the UK. The government simply says 'you must...'

These bodies, established by statute and responsible to some governmental agency, are charged with the task of managing the activities of the membership, supervising the licensing of the membership and performing the legally approved task. The result, in short, is to ensure the profession is firmly embedded within the hierarchy of influence that we know as the 'establishment'. It is usually claimed that statutory accreditation has the following benefits:

1. **Safety and protection of the public**. Yet we have only to think of the case of the BSE crisis in the UK, where the public was let down by a number of statutory, regulatory agencies, to recognise how flimsy a form of defence this is.

2. **Clarity of where responsibility lies and clear methods of accountability**. However, the fact that the Bristol Hospital Trust took ten years to open an inquiry into infant deaths is a glaring example of how misplaced public confidence can be in such systems.

3. **Providing public reassurance**. In the two above examples we see an increasing scepticism in the public mood that undermines confidence in other institutions and in the sphere of public life itself.

Statutory bodies are often very conservative in relation to embracing new practices or encouraging new forms of practice. The link between statutory bodies and the socio-political establishment means they are often under the control of like-minded people who all share a similar outlook; one considerably removed from that of the population at large.

However you can have **authority** accreditation without it being a statutory requirement. Authority accreditation then is a means of perpetuating dependence upon those who assume the role of authority and who retain power over those who seek the imprimatur to practice: again not something likely to promote innovation and new ways of practice. There is no law that says you have to have such accreditation but, if you don't, it is harder to get work. This is the traditional form of accreditation provided by an external body such as the Institute of Chartered... At some stage of its evolution, a body of practitioners is awarded a charter (or awards one to itself) and then begins to award itself the authority to 'licence' practitioners on the basis of its special claim and powers as the representative agency of the membership association. The authority of the BACP (British Association for Counselling and Psychotherapy), to take another example, is not based upon statutory requirement but upon authority to which they have laid claim.

Such forms of accreditation are at odds with the spirit of the times and the move towards more autonomous groups, network organisations and the empowerment of the individual to make wise choices about their own decisions and any move to develop WPL bodies should bear in mind that:

> What happens originally is that some group of people who are necessarily self or peer accredited as Fs[64] engage in a further, higher order act of self or peer accreditation and authorise themselves to engage in the unilateral authorisation of others to become Fs... Thus experts/professionals maintain their privileged caste; they create in aspiring Fs an appetite for similar status and similar powers such that these aspirants will conform to the imposed accreditation game in order to become caste members. ...The contradiction of the game is that the people who first gave 'properly qualified' this kind of meaning necessarily exempted themselves from the definition imposed on others. The method (of authority accreditation) excludes any kind of self and peer assessment prior to accreditation, and excludes any negotiation between the prospective F and the authorities about the accreditation.   John Heron, 1977: 43.

It is commonly said in defence of authority accreditation that it maintains standards at an intellectual, vocational, organisational and political level. Such an arrangement is often favoured because it implies a strong form of social control. It certainly provides for the psychological and social security needs of many by maintaining a hierarchical social system with power vested very firmly with the accrediting professionals who control entry. Having said that, there are two key limitations to authority accreditation:

---

[64] The initial F is used to represent the facilitator.

1. **It demonstrates a deep internal contradiction inherent in the enterprise**. It purports to be a method of maintaining high standards, of professionalism, training and education, yet the methods that are used are at odds with the educational goal. Self-monitoring and sensitively aware professionals are educated by a method that provides no opportunity for this to find any real expression. At the same time, they are somehow supposed to acquire this ability by a method which actually prevents them holding to the worth of their own experience, as opposed to that of those in power.

2. **It promotes intellectual, vocational and professional conformity, and fear-ridden concerns** about what others *may* think. It necessarily emphasises intellectual and cognitive skills over interpersonal and affective skills, since an authoritarian system is oppressive in the form of its provision, the impositions it places upon the student and the way the system itself operates.

Where individuals have life and death issues involved in their practice there seems a very strong case for such statutory and authority based forms of accreditation. At its best, accreditation can be seen as a rational form of regulation to ensure that practitioners have some body of support behind them, and that their clients have some body to whom they can appeal if they are dissatisfied with the service or the treatment they receive. As we know, this is the theory.

In practice, it is often very difficult for established professional groups to provide this function for dissatisfied clients in satisfactory ways. Professional bodies are often regarded as the equivalent of a PR agency established to defend the interests of its members (and nothing wrong with that, if it's explicit). They take on, in other words, a claim that they rarely fulfil well – the protection of the client – and do rather better at promoting the rights and privileges of their members to special conditions they expect are due to them, such as high fees.

Distinctions need to be made between a person's 'fitness' to practice, being 'licensed' to practice and being 'competent' to practice; distinctions that are often conflated. A practitioner can be licensed to practice but they might be untrustworthy; they might be competent but not officially licensed; they may be competent and embrace the values of others who also practice in that field, i.e. be 'fit for practice', but still be unlicensed. A major weakness of all forms of authority based accreditation lies in the fact that once the person has passed the entry test they are then at licence to manifest all forms of degenerate behaviour that do not exclude them from their right to practice the work itself. Unless a person does something highly negligent or deeply scandalous, there is little to call them to account.

To give an example, from years of working in hospital settings I repeatedly encounter individuals who report incidents where consultants 'act out' their own unresolved authority issues in the most oppressive and exploitative ways upon others. No one is surprised (and no longer am I); the culture expects it; fellow practitioners in junior roles (in a very hierarchical arrangement) put up with it; the newcomer to the profession sees it acted out daily and internalises it as they are socialised into their role; and the whole system perpetuates it.

The accreditation system of such figures is not based on their conduct in the wider sense – in a whole person way – but only in the narrowest technical application. This then ensures that many people who are technically competent but interpersonally abysmal are licensed to have life and death issues in their hands, and no accountability structures within which their conduct is to be examined unless they make a major technical error. Violating the sensitivities of the other is not such an error; gross disrespect to colleagues is not such an error; reducing those you are purporting to serve to silence is not such an error.

This state of affairs will change as more and more empowered and peer-based systems and structures are brought into existence. Such structures will ensure that those who perform on our behalf (those who are paid by the taxes of the citizen to perform esteemed roles, for example), those who receive treatment at the hands of those who have a licence to practice (the citizens themselves), and those who have some standing in arbitrating and adjudicating contentious issues in professional life (respected peers for the purpose) will come together to create peer-based forms of accountability structures about how *you as a prospective practitioner* will operate in *this* setting, given that *we* are *employing* you. Your professional body will guarantee us that you have the requisite skills, but we will determine how you are accountable for applying those skills and how far you fulfil the obligations that are placed on *us all*. All of which will be freely adopted by any new entrant.

The current transition, where we are moving out of hierarchical forms of authority, creates a tension between wanting to allow practice to develop and flourish, and yet establishing and maintaining adequate standards of practice. The internal ambivalence is often resolved by the practitioner claiming that they need to protect someone else by having tight forms of restrictive accreditation. Rarely do they feel *they* need such tight accreditation (because if they did, they are questioning their own competence).

Here we observe distress-based fears of being self-accountable with and to one's peers 'projected out' as a need to look after 'vulnerable' clients from other 'incompetent' practitioners. The steadiness required to resist the temptation to 'act out' one's own authority issues needs vigilant scrutiny. In Oasis, for example, the commitment to the peer principle has been at the cost of seeking accreditation with bodies that reclaim the authority back *over* the practitioner. This is one of the consequences of living the new paradigm and it has cost Oasis a great deal.

The New Paradigm Accreditation: Self and Peer Accreditation

Here, we move to altogether more novel forms of accreditation; ones where those seeking accreditation use their self-assessment for the foundation of their accreditation. Self-assessment, peer assessment and self-accreditation usually precede the process of peer accreditation. In other words, the individual forms their own claim about their own practice before it is examined by their peers. Self-accreditation embodies the concept of personal accountability:

1. I can account for my actions.
2. I can give voice to my experience.
3. I can stand by my thoughts.

Whenever we do something for the first time we are in effect saying that we have chosen to accredit ourselves as competent. Such opportunities and conscious efforts are an impetus to further growth, awareness and vigilance in relation to the process of one's own and another's development.

The accreditation statement an individual makes at the close of a successful programme of development is in addition to the assessment itself and the learning statement, and it is a description of what the individual is laying claim to be competent to do as a result of the programme. It is understood and validated by representatives of the peer group and staff and it is unlikely in any community of peers that an individual will self-accredit in the face of strongly expressed reservations and concerns from their peers – though this could and would be allowed to happen since primacy is being given to self-accreditation.

The crucible for this process is *immersion in the peer principle and self and peer assessment*. Yet there can be places where self-accreditation means little more than that the individual simply puts up a plaque on the wall and waits for clients to come. Alternatively, they may seek some support from others or they may be part of a group who have put real effort into providing a way of evaluating what it is they each do, how they do it, to what standard, over what range of clients and so on; they provide a shared forum to hear and support one another's claims. They may even operate an informal system of support and a means of managing complaints.

Having created my own accreditation statement, I invite my peers to enter into dialogue with me. Practitioners are presented with the challenge of making appropriate claims about their competence, having them rigorously explored and potentially modified in the light of feedback. The key question to ask is:

> What attributes and expertise do I want to claim I have, in order to offer myself before my peers as competent to do this work?

Underlying most forms of self and peer accreditation is the idea of a community of peers: folk who share a commitment to practice and to being openly accountable to others about how they go about that practice. It is voluntarily entered into and becomes a strong source of both personal and professional development in itself. Communities of peers[65] could easily be linked together to provide further levels of accountability and, indeed, such links do exist, such as the Independent Therapists Network (ITN) in the north of England. And, of course, a client is able to contact such a group to verify its validity.

Bearing the above in mind, the claimed benefits of self and peer accreditation include:

1. **It motivates self-preparation**. The rigour of a self and peer assessment and accreditation system is a daunting experience, as those who have entered into it thoroughly will testify, and it requires good preparation.

2. **It honours the primacy of self-assessment and personal authority**. It leaves the learning open to the individual's level of understanding and the maximum degree of self-direction.

---

[65] Oasis has a network of over 100 practitioners who are in various peer-based networks of supervision.

> For the human condition is such that, in the last analysis, each person is her own best judge: the ultimate authoriser of competence within. Competence that *depends* on its legitimation from without is surely less than true competence.   John Heron, 1977: 40.

3. **It preserves and enhances the creativity and self-direction of the individual**. Only by repeatedly affirming the worth of the person and their right to be the judge of their own actions will we begin to shift the dead weight of conformity that restrains us all. Self-assessment is a primary and a necessary precondition for any valuable creativity.

4. **There is accountability to a wider group and a community of peers in a shared endeavour**. For those agitated by concerns relating to the protection of the client, it is straightforward to explain that the practitioner is accredited to practice with a group of other practitioners who meet regularly to renew their commitment to practice.

5. **It is a long-term process**. It takes time to prepare, claim and maintain, rather than, say, a one-off 'test' of short duration.

At this point, there are few people who have direct experience of a rigorous self and peer assessment process and, therefore, few who understand its implications because they have not experienced it. But as increasing numbers experience more participative forms of learning, attend participative research and co-operative inquiry type research projects, and generally become more familiar with collaborative styles of working that reduce barriers to sharing information and which encourage more openness to the other, then such methods will become more and more familiar. However, there is no doubt we have a long way to go.

Clearly, at this stage, the way lies open for self and peer accreditation to be no more than the expression of delusional fantasies and half-understood expressions of collusive approval. We know only too well how peer group pressure, partisan intrigue and schisms are significant forces to contend with at a certain stage in the development of any group. This would be especially so if the endeavour in question is an attempt to side-step the conventional world, but remain somehow attached to it. Certain limitations are identified – usually by those who have not yet experienced the rigour of a self and peer accreditation process – that need to be addressed and managed.

1. **Who are to be 'accrediting peers'? How are they to be chosen and by whom?** The selection of the group is clearly a matter for consideration and partly depends upon the activity that is being accredited. Interestingly enough, though, it is not always necessary to know the deep intricacies of the practice in question since what is really being tested out is the sincerity and accuracy of a person making a claim by which their peers will stand. What is important is that there is a willingness to speak up about any disquiet and not to falter when a person is clearly using modesty as a way of hiding their talents even from themselves.

2. **It is open to the manipulative, the deceivers and the charlatans.** The fear is that the process will be taken over and that it will be abused and exploited; however, there are some in-built controls. Self-directing learners can soon distinguish those they wish to work with from those they do not.

3. **The period of learning may be too short.** It is true that the earlier a claim is being made, the less the subtlety of the distinctions of actual practice, as opposed to supposed practice, will be apparent. Length of programme is therefore important in determining the extent to which a full self and peer accreditation process can be undertaken.

4. **The claiming may be too grand.** Over twenty years of experience has shown that under-claiming is a real difficulty in the early stages of self and peer accreditation procedures, far more so than over-claiming. A form of collective collusion to minimise the skills, attributes and understandings can come into play out of the imported fears that any significant claim to effectiveness will be looked upon with suspicion and leave the claimant open to unsupportive challenges 'to prove it'.

5. **Those receiving the service are at the mercy of the practitioner; there is no seal of approval or guarantee of quality.** People are not children and attempts to treat them that way simply infantilise them. It only encourages them to develop, or to maintain, a protracted dependency upon others who are competent in ways they aren't and perpetuates professionalisation and élitism. It runs counter to the whole self-help movement that will increase in other fields – law, education and medical matters. Looking to external bodies to provide the imprimatur inhibits the growth and development of everyone.

Attention to self-direction and attention to honouring the peer principle will go a considerable way to addressing these concerns. No system is foolproof. What we want is a community with the person at its heart, where mistakes can be dealt with judiciously and with mercy, and which is fiercely protective of the accountability of individuals to each other.

Preparation for Practice

Deciding what constitutes effective preparation for any practitioner is not quite arbitrary, but relatively so. Who knows? Who decides? All professional groups in the beginning make relatively arbitrary decisions about what constitutes the prerequisite to practice and then exempt themselves from having to go through the process.

> ...For any domain of human inquiry there is a source point when its originators flourish through self-directed learning and inquiry and through self and peer assessment. ...They thus set up an unilateral assessment and education system from which they exempted themselves.
>
> John Heron in D. Boud (ed), 1988: 79.

As anxieties about accreditation grow, we are likely to see stringent conditions surround many aspects of professional practice, designed, no doubt it will be claimed, 'to protect the consumer' and promote 'high standards'. Such conditions do neither, since the consumer in need rarely knows how to assess the person from whom they are seeking help.

We are now entering a period where the professionalisation of just about every form of help is underway at quite a pace. How far it will get and where it will ultimately lead is anyone's guess. There is every danger that the heart and the mystery of such work may be rationalised out of existence into checklists and competency statements. The increasing number of committees elaborating ever more stringent and rigorous standards will ensure that the heart and the mystery enshrined in the processes that occur between people gathered together to learn will retreat from view to those places where learning is still something that is potentially celebratory and joyous.

As we have seen throughout this work, inherent in the concept of the peer principle is commitment, involvement, engagement and choice from all parties in any endeavour. The view is also held that individuals who are regarded by society as being responsible for themselves and their own actions are adult enough to make decisions governing themselves and their conduct in a caring and supportive environment that promotes challenge.

The starting place is that staff and participants share a fundamental equality that the temporary assignment of different roles within a given context does not undermine. Conventional power differences are thus minimised since the learning group is the vehicle for the process of assessment and accreditation – with support and challenge from facilitators or staff.

This doesn't sound anything startling put like this, but in terms of authority and power it has enormous implications for those attending such programmes for the first time. They are expected and encouraged to make decisions, take responsibility, to 'own' and set about meeting their own learning needs. They are given every expectation that they can do it, can collaborate and that the staff will facilitate rather than teach them what they have come to learn. Out of such a base of practice and commitment to developing a set of internal beliefs, which are open to revision and challenge, a form of accountability to match such a form of preparation must necessarily question traditional methods of accreditation and the procedures that accompany it.

The crucial issue for practitioners who claim a strong element of human relations in their practice is to remain committed to finding ways of operating that:

- Are internally consistent
- Honour the peer principle
- Can be described to the uninitiated so they are reassured that practitioners are able to offer what they claim.

The new paradigm challenges us to find that place of congruence where the practitioner's way of working with others is honourable and respects their client's self-reliance and choice whilst remaining in harmony, both with the assessment and accreditation procedures of the practitioner and the practitioner body to whom the individual belongs.

CONCLUSION

Whole Person Learning: The Way Ahead

WPL calls for more collaborative approaches towards many aspects of personal, social and organisational life; including aspects of leadership and management. It holds the potential for radically transforming how people work together, how they respond to each other, how they view their own role in the world of work as well as in their wider life.

WPL is a way of being and relating that will continue to evolve; it is not fixed or 'set in stone' at this point or with this publication. Inherent within its very nature is openness to experience from all spheres and arenas of our senses, our world and the cosmos itself. This experience then informs knowing that, in turn, leads to reviewing and possibly adapting, modifying or extending understanding of what it means to live from a WPL perspective.

And this is about living WPL rather than it being a mode of operating that is switched on when walking into a group, or taking on the role of facilitator, say. Living WPL is a commitment to viewing others as peers and being willing to meet them in a real way. Meeting them in our vulnerabilities as well as our strengths; meeting them in agreement and in difference; meeting them as fully as we are able. It means, too, being willing to challenge many traditional and fiercely-held views around such issues as power, authority, gender roles, prejudices of all kinds and self-accountability.

This account is far from complete but the foundations have been laid. Already, there are many groups, individuals and communities who are grappling with the intricacies and implications of operating from a whole person perspective in a wide variety of settings. This can only grow as they have influence within their wider communities and as more and more people come to recognise the value and necessity of the transition from 'power over' hierarchical systems to ones that embrace 'power with': self-generating and self-directing approaches. It is clear that we are only at the edge of a new chapter for the human potentiality of learning and making this transition into a new state of consciousness; one where the transpersonal dimension will become increasingly recognised and acknowledged.

For over twenty years, Oasis has been involved with introducing and implementing various forms of WPL events through two-year Diploma courses, countless short-term courses, facilitator training courses, in its work with organisations and co-operative inquiries. Co-operative inquiries have been undertaken in the following areas:

- Leadership, with the UKLI
- Integrated Practice and Holistic Learning (IPHL)
- Difference
- WPL in a WPL organisation
- Transforming the World and Transforming the Self.

Oasis has developed links with other people and groups that are interested and involved in similar approaches. We have a long-standing relationship with John Heron, now at the South Pacific Centre for Human Inquiry in New Zealand, and connections with Ed O'Sullivan (OISE) in Canada, the Omega Institute in the US, past graduates of the IDHP, Doug Paxton of CIIS in San Francisco, Jorge Ferrer, and Estella in Barcelona.

Anyone interested in connecting to WPL through Oasis is most welcome to do so through the website www.oasishumanrelations.org.uk

APPENDIX 1

UNESCO Draft of Universal Declaration of Identity, Diversity and Pluralism

Article 1 – Cultural diversity: the common heritage of humanity

Culture takes diverse forms across time and space. This diversity is embodied in the originality and plurality of the identities that characterize the groups and the societies that make up humanity. Because it makes for exchange and mutual enrichment between these identities which are themselves dynamic and increasingly composite, cultural diversity is a source of innovation and creativity. It is as necessary for the human race as bio-diversity in the natural realm. In this sense, it is the common heritage of humanity and should be recognized and affirmed for the benefit of present and future generations.

Article 2 – From cultural diversity to cultural pluralism

In our increasingly diverse societies, it is essential to design policies aimed at ensuring harmonious interaction and a willingness to live together among people and groups with very varied cultural identities. Policies for the inclusion and participation of all citizens are guarantees of social cohesion, the vitality of civil society, and peace. Cultural pluralism as thus defined is the political response to the reality of cultural diversity. Indissociable from a democratic framework, it is conducive to cultural exchange and to the flourishing of creative capacities that sustain public life.

Article 3 – Cultural diversity as a factor in development

Cultural diversity is one of the driving forces of development, understood not simply as economic growth, but also as a means for individuals and groups to achieve a more satisfactory intellectual, emotional, moral and spiritual existence. By broadening the options open to them, it may lead to their full empowerment.

Cultural Diversity and Human Rights

Article 4 – Human rights as guarantees of cultural diversity

The defence of cultural diversity is inseparable from respect for human dignity. It implies a commitment to human rights and fundamental freedoms, in particular the rights of persons belonging to minorities and that of indigenous peoples. No one may invoke cultural diversity to infringe upon human rights and fundamental freedoms, as defined in universally recognized international instruments, nor to limit their scope.

Article 5 – Cultural rights as an enabling environment for cultural diversity
Cultural rights are an integral part of human rights. The flourishing of creative diversity requires the full implementation of cultural rights as defined in Article 27 of the Universal 31 C/44 Annex – page 3 Declaration of Human Rights and in Articles 13 and 15 of the International Covenant on Economic, Social and Cultural Rights. All persons should therefore be able to express themselves and to create and disseminate their work in the language of their choice, and particularly in their mother tongue; all persons should be entitled to quality education and training that fully respect their cultural identity; and all persons should be able to participate in the cultural life and cultural practices of their choice subject to respect for the fundamental rights of others.

Article 6 – Towards access to cultural diversity for all
The free flow of ideas by word and image should be guaranteed, while ensuring that all cultures can express themselves and make themselves known. Freedom of expression, media pluralism, equal access to art and to scientific and technological knowledge, including in digital form, and the possibility for all cultures to have access to the means of expression and dissemination are the guarantees of cultural diversity.

Cultural Diversity and Creativity

Article 7 – Cultural heritage as a source of creativity
Creation draws on the roots of cultural tradition, but flourishes only in contact with other cultures. For this reason, the heritage, in all its forms, must be preserved, enhanced, and transmitted to future generations as testimony to human experience and aspirations, so as to foster creativity in all its diversity and to inspire a genuine dialogue between cultures.

Article 8 – Cultural goods and services: commodities of a unique kind
In the face of present-day economic and technological change, opening up vast prospects for creation and innovation, particular attention must be paid to the diversity of the supply of creative work, to due recognition of the rights of authors and artists and to the specificity of cultural goods and services which, as vectors of identity, values, and meaning, must not be treated as mere commodities or consumer goods.

Article 9 – Cultural policies as catalysts of creativity

Without hampering the free circulation of ideas and works, cultural policies must create conditions conducive to the creation and dissemination of diversified cultural goods and services through cultural industries that have the means to assert themselves at the local and global level. It is for each State, with due regard to its international obligations, to define its cultural policy and to implement it through the means it considers fit, whether by operational support or appropriate regulations.

Cultural Diversity and International Solidarity

Article 10 – Strengthening capacities for creation and dissemination world-wide

Current imbalances in flows and exchanges of cultural goods and services at the global level threaten cultural diversity. To avert this threat, it is necessary to reinforce international cooperation and solidarity aimed at enabling developing countries and countries in transition 31 C/44 Annex – page 4 to establish cultural industries that are viable and competitive at national and international level.

Article 11 – Building partnerships between the public sector, the private sector and civil society

Market forces alone cannot guarantee the preservation and promotion of cultural diversity. Therefore, in promoting sustainable human development, the key role of public policy, in partnership with the private sector and civil society, must be reaffirmed.

APPENDIX 2

The Ten Principles of The Global Compact

The Global Compact's ten principles in the areas of human rights, labour, the environment and anti-corruption enjoy universal consensus and are derived from:

The Universal Declaration of Human Rights

The International Labour Organization's Declaration on Fundamental Principles and Rights at Work

The Rio Declaration on Environment and Development

The United Nations Convention Against Corruption

The Global Compact asks companies to embrace, support and enact, within their sphere of influence, a set of core values in the areas of human rights, labour standards, the environment, and anti-corruption:

Human Rights

Principle 1: Businesses should support and respect the protection of internationally proclaimed human rights; and

Principle 2: make sure that they are not complicit in human rights abuses.

Labour Standards

Principle 3: Businesses should uphold the freedom of association and the effective recognition of the right to collective bargaining;

Principle 4: the elimination of all forms of forced and compulsory labour;

Principle 5: the effective abolition of child labour; and

Principle 6: the elimination of discrimination in respect of employment and occupation.

Environment

Principle 7: Businesses should support a precautionary approach to environmental challenges;

Principle 8: undertake initiatives to promote greater environmental responsibility; and

Principle 9: encourage the development and diffusion of environmentally friendly technologies.

Anti-Corruption

Principle 10: Businesses should work against all forms of corruption, including extortion and bribery.

ADDENDUM TO APPENDIX 3

Globally Responsible Leadership Initiative Partners

China Europe International Business School – CEIBS	China
ESSEC Business School	France
Fundação Dom Cabral	Brazil
IBM	USA
IESE Business School	Spain
INSEAD	France & Singapore
Lafarge	France
London Business School	UK
Merryck & Co	UK
Pepperdine University Graziadio School of Business and Management	USA
Petróleo Brasilero SA – PETROBRAS	Brazil
Queen's University School of Business	Canada
The Foresight Group	Sweden
University of South Africa, Centre for Corporate Citizenship	South Africa

APPENDIX 3

Globally Responsible Leadership Initiative Partners

Aviva	UK
AIM (Asian Institute of Management)	The Phillipines
Audencia Nates Ecole de Management	France
Barloworld Limited	South Africa
Bordeaux Business School	France
Caisse d'Epargne Aquitaine Nord	France
CCL (Centre for Creative Leadership)	USA and Belgium
Deutsche Bank	Germany
EFMD	Belgium
ESADE Business School	Spain
GlaxoSmithKline Biologicals	Based in Belgium
Griffith University Business School	Australia
Groupe ESC Rouen	France
IAG (Louvain School of Management)	Belgium
Instituto de Empresa	Spain
Leeds Metropolitan University	UK
Mannheim University	Germany
National Australia Bank	Australia
Northern Institute of Technology Hamburg	Germany
Responsible Business Initiatives	Pakistan
Schneider Electric	France
Stellenbosch Business School	South Africa
Sunland Group Ltd	Australia
Telefonica	Spain
The Oasis School of Human Relations	UK
United Nations Global Compact	
University of Management and Technology	Pakistan
University of Notre Dame, Mendoza School of Business	USA
Universidad del Pacifico	Peru
Wake Forest University, Babcock Graduate School of Management	USA
Welingkar Institute of Management Development and Research	India

Bibliography

Bateson, G: in *World Futures. Journal of General Evolution* (ed E Laszlo) *Traps for Sacrifice: Bateson's Schizophrenic and Girard's Scapegoat; Sergio Manghi.* Vol 26, No 6, Dec 2006.

Berne, E: *The Structure and Dynamics of Organisations and Groups.* New York: Grove Press, 1958.

Blumberg, A & Golembiewski, R: *Learning and Change in Groups.* Harmondsworth: Penguin, 1976.

Boldt, L G: *The Tao of Abundance.* Penguin Compass, 1999.

Bushe, G R: *Five Theories of Change Embedded in Appreciative Inquiry* in Cooperinder, DL; Sorenson, P Jnr; Whitney, D & Yaeger, T F (eds), *Appreciative Inquiry – Rethinking Human Organization. Toward a positive theory of change.* Champaign, Illinois: Stipes Publishing LLC, 2000.

Cartwright, D & Zander, A (eds): *Group Dynamics: Research and Theory. 3rd Edition.* New York: Harper and Row, 1968.

Clarkson, P & McKewan: *Fritz Perls.* London: Sage, 1993.

Cooperinder, D L & Whitney, D: *Appreciative Inquiry.* Berrett-Koehler Communications Inc San Francisco, 1999.

Daloz, L A: *Effective Teaching and Mentoring.* Jossey Bass, 1986.

Douglas, T: *Groupwork Practice.* London: Tavistock, 1976.

Egan, G: *You and Me: The Skills of Communicating and Relating to Others.* Monterey, California: Brooks Cole, 1977.

Friedman, M: *Dialogue and the Human Image; Beyond Humanistic Psychology.* London: Sage, 1992.

Fuller, S: *Social Epistemology.* Indiana University Press, 1991.

Girard, R: *The Scapegoat.* Johns Hopkins University Press, Baltimore, 1992.

Gore, A: *An Inconvenient Truth: The Planetary Emergency of Global Warming and What We Can Do About It.* Rodale Books, 2006.

Gray, J: *A Tour of John Heron's 'Feeling and Personhood'.* Oasis Press, 2004.

Greenwood, D J & Levin, M: *Introduction to Action Research*. London: Sage, 1998.

Heron, J: *Experience and Method: An Inquiry into the Concept of Experiential Research*. Human Potential Research Project, University of Surrey, 1971.

Heron, J: *The Concept of a Peer Learning Community*. Human Potential Research Project, University of Surrey, 1974.

Heron, J: *Behaviour Analysis in Education and Training*. Human Potential Research Project, University of Surrey, 1977.

Heron, J: *Dimensions of Facilitator Style*. Human Potential Research Project, University of Surrey, 1977.

Heron, J: *Experiential Research Methodology* in P. Reason & J. Rowan (eds), *Human Inquiry: A Sourcebook of New Paradigm Research*. Chichester: Wiley, 1981.

Heron, J: *Empirical Validity in Experiential Research*. Human Potential Research Project, University of Surrey, 1982.

Heron, J: *Education of the Affect*. Human Potential Research Project, University of Surrey, 1983.

Heron, J: *Six Category Intervention Analysis*. Human Potential Research Project, University of Surrey, 1986.

Heron, J: *Confessions of a Janus Brain*. London: Endymion Press, 1987.

Heron, J: *Assessment Revisited* in D. Boud (ed), *Developing Student Autonomy in Learning*. London: Kogan Page, 1988.

Heron, J: *Feeling and Personhood: Psychology in a New Key*. London: Sage, 1992.

Heron, J: *Co-operative Inquiry: Research into the Human Condition*. London: Sage, 1996.

Heron, J: *Helping Whole People Learn* in D. Boud and N. Miller (eds), *Working with Experience: Animating Learning*. London: Routledge, 1996.

Heron, J: *A Little Book of Co-creating*. Oasis Press, 1997.

Heron, J: *Sacred Science: Person-centred Inquiry into the Spiritual and the Subtle*. Ross-on-Wye: PCCS Books, 1998.

Heron, J: *The Complete Facilitator's Handbook*. London: Kogan Page, 1999.

Heron, J: *Helping the Client: A Creative Practical Guide* (5th Edition). London: Sage, 2001 (5th Edition)

Hobbs, T: *Experiential Training: Practical Guidelines*. London: Routledge, 1992.

Hopson, B and Scally, M: *Lifeskills Teaching*. London: McGraw-Hill, 1981.

Hunter, D; Bailey, A; Taylor, B: *Co-operacy. A new way of being at work*. Tanden Press, 1997.

Johnson, D W & Johnson, F P: *Joining Together: Group Theory and Group Skills*. Alleyn and Bacon, 2002.

Jourard, S: *Disclosing Man to Himself*. New York: Von Nostrand, 1968.

Jourard, S: *The Transparent Self*. Princeton, New Jersey: Van Nostrand, 1971.

Kegan, R: *The Evolving Self*. Harvard, 1982.

Kegan, R: *In Over Our Heads: Mental Demands of Modern Life*. Harvard University Press, 1995.

Klein, J: *Working with Groups*. London: Hutchinson, 1961.

Knowles, K; Holton, E F & Swanson, R A: *The Adult Learner*. Butterworth-Heinemann Ltd, 1998 (6th edition).

Kolb, D A: *Experiential Learning*. Eaglewood Cliffs, N J Prentice-Hall, 1984.

Kopp, S: *If You Meet the Buddha on the Road, Kill Him*! Bantam, USA, 1988 (reissue edition).

Lakoff & Johnson, M: *Philosophy in the Flesh: The Embodied Mind and its Challenge to Western Thought*. Basic Books, 1999.

Le Guin, U: *Earthsea Quartet. Book Two: The Tomb of Atuan*. Penguin Books, 1993.

Merton, T: *The Way of Chuang Tzu*. Barton: Shambala Library, 2004.

Morgan, G (ed): *Beyond Method*. London: Sage, 1986.

Moustakas, C: *Heuristic Research*. London: Sage, 1990.

Moustakas, C: *Phenomenological Research*. London: Sage, 1994.

Mowbray, R: *The Case Against Psychotherapy Registration*. London: Transmarginal Press, 1994.

O'Sullivan, E: *Transformative Learning: a vision for the 21st century*. London: Zed Books, 1999.

Parker, H: *The Enneagram*. San Francisco: Harper, 1991.

Parker I et al (eds): *Deconstructing Psychopathology*, Sage, 1995 in *Self and Society* Vol. 25 No 1 March 1997.

Peden, N (ed): *Doing Cooperative Inquiry: Exploring the Experience and Engaging in Full Personhood*. Lived Learning, Online Guide, 2004.

Postman, N & Weingartner, C: *Teaching as a Subversive Activity*. Dell Publishing, 1987.

Reason, P (ed): *Human Inquiry in Action*. London: Sage, 1988.

Reason, P: *Participation in Human Inquiry*. London: Sage, 1994.

Reason, P & Rowan, J (eds): *Human Inquiry: A Sourcebook of New Paradigm Research*. Chichester: Wiley, 1981.

Reason, P & Bradbury, H (eds). *Handbook of Action Research: Participative Inquiry and Practice*. Thousand Oaks, Sage, 2001.

Rogers, C R: *On Becoming a Person*. Boston: Houghton Mifflin, 1961.

Rogers, C R: *Freedom to Learn*. Columbia, Ohio: Charles E Merrill, 1969.

Rogers, C R: *A Way of Being*. Boston: Houghton Mifflin, 1980.

Rowan, J: *The Reality Game. A guide to humanistic counselling and therapy*. Routledge, 1983.

Rowan, J: *Ordinary Ecstasy: Humanistic Psychology in Action*. Routledge & Kegan Paul, 1976.

Schon, D: *Educating the Reflective Practitioner*. San Francisco: Jossey Bass, 1984.

Schutz, W: *Elements of Encounter*. California: Joy Press, 1973.

Schutz, W: *Profound Simplicity*. Bantam Books, 1986.

Schutz, W: *The Human Element*. Jossey Bass, 1994.

Senge, P; Ross, R; Smith, B; Roberts, C & Kleiner, A: *The Fifth Discipline Fieldbook: Strategies and Tools for Building a Learning Organisation*. Nicholas Brealey Publishing, London, 1994.

Swimme, B: *The Hidden Heart of the Cosmos: Humanity and the New Story* New York: Orbis Books, 1996.

Taylor, B: *Forging the Future Together: Human Relations in the 21st Century* Oasis Press, 2003.

Taylor, B: *Working with Others: Helping and Human Relations*. Oasis Press, 2004.

Taylor, B: *Transformative Learning through Participative Knowing*. Oasis Press, 2006.

Torbert, W: *Learning from Experience: Toward Consciousness*. New York: Columbia University Press, 1973.

Torbert W R et al: *Action Inquiry: The Secret of Timely and Transforming Leadership*. Berrett-Koehler Publishers, 2004.

Vonnegut, K: *Cat's Cradle*. Dial Press, 1998.

Watkins, J M & Mohr, B J: *Appreciative Inquiry: Change at the Speed of Imagination*. Jossey Bass/Pfeiffer, 2001.

Wilber, K: *No Boundary: Eastern and Western Approaches to Personal Growth*. Boston and London: Shambhala Publications, 1979.

Williams, H: *Cassell's Chronology of World History*. Weidenfeld and Nicolson, 2005.

Witkin & Altschuld: *Planning and Conducting Needs Assessments*. London: Sage, 1995.

INDEX

accreditation, 36, 37, 84, 97, 104, 113, 166, 168, 203, 208, 215, 227-230, 235, 240-241
– authority, 231-234
– peer, 228, 233, 236-239
– self, 228, 237
– statutory, 231-234
Action Inquiry (AI), 31, 79, 80, 254
Action Research (AR), 31, 38, 40, 251, 253
Affective competence, 85-87, 163
androgogy, 28
Appreciative Inquiry, 31, 250, 254
assessment
– criteria, 25, 212
– peer, 36-39, 84, 117, 166, 200, 202, 210-219, 224, 225, 227, 230, 233, 236, 238, 240
– self, 25, 168, 219, 221-225, 236, 238
authenticity, 32, 33, 44
authority
– personal, 44-46, 54, 146, 231, 237

Bannister, Don, 40
Bateson, Gregory, 20, 35, 58, 250
behaviours
– maintenance, 158, 159
– task, 158
Berry, Thomas, 69
Blagdon Marks, David, 36
Bradbury, H, 80, 253
British Association for Counselling and Psychotherapy (BACP), 233
British Holistic Medical Association, 39

CARPP, 38, 39
cathartic skills, 81, 162
challenge, 56, 69, 105, 116, 140, 142, 149, 151, 167, 178

change
– learning and, 135, 250
– personal, 115
Chapman, Eva, 40
choice, 32, 49-53, 57, 59, 67, 68, 70, 72, 75, 89, 113, 138, 147-9, 163
Chrysalis, 38
co-creation, 107, 111
cohesion – group, 127, 136, 145, 149, 150, 158, 211
collaboration, 4, 26, 70, 84/5, 87, 95, 108, 115, 143, 147-149, 162, 164-167, 171, 200, 203, 210
commitment, 25, 52, 59, 68, 79, 106, 110, 145, 148
– in groups, 37, 85, 100, 113, 136, 140, 141, 151, 167, 238
communication skills, 34, 189, 190
conflict
– in groups, 112, 124, 137, 144, 150, 152, 153, 155, 173
– managing, 85, 92, 113-115, 158, 170, 177, 181
control, 52, 77, 145-147, 180, 233
conventional or self-managing ego, 67
Coombs, Brian, 40
cooperative inquiry, 79
Cowan, John, 93

decision-making, 140
Declaration on Fundamental Principles & Rights at Work, 247
drives, social, 52, 144
Drucker, Peter, 35

educated person, 42
education, 19, 25, 28, 36, 40, 42, 47, 71, 72, 86, 92, 95, 99, 105, 111, 112, 117, 162, 174, 179, 180, 203, 211, 234
Egan, Gerald, 35, 250

ego consciousness, 61, 64-66
Encounter, 36, 253
engagement, 29, 49, 79, 84, 95, 104, 112, 123, 149, 167, 175, 240
Enneagram, 34, 253
equality
– of consideration, 88, 117
– of opportunity, 88, 117
Esalen Institute, 30, 31
evaluation, 29, 81, 90, 165, 193, 194, 223
experience, 33, 116, 135, 152, 169, 191, 219, 220, 223
experiential learning, 15, 28, 33, 34, 37, 39, 46, 78, 79, 81, 179

facilitating
– groups, 182
– self-as-instrument, 15, 174, 175
facilitator, 37, 82, 84, 85, 90, 95, 102, 107, 110, 115, 123, 131, 135, 143, 145, 161-164, 167, 170, 173-199, 209, 215, 225
– guidelines, 192, 195
Feldberg, Tom, 40
Ferrer, Jorge, 243
FIRO-B, 52
freedom, 31, 75, 114, 141
Friedman, Maurice, 100, 146

gender, 19, 20, 27, 37, 84, 85, 115, 138, 176, 178, 242
Gendlin, Eugene T, 55
General Medical Council (GMC) for doctors, 232
Gestalt, 66
Girard, Rene, 114, 250
Gore, Al, 101, 250
Grandin, Temple, 108
Grof, Stanislav, 32
group
– dynamics, 28, 36, 114, 123, 162, 176, 184
– facilitation methods, 172

– models, 123
– norms, 150, 154, 155
– process, 173
– security, 142, 146, 147, 150
– stages, 123, 124, 137, 145, 151, 152, 170
groups – types of, 119

Harre, Rom, 40
Hawkins, Peter, 40
Heather, Beryl, 40
Heron, John, 24, 36, 38, 39, 41, 50-61, 68, 74, 81-83, 86, 87, 89, 94, 96, 101, 108, 111, 136, 162, 170, 174, 179, 200, 206, 233, 238, 240, 243, 250, 251
hidden agenda, 179, 180
hierarchy, 19, 45, 82, 100, 146, 232
holistic learning, 82, 94, 163, 164, 243
Hopson, Barry, 40
Human Potential Movement, 30, 32, 33, 95, 103, 105
Human Potential Research Project (HPRP), 36, 38, 251
Human Potential Research Project/ Group (HPRG), 38
Humanistic Psychology, 31, 32, 35, 37, 39, 40, 66

imaginal, the, 82, 83, 85, 136
inclusion, 52, 141, 144-147, 244
inquiry based learning, 80
Institute for the Development of Human Potential (IDHP), 37, 39, 40, 230, 243
interpersonal
– needs, 52, 138, 144, 145
– skills, 28, 30, 36, 110, 112, 113, 129, 130, 152, 157, 162, 180, 189, 190, 207, 213, 234
involvement, 29, 30, 46, 47, 77, 84, 95, 101, 104, 108, 110, 166,173

Jackins, Harvey, 38
Jenkins, David (Bishop), 73
Johnson, D W & Johnson, F P, 81, 82, 121, 252
Jourard, Sidney, 19, 20, 58, 59, 72, 77, 120, 135, 147, 252
journal, 216, 219, 220, 223

Kegan, Robert, 69, 250
know what – know how, 33
Knowles, K, Holton, E F. and Swanson, R A, 28, 42, 252
Kolb, D A, 81, 82, 252
Kopp, Sheldon, 104, 252

Lake, Frank, 40
Lancaster University, M.A., 38
Lao Tzu, 62
le Guin, Ursula, 49
Leading Edge, 38
learning
    – contract, 26, 84, 110, 112, 133, 165, 168, 178, 200, 213, 219, 221, 223
    – personal, 172, 213
    – statement, 200, 226, 228, 230, 236
    – style, 77, 82, 97
Learning Edge, 38
Lewin, Kurt, 28
Lifeskills, 40
Lindeman, E C, 28, 42

Marshall, Judi, 40
Maslow, Abraham, 32
Merton, Thomas, 42
mindfulness, 55, 65
Minster Centre, The, 40
modelling, 161, 162, 181
monitoring, 103, 192, 194
Moustakas, C, 79, 252

negotiation, 26, 69, 84, 107, 166, 170, 224
Neuro Linguistic Programming, (NLP), 35, 95

New Paradigm Research Group, 39

O'Sullivan, Edmund, 101, 243, 253
Oasis School of Human Relations, 38, 40, 82, 99, 114, 115, 170, 174, 200, 211, 213, 230, 236, 237, 242, 243
Omega Institute, 243
Open Centre, The, 40
open ego, 68
Open Encounter, 32, 39
Open Space Technology, 108
openness, 33, 41, 52, 69, 90, 113, 119, 145-149, 160, 185, 242
other, role of, 44, 90, 150, 224

paradigm, 19, 27, 47, 64, 104, 108, 228, 230, 236, 241
participation
    – influence upon individuals, 113, 122, 144, 145, 151
participative learning, 28, 77
Participatory Action Research (PAR), 31
Paxton, Doug, 111, 243
Peden, Nancy, 108, 253
peer
    – learning, 15, 38, 90, 107, 108, 113, 117, 138, 148, 210
    – paradigm, 92, 95, 102, 163, 165, 181
    – principle, 38, 54, 91, 95, 99, 102, 107, 200, 236, 240, 241
personhood, 27, 42, 50, 52, 57, 59, 61, 64, 65, 68, 71-73, 84, 92, 95, 97
    – and freedom, 75
Pirani, Alix, 40
planning and design, 191, 192
portfolio career, 22
Postman, N & Weingartner, C, 179, 180, 253
power
    – personal, 45, 54, 138, 154, 162, 201

power over, 27, 54, 69, 102, 170, 232, 242
power with, 45, 53, 100, 170, 242
presence, 49, 50, 56, 95, 123
programme design, 191

Quaesitor, 36
qualitative research, 79, 80

Rajneesh, 37
Reason, Peter, 38-40, 80, 108, 253
Re-evaluation Counselling (RC), 38
reflection, 25, 26, 46, 81-83, 90, 93, 94, 104, 110, 136, 174/5, 185, 193, 196, 201, 208, 215, 220, 223
Research Center for Leadership in Action (RCLA), 111
review, 25, 39, 73, 82, 103, 160, 167, 192/3, 201, 220, 224, 225, 242
Rio Declaration on Environment and Development, 247
Rogers, Carl, 20, 29, 32, 46, 47, 59, 146, 253
Rowan, John, 39, 40, 128, 253

Scally, Mike, 40
Schon, Donald, 25, 26, 35, 101, 253
Schutz, Will, 30, 32, 39, 52, 253
Schweitzer, Albert, 62
Scientific and Medical Network, 65
self-creative person, 68
self-esteem, 50, 56, 63, 87, 143, 176, 213
self-transfiguring person, 68, 69
Seven Modes of Being, The, 69
Sinclair, Upton, 101
structuring skills, 189, 190
Swimme, Brian, 83, 254

Taylor, Bryce, 15, 19, 174
T-Groups, 130
Theory X, Theory Y, 35
Torbert W R, 40, 80, 204, 254
Transactional Analysis, 66

transpersonal, 32, 33, 49, 85, 114, 162, 242
Transpersonal Learning Community (TLC), 114
trust, 57, 65, 75, 102, 142, 146, 149/50 150, 156, 160, 185, 198, 206, 211

UK Central Council (UKCC) for nursing, 232
United Nations Convention Against Corruption, 247
Universal Declaration of Human Rights, 247
unknowable, the, 21

visibility, 116, 147, 148, 149
Vonnegut, Kurt, 92, 254

Walton, Joan, 65
Whole Person Learning Community (WPLC), 47, 106, 114/5, 117, 163
Wilber, Ken, 63, 65, 252
Williams, Hywell, 31
wounded ego, 66
written work, 213, 215, 217, 218